VOLUPTUOUS PANIC
THE EROTIC WORLD OF WEIMAR BERLIN
EXPANDED EDITION
BY MEL GORDON

FERAL HOUSE

ISBN: 1-932595-11-2

10 9 8 7 6 5 4 3 2

Feral House
1240 W. Sims Way Suite 124
Port Townsend, WA 98368

Send SASE for complete catalogue of publications

www.feralhouse.com — a site for sore eyes

Book and Cover Design: Sean Tejaratchi
Printed in Korea.

This book is dedicated to Barbara Ulrich, my co-conspirator. It is also dedicated to three Weima
wildchildren, Henry Marx, Felicity Mason, and Tonio Stewart. Each was a master raconteur. They spen
much precious time with me, telling me about their Berlin years and their many adventures there
and in exile. All of them passed away before I finished this project. They will be sorely missed

CONTENTS

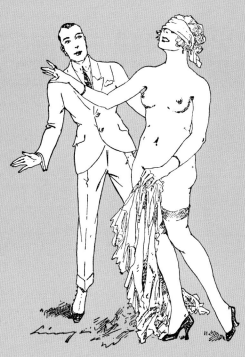

PREFACE

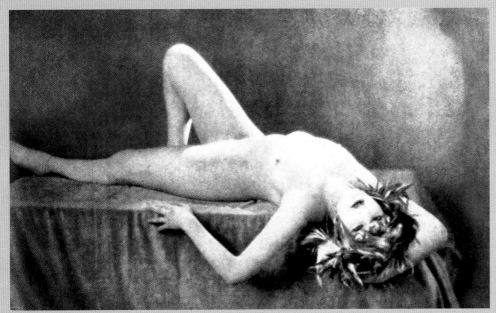

Voluptuous Panic began as research for an out-of-control theatre piece. In 1994, I wrote and directed a nightclub extravaganza for the German Queen of Punk Rock, Nina Hagen, entitled *The Seven Addictions and Five Professions of Anita Berber*. The theme of the production was the tragic and dreamy life of Anita Berber, the most glamorous decadent personality from Berlin's Golden Twenties.

Berber consciously broke every social and theatrical convention of her time, and then proclaimed some startling theory to justify her provocative, outlaw behavior. She haunted the Friedrichstadt quarter of Berlin, appearing in hotel lobbies, nightclubs, and casinos, radiantly naked except for an elegant sable wrap that shadowed her gaunt shoulders and a pair of patent-leather pumps. One year, Berber made her post-midnight entrances looking like a drugged-out Eve, clad only in those heels, a frightened pet monkey hanging from her neck, and an heirloom silver brooch packed with cocaine.

On Berlin's cabaret stages, Anita Berber danced out bizarre erotic fantasies—scenic displays, fueled by noxious concoctions of ether-and-chloroform, cognac, morphine injections, and a chic, pan-sexual disposition. Satiated Berliners, after a few riotous seasons in the early Twenties, finally tired of Berber's libidinous antics. The high priestess of choreographic decadence died a pauper's death in 1928, the result, more or less, of a desperate attempt to quit cold-turkey from her most beloved of addictions, cognac.

Nina Hagen and I rejected the notion of Anita Berber as a doomed flapper or artistic victim of Berlin's uncaring, patriarchal public, For us, she was the first postmodern woman: a vibrant Marilyn Monroe with the devious, adolescent mind of Norman Mailer. Her life needed to be celebrated.

I decided to organize the performance like an invented German cabaret evening with discrete units of wild 1920s-going-into-the-1990s, Weill-Hollaender music; erotic Expressionist sketches, hardcore Berber dance (with sacred dildos and morphine syringes as props); smutty poetry-recitations-in-the-nude, and loops of Weimar pornography—all running in a side-show sequence and introduced by an evil, beyond-Joel-Grey MC, delivering witty, narrative commentary.

Finding authentic erotic images of Twenties Berlin for my show would be the simplest of a dozen directorial tasks. I figured two of three days (tops) in the public library would suffice. To my initial surprise, there were relatively few lurid Weimar pictorials, other than the obvious George Grosz and Otto Dix etchings of grotesque whores, war-cripples, and bald-headed exploiters.

The authoritative history of racy men's periodicals, Mark Gabor's *The Pin-Up* (Bell Publishing: New York, 1972) maintained, "In Germany, there were no girlie magazines of consequence until after 1945." [In fact, I later learned over 80 such mags could be found in Berlin kiosks in 1930.] The researchers for Bob Fosse's film *Cabaret*, which was shot on location in Berlin in 1971, also reported a remarkable lack of erotic documentation; one of them complained to *The New York Post*, only literary routines and political satires remained of the old cabaret milieu. Even contemporary German-language books on the subject of interwar Berlin contained pitiful numbers of the provocative visuals that the production concept demanded.

My brain reeled. Did the Nazis or frightened Berliners destroy every suggestive publication during the politically sobering Thirties and Forties? Were Allied firebombings equally responsible for the incineration of Berlin's debauched past? Or maybe such print or photographic material from the orgiastic Weimar era never really existed as I imagined them.

Relying on private European contacts and antiquarian bookstores, I launched a feverish search for all bits of data and representations from pre-Hitler Germany. Within a few months, I had acquired dozens, then boxes, of extraordinary Weimar Berlin paper items, erotic news magazines, cabaret postcards and playbills, sexy hotel brochures, *Galante* journals, *verboten* travelogues, illustrated "Moral Histories" (*Sittengeschichten*), underground tabloids, popular crime weeklies, and naughty, what-to-do-after-midnight guidebooks. These saucy remnants contained not just pictures and photographs but descriptions, exposés, and print enticements of every sort.

The living ephemera of a lost Berlin, if only a few hundred scraps, had fallen into my hands. Now I had considerably more than a cache of weird material to brighen up a wild performance project. Scattered around my copy stand was enough arcane junk for a book. Or two. ■

hohe Politik.
Volkswirtschaft
Devisenkurse.
und Kunst
Bühne
Sport
Selbstmord
Filmnachrichten.
Eine Lebenstragödie
Theater.

A disgusting city, this Berlin, a place where no one believes in anything.

Cagliostro, 1775

And now we come to the most lurid Underworld of all cities—that of post-war Berlin. Ever since the declaration of peace, Berlin found its outlet in the wildest dissipation imaginable. The German is gross in his immorality, he likes his Halb-Welt or underworld pleasures to be devoid of any Kultur or refinement, he enjoys obscenity in a form which even the Parisian would not tolerate.

Netley Lucas, *Ladies of the Underworld*, 1927

ONCE IN BERLIN

Berlin means depravity. Moralists across the widest spectrum of political and spiritual beliefs have condemned by rote this chimerical metropolis as a strange city, built on strange soil. Even the alkaline air around the Prussian capital (*Berliner Luft*) was said to contain a toxic ether that attacked the central nervous system, stimulating long-suppressed passions as it animated all the external tics of sexual perversity. In the center of Europe, mesmerized audiences were warned, sits a nightmare municipality, a human swamp of unfettered appetites and twisted prurient proclivities. The American writer, Ben Hecht, self-described bon vivant and one-time foreign corespondent for the *Chicago Daily News*, characterized the expansive pre-Nazi cityscape succinctly as the "prime breeding ground for evil."

Amazingly, the legend of wicked Berlin, the international sex-tour-

Mythological Roots of Weimar

Contemporary knowledge of life in Twenties Berlin principally springs from mass-market films and plays. But the number of Lost-in-Weimar costume-dramas is surprisingly small. Motion-picture shorthand normally brings to mind the haughty personas of Marlene Dietrich, Lotte Lenya, Joel Grey and Liza Minnelli—each iconically attired in a lacy garter belt, black silk stockings, and shiny, elevated footwear.

Although Josef von Sternberg's early talkie *The Blue Angel* (shot simultaneously in German, English, and French in 1930) was based on Heinrich Mann's 1905

ist Mecca of the Twenties and early Thirties, endures into the twenty-first century. Two full generations after its Sodom and Gomorrah-like demise in March 1933, hundreds of American and British filmmakers, pop novelists, fashion photographers, playwrights, academics, and twenty-something website designers still play out the enchanting tale of a debauched, twentieth-century Eldorado that disappeared in flames. With Babylon and Nero's Rome, Weimar Berlin has entered into our topological thesaurus as a synonym for moral degeneracy.

novel, its dark atmospheric rendition of sexual debasement at least belonged to a then present-day Berlin. In fact, the Blue Angel cabaret of the movie title was directly modeled on a Berlin North dive known as The Stork's Nest. Even Marlene Dietrich's chair-straddling Lola-Lola character had more than a passing physical likeness to the Nest's real-life star fatale, Lola Niedlich, who was not above hawking her own dirty postcards between other singers' acts.

(Dietrich, of course, later claimed her glamorous, cold-hearted inspiration was sparked by a nameless male transvestite, an anonymous fashion-plate she admired at the Silhouette, Berlin's HQ for glam-dom gender-benders. Maybe, maybe not.)

Another émigré, Lotte Lenya, the diminutive Viennese chanteuse, arrived in New York in 1936 with equally high hopes. Although her composer husband Kurt Weill dutifully pushed her career forward, Lenya's star rose only in the post-World War II period when the Weill/Brecht Weimar confection *The Three-Penny Opera* became the surprise Off-Broadway musical hit of 1954. Lenya achieved immediate cult status as a novel avatar of Berlin sexuality—the saucy shrew with the delectable, whiskey-and-cigarette rasp. Everything about Lenya radiated High Camp (not yet defined but rapturously appreciated in the Greenwich Village habitat of the time) from her ironic stage delivery to

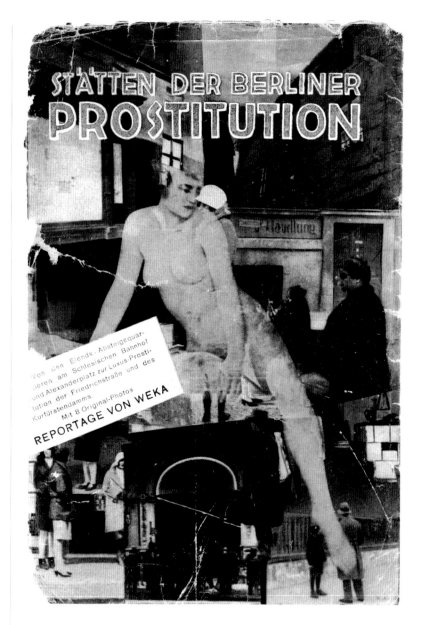

Above:
Sites of Berlin Prostitution, 1930

her evil-if-matronly bisexual predilections. Moreover, Lenya herself disturbingly epitomized the cartoonish whores from George Grosz' pornographic oeuvre, another Weimar import that was gaining popularly in the Eisenhower-Marlborough Book Club-Kennedy era.

The writer most responsible for the myth of "Sodom on the Spree" was, of course, the British Peter Pan, Christopher Isherwood. His semi-autobiographical *Berlin Stories* were written in the Thirties but only found a wide readership decades later when they were appropriated for Broadway and Hollywood vehicles.

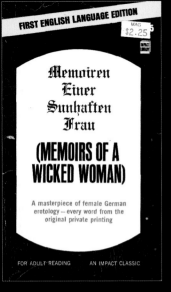

FIRST ENGLISH LANGUAGE EDITION

$2.25

Memoiren
Einer
Sunhaften
Frau

(MEMOIRS OF A
WICKED WOMAN)

A masterpiece of female German
erotology — every word from the
original private printing

FOR ADULT READING   AN IMPACT CLASSIC

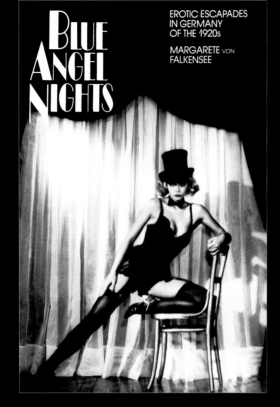

BLUE
ANGEL
NIGHTS

EROTIC ESCAPADES
IN GERMANY
OF THE 1920s

MARGARETE VON
FALKENSEE

Carmin Capalbo and Stanley Chase present

Kurt Weill's
THE THREEPENNY OPERA
(Die Dreigroschenoper)

ENGLISH ADAPTATION OF LYRICS BY MARC BLITZSTEIN

MUSIC BY KURT WEILL   ORIGINAL LYRICS BY BERT BRECHT

THE COMPLETE SCORE

featuring

SCOTT MERRILL   MARTIN WOLFSON   JO SULLIVAN

CHARLOTTE RAE   GERALD PRICE   BEATRICE ARTHUR   GEORGE TYNE

and Lotte Lenya

as produced at the Theater de Lys, New York City

Musical Director: SAMUEL MATLOWSKY

MGM RECORDS

937
SIGNET BOOKS

Bohemian Life in a Wicked City

Goodbye to Berlin

CHRISTOPHER
ISHERWOOD

A SIGNET BOOK
Complete and Unabridged

THE HUSTLER

JOHN HENRY MACKAY
TRANSLATED BY HUBERT KENNEDY

JOSEF VON
STERNBERG

THE BLUE ANGEL

INSIDE
THIS BOOK IS
INCLUDED
A SPECIAL
RECORD
OF EXCERPTS FROM
THE COLUMBIA
ORIGINAL CAST
ALBUM

the new musical
CABARET

AVON
25¢
675

ROOM in
BERLIN

Forced by
Squalor and
Poverty into
Abnormal Love

Günther Birkenfeld

Complete and Unabridged

The first dramatization of the Isherwood vignettes, *I Am a Camera* (staged in 1951; filmed in 1955) introduced the American public to the character of Sally Bowles and the sinister "demonic Berlin-Nazi takeover" theme. These adaptations, however, were essentially cerebral renderings—in the inimitable "Playhouse 90" black-and-white television style—not helped by their tame erotic imagery (nary a nipple or garter in sight) and conventional Fifties scenario: serious, artistic type lands in a dangerous and sexually-charged environment (usually a foreign stand-in for Manhattan), becomes involved with a promiscuous female, realizes the folly of his ways, and returns with newly-minted enthusiasm

ROGER SALARDENNE

HAUPTSTÄDTE DES LASTERS

Eine Reportage aus den dunkeln Vierteln der Großstädte

to his trustworthy wife/fiancée/home (that is, the domestic tranquility of Levittown).

Hal Prince's Broadway musical version of the Isherwood stories, *Cabaret* (staged in 1966) provided an entirely fresh and titillating look at nocturnal Berlin. His scenic designer, the Russian-born Boris Aronson, actually spent several months in the city during the depths of the 1923 Inflation. And the book by Joe Masteroff attempted to both restore the "divine decadence" of Isherwood's about-to-be-fascist Berlin while updating

Opposite:
Popular representations of wicked Berlin

Above and left:
Contemporary accounts of Berlin's nightlife, 1929 and 1931

its obvious message toward a middle-class/middle-aged (largely Jewish) New York audience.

Prince's *Cabaret* was shot through with the anxieties of 1966 America in Year Three of the Great Society. Counterculture live-in arrangements, drug use on campus, The Factory, and debutantes-gone-wrong were already stock-in-trade *Life* magazine features. Censorship in Hollywood and on the newsstands was fast eroding, thanks to the ACLU, which helped suburbanize the Sexual Revolution. Halloween-masked radicals paraded down Fifth Avenue while Silent Majority hardhats menacingly chewed their hoagies. Inner-city teens

torched and looted without consequence. Feminists talked a lot about their bodies. Towering drag queens in ever-swelling groups sauntered through the big-city night. Prince's *Cabaret* really hit home. Sally Bowles could have been any investor's (or reviewer's) daughter from the suburban North Shore.

Nazi Sexuality expanded into a hot S&M and leather subset of mail-order pulps and 16mm smokers. The backstreet Ventura County shlockmeisters, naturally, were just following in the footsteps of Fifties' Men's magazines, which long bandied about the sick-sex by Germans-in-wartime scenario. Finally, highbrow European film directors mounted the Berlin-to-Auschwitz bandwagon, notably with *The Damned* (1969), *The Night Porter* (1973), and *The Serpent's Egg* (1976). Like Edwin S. Porter, Christopher Isherwood had unwittingly devised a free-wheeling multinational staple that knew no cultivated bounds or embodied much historical truth.

Fosse's Hollywood musical *Cabaret* (1972) jettisoned the sweet comic interludes of the Masteroff stage script. He sharpened the juxtapositions of fetish-strewn Berlin with the smartly-uniformed avengers of the New Germany. Yet again mass audiences were allowed to partake in the polymorphous confusion of old Weimar—via a doll-faced Joel Grey in nifty drag and big-eyed Liza in shameless, junior Marlene getup—while rationally condemning it. Although the Fosse film laboriously plotted out the dangers of female promiscuity and predatory homosexuals (of the duplicitous cross-dressed or monocle-wearing varieties), its harsh social message was less apparent to Seventies adolescents. *Cabaret* (and, by extension, Weimar Berlin) signified nothing more than wild clothing and wild sex. Bad Boy, Bad Girl, mean, mocking, in-your-face Sex.

This newest trend in Weimarism was a kick, imparting graphic life to Karl Lagerfeld, David Bowie (on his third go-round), German neo-noir costume film-epics, the Plasmatics, Macy's lingerie ads (especially preceding Mother's Day), *Marquee-"O"-and-Skin* glossies, Madonna-in-Gaultier-garb, a mini-genre of gay Holo-

caust weepies, Marilyn Manson, and a smash, brothelized import of that old workhorse, *Cabaret*.

For the erotic trailblazers of the pre-millennium, the reimagined Weimar Berlin remained a cutting-edge, mythic terra firma. But even their heightened visions were still not as fantastic as history's erotic metropolis.

Above:
So It Seems— Berlin! 1927

Left:
Berlin: What's Not in the Baedeker Guide, 1927

"Berlin is Still Berlin"

How Berlin transformed from a minor neoclassical outpost in Goethe's time to the third largest city in the world (with over four million registered citizens in 1930) is the subject of an immense body of urban-studies literature. While the external and sociopolitical factors

BERLINS LESBISCHE FRAUEN

von Dr. Magnus Hirschfeld

Above:
Ruth Margarete
Roellig, *Berlin's
Lesbians*, 1928,
a guidebook
with an intro-
duction by
Dr. Magnus
Hirschfeld

Opposite:
Manassé,
*The Forbidden
Book*

of Berlin's development have been analyzed in stupendous detail, one ineffable aspect has been largely ignored in these academic tomes: the unconventional religious profile of native Berliners throughout the nineteenth and twentieth centuries.

If it was possible to objectively measure the spiritual life of a city—through the language of its municipal charter, the legislative influence of its church leaders, the ratio of religious institutions to residents, its weekly church attendance, the judicious enforcement of Blue Laws, and so forth—then Berlin (with Montevideo and San Francisco) would have to be considered as one of the most faithless—or heathen—cities in the Western world. Much of the unvirtuous Berlin ethos can be explained by global events (the mass influx of French Huguenots and Central European Jews; the rise of modern capitalism) and ideological shifts (the weakening of Lutheran doctrine; trickle-down faith in scientific inquiry and Nietzschean vitalism); but, mostly by the creation of a self-conscious urban identity.

Before 1900, the archetypal Berliner was characterized by his crude—almost American—demeanor and breezy attitude toward aristocratic codes of conduct. He was deadly cynical, possessing a *Berliner Schnauze* (Berlin snout or "trap"), spoke in a side-of-the-mouth patois, and never missed an occasion to deliver a *schpritz* of wiseguy wisdom. A city of such characters was a distinct liability to the stodgy monarchy.

The harsh imposition of Wilhelmian law and threats of Prussian discipline kept the anarchistic urban-swamp in check. But in 1919, with the Kaiser gone and a democratic constitution about to be proclaimed in Weimar, those legal strictures basically expired. The tapped-down moral restraints of bratty Berlin suddenly burst at the seams. The once quaintly roguish German metropolis was now an open city—open for sex. Or, as its many provincial detractors decried, "a new Hell on earth." ■

THE COLLAPSE

All wars, in the iron cosmology of Berlin's leading sexologists, were a function of the male sex impulse and civilization's attempt to manipulate it. Even the declarations of hostility, victory, conquest, and defeat have been oedipally recast into clear eroticized language and imagery. National opponents were said to be not mere adversaries but rampaging savages and demons, hell-bent on torture, violation of defenseless communities, and mass rape. Armed teenagers fighting in the service of their motherland were praised by writers of epics (or modern propagandists) as de facto protectors of the race, guardians slumped up against the bedroom doors of frightened mothers.

The Kaiser's Wand

The Great War, World War I, exaggerated the erotic fears and longings of its warring nations. For one, the heroic enterprise stretched out endlessly, endangering the morale and mental stability of both the conscripted soldiers and civilian populations. What was to be a five- or six-month, lightning-like military campaign, according to the Central Powers and Allied High Commands, soon stagnated into a battlefield morass. The wholesale human slaughter, thanks to the new technology of weaponry, actually hardened political attitudes and impeded the war's conclusion. Given the astronomical numbers of casualties sustained in combat, no government could tolerate a defeat. There were also the perceived sexual issues, heightened by skilled propagandists.

When the Archduke Ferdinand and his wife Sofia were assassinated by Serbian nationalists in Sarajevo in 1914, much was made in the world press about the fanatical character of Balkan politics, Austrian arrogance (Ferdinand deliberately chose June 28th, the Serbian national day of mourning, to tour newly incorporated Bosnia), and the Great Power consequences. But during the six weeks between the shooting of Austro-Hungary's heir apparent and the actual war, German propaganda played up one minor aspect of the Saravejo event: the Serbian Black Hands had needlessly murdered an

Few national conflicts have been fought without these psych-war stratagems, or, more to the point, erotic inducements and rewards for its soldiers. The elevated levels of testosterone that biologically steel post-pubescent bodies and cloud the instinct for self-preservation also increase sexual desire in young men. So it is little wonder that societies have traditionally accorded their warrior class (and consorts) dispensation from chastity and monogamous regulation.

Right:
Ernst Hiller,
Revolution

Below:
Doodles by
a German
soldier on the
Western Front,
1915

aristocratic woman. This was further proof of the sexual perfidy of Slavic men. Serbs, Russians, Ukrainians, Macedonians, Poles, and all their lesser cousins were in need of the civilizing canon of the German army and its partners.

More than any country in Europe, Imperial Germany was prepared for war. Its High Command, over a tense decade, assiduously mapped out the grand project. And a circus atmosphere reigned in Berlin during the August mobilization. Kaiser Wilhelm II waved madly to the enlistees while a tennis racket dangled listlessly from his withered left hand. Yet the conflagration that erupted in September was anything but sporting.

The Home Front

The war years of 1914–1918 upended everything in Germany proper. Trainloads of young women from the provinces were delivered to work destinations in Berlin's war ministries and federal bureaus, filling minor positions once held by male secretaries and clerks. A kind of radical feminism and shared sisterhood, long dreaded by conservative elements in the German government, began to form in the epicenter of the Wilhelmian Empire. No longer wide-eyed innocents, these newly enfranchised women had also witnessed an implosion of moral values in their own native villages and cities.

As the national euphoria and jingoistic enthusiasm for modern warfare waned, even in the patriotic countryside, an insidious Chicago-style corruption spread. Butchers who honorably served families for generations were noticeably pressing their thumbs on the

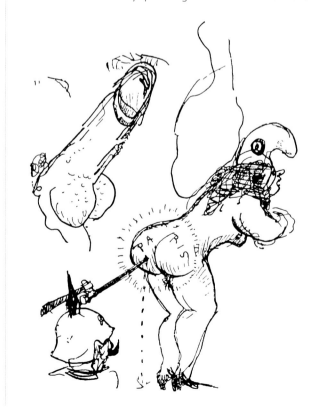

14

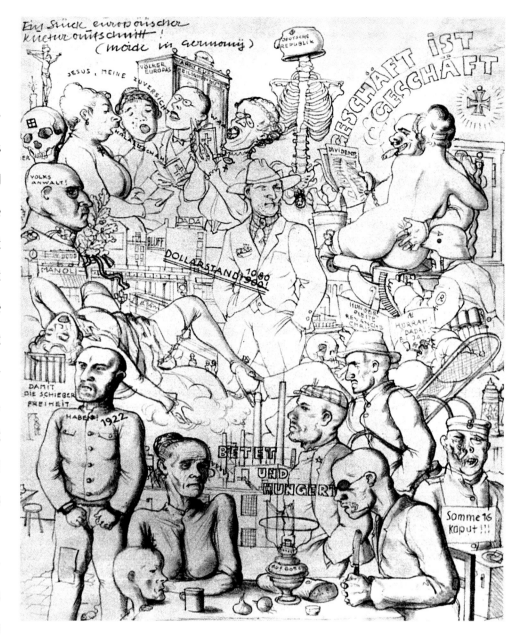

edges of regulated meat scales; formerly virtuous small-town mayors and church officials were implicated in preposterous scams and bizarre sexual improprieties. For the first time in a century, black-market survival and fears of illegitimate pregnancies became more than just neighborhood gossip for middle-class households. Worst of all, Germanic faith in the sacrosanct world of mustached, steely-eyed men—that is, the Kaiser and his General Staff—began to erode.

The pernicious hypocrisy and murderous bluster of the ruling patriarchs at every social level, the inescapable sights of disfigured and hollow-eyed soldiers wandering Berlin's streets and parks, the long-delayed (if heavily censored) official postings of the millions dead, missing, or captured created a novel and creepy psychosexual vacuum. The realm of shared national purpose and manly virtue was challenged by more primitive philosophies of day-to-day survival.

For most German families, trade—either in heirlooms or stolen merchandise—earned subsistence to endure the month or week. But eventually these items became scarce or obsolete. Only foodstuffs mattered. The profiteering and theft of them were abetted by a distracted government, intent on victories in the field. Those poor souls without food sources or connections had just one other commodity to haul to the public market: sex.

At first, young war brides, branded "straw-widows," offered their carnal services to the available males of Berlin, then it was the provincial youth of both sexes, and finally the children of bourgeois families. Prostitution lost its exact meaning when tens of

Above:
*Otto Griebel,
A Slice of
European
Ham (Made in
Germany),
1922*

thousands were involved in complex sex attachments, all of a commercial nature. The vaguely Wilhelmian underpinning of middle-class Berlin slowly cracked and, over time, collapsed.

Venereal disease, not flesh-peddling, threatened the immediate well-being of the capital. Syphilis and gonorrhea spread at an alarming rate. The city fathers, once proud watchdogs of the moral code, turned to Berlin's

public health officials and social workers for help. The war had spiritually corroded the old order at home.

Trench-Life and the *Etappe*

In the conquered areas of Belgium and Polish Russia, German servicemen behaved strangely, too. Hundreds, then thousands, experienced a headlong release from all peace-time constraints. Homosexual affection and cross-dressing amusements became commonplace activities in the musty trenches and isolated campsites. Instead of pictures of their sweethearts to inspire them, pockets of combat-weary troops stared in frozen rapture at S&M and fetishistic photographs that they cradled in their palms. Public and habitual masturbation, manifestations of shell-shock, grew to epic proportions, shaking morale as well as becoming an embarrassing disciplinary problem. In the countryside, the brutal corralling and rape of foreign women, usually peasant girls, by German recruits was reported with some frequency in the early dispatches. Some nationalistic officers defended their underlings' misbehavior as a healthy discharge from the tedium of building fortifications and other noncombatant duties.

The High Command, alarmed that the Imperial Army was aping the uncouth ways of their despised Serb and French brethren, responded with Prussian efficiency. They permitted local brothels to open under the strict supervision of military physicians. Every frontline soldier was issued a ration book of sex coupons; the frequency of contact, number of minutes, time of day, and class of whores allowed was determined mathematically by rank and combat unit. The booklets were as treasured as tobacco.

In the staging grounds behind the active theatres of war, or the *Etappe*, senior officers also engaged in nightly debaucheries. Local pretties were treated to luxurious outings, champagne dinners, risqué naked recitals, and crates of pilfered goods. Roman-style orgies became synonymous with *Etappe* life. Female

spies, like the legendary Mata Hari, sometimes frequented these command centers, wrangling battlefield secrets from lust-smitten German administrators and military leaders.

Sex, the historical lubricant for rallying a nation to armed conflict, was destroying the Kaiser's war.

Other unforeseen factors, like the American Expeditionary Forces and mutiny in the hinterlands, also undermined General von Hindenburg's scheme for the occupation of eastern France and military triumph. By 1918, it was evident that the Central Power alliance had splintered irrevocably under the onslaught of Allied armies. Each nation was ready to sue for a separate peace.

The Paper Republic

On November 9th, 1918, a German republic was declared, replacing the Wilhelmian Second Reich. Within 24 hours, the Kaiser abdicated his monarchy and fled

Opposite Above:
Alexander Szekely, *Scene from a German Brothel in Ghent*

Opposite Below:
Postcard, *Behind the Lines*

Above:
Postcard, *The Price of Flesh Has Fallen*

with his family to the Netherlands. Two days later an Armistice was signed with the Western powers. All fighting ceased. Germany had lost the Great War.

Now a stunned populace, reeling from new economic chaos and terror in the form of revolution and counter-revolution, watched in disbelief as top-hatted politicians attempted to transform their vanquished nation into a model constitutional republic. Germany in 1919 had no traditions of democratic consensus, only an embittered electorate in search of quick political fixes. Extremist parties of the left and right attained immense power in the first national election and ultimately dominated the workings of the Weimar Assembly.

Some radicals opted for a Soviet solution. But Lenin, the supreme revolutionary commander, already knew what the seditious leaders of Bavaria and Hamburg would soon discover to their regret: Germans were incapable of fomenting Socialist revolution; when ordered to storm a railroad station, they would stand in line first to buy tickets. By March 1919, the period of romantic left-wing insurrection had been checked. Private Nationalist militias, in league with the centralist authorities, had assassinated the Red leaders and overturned their "peasant-proletariat" communes. Berliners then returned to their business of pleasure.

The municipal chiefs of the great city had little to say about prostitution, which, resulting from an oversupply of females (primarily war-widows), had shown a massive increase since the Armistice. The dignitaries had other moral concerns. Two public acts were now strictly forbidden: fishing by hand grenade in the lakes and rivers around Berlin, and social dancing inside the city bounds. On a single day in January 1919, five dance halls were raided by Berlin vice squads while frumpy streetwalkers and *cocaine-Schleppers* watched in bemused stupefaction.

Through much of 1919, Berlin waged a war against the promoters of popular dance. But the universally reviled campaign was doomed from the start. A delirium for social dance (*Tanztaumel*) had swept the city and much of Germany since the cessation of fighting. Klaus Mann, the son of the Nobel Prize laureate, recalled the choreographic outbreak as "a mania, a religion, a racket." Secret dance parlors, hidden in the Friedrichstadt and in Berlin North, became the craze. In workers' quarters, Apache-like tango dances, cakewalks, and foxtrots played out under streetlights and in parks. Life in postwar Berlin had become bizarrely eroticized and dance-madness was its improbable visible symptom.

Social and popular dances took place in an array of venues: at lavish balls (like the Bad Boys' Ball or the Pretty Leg Festival), in sleazy corner bars, at private clubs near resort areas, but mostly it was stimulated by

imported American music and the new women's fashion that emphasized silk stockings and revealing skirts. What was once the shocking mode of film stars and drunken aristocrats now availed itself to everyone. Even at formal dances, clothing shrank to practically nothing. Variety houses and cabarets featured rows of naked women, but many found it impossible to compete with the risqué styles in the audience.

At first the city made a purely Kantian appeal: if every Berliner tripped the light fantastic, full economic recovery could never be achieved. But there was a growing sense of prosperity in Berlin anyway. Despite the ubiquitous presence of beggars and hideous

Above:
Carlo Jung,
A Fine Family

war-wounded, demobilized aristocrats and the children of Germany's affluent classes gravitated to the country's financial and cultural center.

Then thousands of posters from the health ministry warned, "Berlin, Your Dance Partner is Death!" The admonishment in garish Expressionist script weirdly coupled brain-damaging syphilis with all-night tangos. In no time, the slogan inspired trunkloads of caustic sketches by cabaret artists and provided the ideal catchphrase-refrain for dozens of dialect song parodies.

In April 1919, a new tactic was tried. A few of the largest dance halls were allowed to reopen. However, ballroom dance remained *verboten* elsewhere in Berlin. Closures of defiant bars, mass arrests, and costly lawsuits resulted. By late fall, the entire civic enterprise had to be abandoned. The city fathers discredited them-

selves with their silly exercise in extreme social rectitude. Dance was made legal and censorship in Berlin basically ceased.

A dizzying panic overtook Berlin in October 1919. Not since Paris in the 1860s had a European city experienced the Edenic flush of total erotic freedom. With prostitution and all-night dancing already accepted features of contemporary Berlin life, what else could be added? Drugs and over-the-counter pornography appeared first.

Cocaine powder, morphine solution in vials, and opium balls were hawked on street corners. Chinese entrepreneurs from the former German concession of Kiaochow installed a string of opium dens in Friedrichstadt cellars, but these were far too claustrophobic for German tastes. Invented sedatives—like Anita Berber's breakfast elixir, chloroform and ether—seemed more modern and daring. (The C-and-E cocktail was ingested by swirling white roses in the potion and then biting off the frozen petals. Really the designer drug of its time.)

The most sought-after pornographic postcards and films had been imported from Paris or Budapest before the war. Now Berlin was patriotically producing its own brands in oversized graphic portfolios, "bachelor" *Galante* magazines, photo-sheets, and smokers. Even German nudist journals that were published for decades took on darker tones. The sweet qualities of Gallic porno were supplanted in Berlin studios by the psychopathic scenarios from Krafft-Ebing. Forced, intergenerational, scatological, and obsessive fetish sex prevailed. Sunny pics of bob-haired, smiling French beauties in nude repose (often in sylvan settings before gleaming, immobile sedans) gave way to queasy, regressive fantasies—Gymnasium masters and nannies administering instruments of torture and humiliation to their naked charges. The distinct erotica of Berlin was sold in specialized bookstores and here and there on the street.

The *Nachtlokal*, or private nightspot, was another crude expression of the new era. In 30 or so Berlin hideaways, gentlemen and sophisticated couples could encounter the latest erotic sensation, the Naked Dance. Cynical journalists compared these postwar Berlin "nightclubs" to *Tingel-Tangels*, ugly Wilhelmian whorebars where honky-tonk entertainers intermingled with

their equally lowbrow clients. In truth, the *Nachtlokals* catered to a much more naive class of patron.

Usually the potential customer was discovered on a midnight *Bummel* (urban stroll) somewhere near the Friedrichstadt. A scruffy teen working for the *Lokal*, the *Schlepper*, would then approach the target, luring him with promises of covert erotic entertainment and, if alone, female companionship. A picturesque journey through a Byzantine circuit of courtyards and passageways followed. Finally, the disoriented sucker was delivered to the secret club hidden in an out-of-the-

Above:
Erich Schütz,
*Raiding the
Nacktlokal*

21

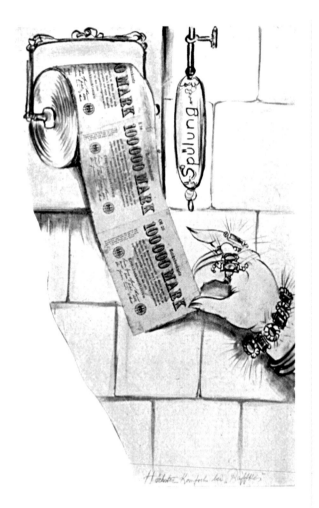

way apartment complex. Once inside, the *Suitor* paid a horrific tariff (in the form of an overpriced bottle of German champagne, *Sekt*) just to sit at a table. An improbably upbeat Russian balalaika band normally filled the air with musical static.

Around one or two in the morning, a smutty revue commenced. The nature and duration of the show varied considerably, mostly consisting of few naked whores and their daughters, prancing in mock Isadora abandon. Poor sightlines and erratic seating arrangements were offset by the itinerant activities of the performers, who would erotically tease *Suitors* at their tables and join free-spending customers for more brazen contact. Genital frisson in the form of lap-dancing or foot-sex (with the woman perched on the tabletop) was a customary enticement.

Newspapers and magazines had a field day exposing these tourist traps. The kitschy symbol of a nineteenth-century orgy, bald-headed men downing *Sekt* from the shoes of giggling whores, appeared repeatedly in their pages as sidebar photographs and sketches. (Waggish columnists opined that such a practice must have enhanced the inferior quality of the foaming swill.)

Neither a source of fine entertainment nor a legitimate venue for intercourse, the *Nachtlokals* were lambasted as embarrassingly ersatz. But they provided Berlin with a psychic opening. Wild sex and all-night antics could be made anywhere. In private flats, hotel rooms, and rented halls, drug parties and nude "Beauty Evenings" were constantly announced and held. A gala atmosphere enveloped 1919 and 1920. The entire city transformed into a *Nachtlokal* for its liberated youth and still comfortable bourgeoisie.

The stimulants and fashions changed too. "Radium cremes" and tincture of yohimbé bark from West Africa, which augmented female and male desire, were manufactured in little shops and advertised in *Galante* monthlies. Seamstresses—mostly White Russians and former noblewomen—added a Berlin touch; they reinvigorated Flapper-era couture by utilizing materials associated with male fetishism and slashed dresses to mimic pornographic renderings. Exhibitionism competed with voyeurism as the city's outrageous draw. Every single Berlin night before June 1920 began to resemble New Year's, or Sylvester's, Eve.

The Great Inflation

When the Weimar Republic signed the Treaty of Versailles in 1919 there was a mutual understanding that the emotional issues of German national boundaries, demilitarization, and war reparations would be negotiated at future parleys. But the subsequent conferences in the early Twenties proved disastrous for the Republic. Angered by German bickering that rejected their resolute demands for immediate disarmament and sharply redrawn borders, French and English politicians tripled the amount Germany would owe the victors—six billion gold marks in raw materials and industrial goods to be paid over a 42-year period.

The terms of the 1921 Reparation Act more than bankrupted the German federal treasury; it ensured the end to any hopes for a stable commercial life in the struggling Republic. Its currency would eventually become worthless. But the scope of the monetary freefall was not clear at first. Seven marks bought one American dollar in January 1921, then the rate of

exchange tumbled to 550/1 in August. In the summer of 1922, a mere dollar traded for 7,500 German marks. By January 1923, the official rate was 22,400/1, then in May the mark slid further to 54,300 per dollar. An all-time low was reached on October 12, 1923 when the once-vaunted German note plummeted to the staggering equation of 4.2 billion marks to the dollar.

Germans on fixed incomes and pensioners lost everything in those years. Once again wartime barter was a favored means of livelihood. Religious charities, like the Catholic Relief and the comically American Salvation Army, fanned out across Berlin. Crank indigenous cults also dished out thin soup with apocalyptic homilies.

Above:
Paul Kamm,
1923

23

rows of marks to pay taxes or purchase bread while their grandchildren built toy fortresses in alleyways, using stacks of the discarded bills as architectural blocks.

The Great Inflation complicated Berlin's sexual folkways but did not really alter them. The so-called moral collapse had already occurred. Erotic amusements, prostitution, and narcotics were all readily available before the inflationary madness. But now the purveyors of commercial sex and other decadent offerings had a more acute economic incentive. Berlin was suddenly inundated with hard-currency tourists, looking for Jazz Age bargains. Swedes, Dutch, French, and detested hordes of Turks and Japanese flocked to the open city. Their modest assets in the form of kronen, guilders, francs, lira, and yen metamorphosed the plucky foreigners into multimillionaires the

Most urban employees were paid by the day and scurried to exchange-banks in the morning before the value of their salaries declined by half in the late afternoon. German towns issued emergency paper scrip for its bewildered citizens; by the bitter fall of 1923, the nationwide legal tender was valued chiefly as a combustible for apartment furnaces. French newsreel-cameramen captured mustached Burgers hauling wheelbar-

moment they disembarked at the Stettiner Bahnhof.

In postwar Paris, a traveler could engage the services of a streetwalker for five or six dollars; but during the Inflation in Berlin, five dollars could buy a month's worth of carnal delights. The most exquisite blowjob or kinky dalliance with a 15-year-old never cost more than 30 cents, or 65 million 1923 marks. The widows of famous *Wehrmacht* generals rented their bodies and bedrooms for a few precious kronen. Even upright bourgeois couples exhibited themselves in marital embrace for a solid hour if anyone was interested in that kind of theatre.

Ilya Ehrenburg, the Russian writer, remembered going to a flat in a respectable neighborhood during the Inflation and discussing Dostoyevsky with the excited middle-class residents. After a glassful of lemonade mixed with spirits, the staid Berliners brought out their young, nubile daughters, who promptly executed a striptease before the shocked eyes of their celebrated guest. For American money, the mother proposed to the Communist ideologue, there was much more to be had that evening.

The *Nachtlokals* in particular teemed with non-German speaking thrill-seekers. For the newest clientele, humiliation and sexual degradation served as an equal attractant as the old Naked Dance revue itself. In one *Lokal* favored by Dutch vacationers, businessmen and their wives tossed foreign coins to any female German in attendance willing to strip completely nude. Outside the tourist hotels and downtown pensions, knowing gigolos and pretty boys, dolled up in rouge and mascara like wax mannequins, displayed their androgynous wares. To the merry-making *Ausländer*, Berlin was conducting a clearance sale in human flesh. Sex was everywhere and obtainable on the cheap. The

Kaiser's Germany, in the minds of many, was finally repaying its war debts.

On November 20th, 1923, the financial dementia lifted. The administration in Weimar introduced a new currency, the Rentenmark, which overnight stabilized the internal economy and Germany's standing in the international marketplace. Worth about 20 cents, or one trillion marks, the Rentenmark was itself replaced by the Reichsmark in 1924. But confidence in Weimar governance, at least until 1929, was restored. The glorious period known as Germany's "Golden Twenties" catapulted into history with champagne toasts and an intoxicating roar. ■

> Sex is the business of the town.
>
> **Anita Loos, 1923**

> There were men dressed as women, women dressed as men or little school-girls, women in boots with whips (boots and whips in different colors, shapes, and sizes, promising different passive or active divertissements). [...] Young, well-washed, and pretty females were abundantly available. They could be had for the asking, sometimes without asking at all, often for the mere price of a dinner or a bunch of flowers: shopgirls, secretaries, White Russian refugees, nice girls from decayed good families. Some of them pathetically wept on the rumpled bed after making love when they accepted money.
>
> **Luigi Barzini,** *The Europeans,* **1983**

CITY OF WHORES

The end of the Great Inflation did not stanch the perv invasion of Berlin. In fact, fascination with the amoral city intensified as soon as the Reichsmark proved a stable currency. Weimar Berlin, while shedding the scintilla of menace and social volatility, retained its transcendent reputation as Europe's newest illicit playground. Along with cruises down the Rhine and Munich's Oktoberfest, the *Grieben* guidebooks added Berlin's Friedrichstadt at midnight as a must-see tourist adventure.

The very first thing foreigners noticed in Berlin were whores, thousands of tarted-up females on the streets, in hotel lobbies, and seated at cafés and clubs. How many *Beinls* made their living in Berlin during the Golden Twenties was impossible to calculate. The estimates ranged from a low of 5,000 to the oft-published figure of 120,000 (which didn't include the 35,000 male

BERLIN PROSTITUTE TYPES (OUTDOORS)

—Identified by their furs and calf-length, Wilhelmian-era, black-leather boots or (after 1926) in shiny, patent leather versions. Lacquered gold, cobalt blue, brick, "poisonous" green, or maroon, the iridescent footwear indicated the Girl's specialty. Freelance *Dominas*, they attracted frugal provincial German *Suitors*, who were led to nearby pensions. Estimated numbers (in 1930): 300–350.

—Lowly streetwalkers without "room money," who serviced men in the corners of the Tiergarten and around Bülowplatz. [Ironic variant name: FRESH-AIR WOMEN.] Estimated numbers: 600.

—Unattractive sex-workers on Oranienburgstrasse. Included women with missing limbs, hunchbacks, and other deformities. [Also known as WRECKS.] Estimated numbers: 400.

—[literally "Half-Baked"] Amateur, occasional prostitutes, the vast majority of the Friday-night trade. Often secretaries, shopkeepers, and office clerks supplementing their incomes after work. [During the Inflation Era, they were called DANGERS, due to their unregistered status and FIVE O'CLOCK LADIES because of their preferred time of contact.] Estimated numbers: 40,000–55,000.

—Three defined classes of legal prostitutes who reported to the Berlin vice authorities on a regular basis and were checked for venereal disease by police physicians. Before 1927, they were concentrated in the Friedrichstadt and Berlin North. Typical romantic opening: "So, sweetheart?" [Variant names: BONG-STRASSE, TRS-GIRL, and KONTROLL.] Number of Berlin "Control Books" issued to street prostitutes and CONTROLS in 1930: 8,750.

—Pregnant girls and women who waited under the lampposts on Münzstrasse for "old money" clients in search of this erotic specialty. Very expensive sessions. [Also known as KASSUBE (from Viennese Romany argot)]. Estimated numbers: seasonal, under two dozen.

—Boyish, teenage girls. Coquettishly dressed and working in secret from their families, they treated prostitution as a form of dating. Often traveled in pairs. Thought of as primarily gold diggers. Standard pickup line: "Don't you think we should have a coffee first?" Estimated numbers: 25,000–30,000.

—*Bubikopfed* streetwalkers in the latest fashions (sometimes in mother-and-daughter teams), who silently solicited customers on

prostitutes). It all depended on one's definition of the term. Berlin was like no other European city when it came to the sheer magnitude of sexual possibility.

"Controlled" Prostitution

During the late Renaissance, most German towns established boundaries for free-wheeling bathhouse-taverns, brothels, and street prostitution. These areas were marked by *Striche*, painted lines or stripes. Draconian punishments awaited sex traffickers and adulterers caught outside the Line. Wayward prostitutes

were tied naked to a pillory, which usually stood in the village commons. Special constables administered public floggings. And afterward, citizens could taunt the culprits, beat them, spit on them, or even urinate on them.

In western and southern cities, female violators of the *Strich* were confined to stocks. A thick leather strap was laced around the woman's neck and hollows of her knees, and then tightened. In this excruciating, fetal-like position, the offender was placed in a wooden-stock frame, which had openings for her head and naked posterior. The sex criminal was finally subject to a hail of brutal blows and kicks to her exposed areas during the course of an afternoon. The upright Burgers and their women often inflicted permanent damage to the prostitute's body.

Inside the *Strich*, a counter-ecclesiastic world reigned. Pleasure enterprises, although controlled and highly taxed, provided a bit of heaven for sinners. Food and intoxicants, gaudy entertainment, and sex were all available for a price. A furtive jargon—a mix of vulgar Yiddish, thieves' argot, Romany, and low-German dialects—developed into the *Strich*'s lingua franca. In each town, separate rules and folkways emerged.

During May celebrations in Mainz and Nuremberg, a "Whore-Queen" was chosen in a free-for-all competition. According to the upside-down culture of the *Strich*,

Previous Left:
Böhm,
Stocking Gold

Previous Right:
Kamm, *Minette*

Left:
Hans Baluscek,
A Nutte at the Carnival, 1923

the foremost attributes of a Queen revolved around her sexual mastery (evidently vaginal and manual skills) and a quick wit; the conventional standards of physical beauty were eschewed here. Interestingly, the local lawmakers recognized the authority of the Queen and made her responsible for enforcing their ordinances throughout her sovereign rule.

Municipally-confined areas for commercial sex traffic in the German-speaking world evolved naturally from the *Strich* concept. A single neigh-

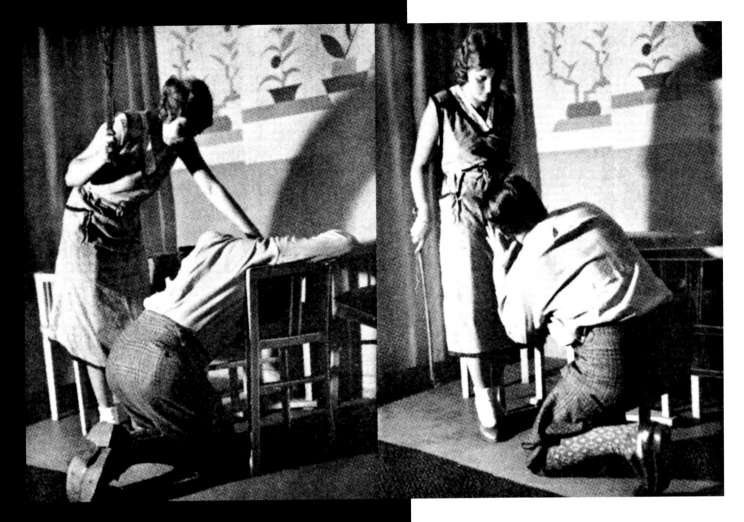

Tauentzienstrasse, south of the Memorial Church. *T-Girls* were celebrated for their down-to-earth, brash attitude. Beloved species to Berlin's press corps, even those working for Conservative and Nationalist dailies. Estimated numbers: 2,500.

BERLIN PROSTITUTE TYPES (INDOORS)

——[From Galizianer-Yiddish] Low-grade Jewish whores. Polish-born. Mostly found in the Alex near the police station or in Transient-Quarters. [Also known as (illegal immigrants from the Polish industrial city)].

——[From French underworld jargon—literally: "half-beavers," or "amateur hookers."] Young women from good families who supplemented their allowances by working in secretive, high-class houses in Berlin West. Normal hours of operation were late afternoon/early evening. [Variant name: .] Estimated numbers: 500.

——Leather-clad, mesomorphic women who specialized in whipping,

borhood, under police supervision, delimited and contained all the city's lewd merrymaking. Urban centers elsewhere in Western Europe designated similar "Zona Rosas" to control their vice problem. Most endured into the 1930s.

No visitor doing the town in Paris, Rome, Barcelona, Hamburg, Vienna, Budapest, Antwerp, or Marseilles in pre-World War II Europe could avoid traversing these notorious "Red" or "Chinese" districts. Depending on the current political climate, their integration into the local culture, and financial boon to the civic coffers, each of these Zonas varied considerably in size and public toleration. To a great degree, they defined the secret and cosmopolitan life of the city. And among

humiliation, and other forms of erotic punishment. Active in lesbian nightclubs that permitted kinky heterosexual couples and free-spending male clients. Also found in phony "Body-Culture" clinics. Estimated numbers: 1,500.

TOISES—[Corruption of French underworld argot for "vaginas."] Independent whores, who advertised in newspapers and magazines as manicurists and masseuses. Sometimes seen by Kudamm outdoor display cases. [Also known as DUALITY WOMEN.] Estimated numbers: 2,500.

MEDICINE—Child prostitutes, ages 12-16, who were "prescribed" by pimps, posing as physicians. The "patient" indicated the "length of his illness" (requested age of the girl) and color of pills (hair tint). Transaction took place in Berlin West "pharmacies." Estimated numbers: less than 100.

MINETTES—[French for "female cats." A common Parisian expression for independent, sexually active women.] Exclusive call girls who enacted S&M fantasy scenes, often involving foot worship, bondage, and forced transvestitism. Located in all the large Friedrichstadt hotels. Estimated numbers: 350.

RACE HORSES—Masochistic prostitutes who enjoyed being beaten or whipped. Worked in "Institutes for Foreign Language Instruction," where the "schoolrooms" were equipped with instruments of torture and bondage furniture. Patrons were carefully screened before their first session. Estimated numbers: 200.

TABLE-LADIES—Berlin's version of the Geisha. Employed in private nightclubs on the Kudamm, Table-Ladies were reputed to be ravishing and multilingual. Each conformed to a specific national type: Demonic German, Exotic Eurasian, dark-eyed Gypsy-Girl, blonde Nordic, or Spanish Aristocrat. A favorite of politicians, movie moguls, bigtime capitalists, and Scandinavian tourists. Customers paid "table-money" to the club—often in excess of 100 marks—for an evening of champagne, fancy canapés, scintillating gossip, and a private backroom encounter. Estimated numbers: 400–500 before the 1929 Crisis; half as many after.

TELEPHONE-GIRLS—Child prostitutes, ages 12-17, who are ordered by telephone and then delivered to clients in limousines or taxis. Usually given the names of stage or film stars, like Marlene Dietrich or Lilian Harvey, that described their prepubescent physical features. Often billed as "virgins." Extremely expensive. Estimated numbers: 3,000.

them, Pigalle (in Paris' colorful Montmartre quarter) bustled with the most naughty panache, Ooh-la-la fashion, and Bohemian picaresque charm. One could honeymoon there.

Only Berlin, among the great metropolises, lacked a *Strich* or Zona Rosa.

"Berlin Is Becoming a Whore"

A 1792 statute (with 24 clauses) from the time of Friedrich II gave rise to Berlin's exceptionalism in all matters sexual. In keeping with strict Prussian decorum, no brothel quarter could be legally sanctioned within the city proper. Commerce in sex was declared illegal but—according to the confusing edicts—female and male prostitution itself was to be placed "under government surveillance" (in effect, authorized). The unin-

tended consequence was whimsically clear to the inner-city inhabitants and the newly-arrived Napoleonic authorities: by default, unregulated street vice and whorehouses surfaced everywhere in city (although they were most visible in the Friedrichstadt and the areas just north of it).

Sex for hire was stated to be unlawful but, bafflingly, also technically permitted. The city administrators were of several minds in dealing with this judicial conundrum. Whoring was, through the Wilhelmian era, alternately tolerated, then banned, then yet again "placed under surveillance." No matter what was decreed, however, prostitutes and the citizenry who engaged their services always found ingenious ways to circumvent the murky codes. Only two sanctions were consistent: 1) Berlin refused to allot a legal district for the practice of harlotry—the "Mediterranean" solution, and 2) public solicitation for sex was strictly prohibited.

A relatively small number of prostitutes—around 4,000 in 1914—were granted *Kontroll*-cards, which subjected them to monthly inspections by eight vice-doctors, or *Pussy-Pressers*. This allowed the certified sex-workers to maintain their vocation on the Line

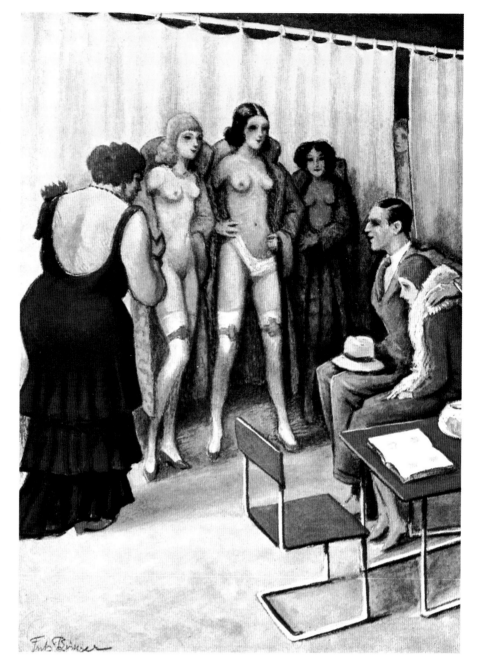

(which in Berlin was anywhere). How they were supposed to drum up business in outlying or unfamiliar quarters was solved with inimitable Berlin logic: because streetwalkers could only be arrested for verbal solicitation, an elaborate gestural and dress code quickly arose. Customers could recognize the compliant goods instantly by their characteristic packaging. In other words, whores would promote themselves by looking like whores.

Previous Left:
Minette at work, 1932

Previous Right:
A *Half-Silk*, 1926

Opposite Left:
Jeanne Mammen, *Boot-Whores*

Above:
Fritz Burger, *Off the Track*

example, advertised their services pedalogically through a semaphore-like language. Black, green, scarlet, red, and brown leather footwear promised different mise en scènes of sexual torment and debasement (i.e., green boots and gold shoelaces meant an evening of enslavement with a scatological conclusion; red-on-maroon denoted flagellation and discipline; and so forth). Naturally only devoted aficionados could decipher such specific messages with confidence. Other potential clients had to buy special primers, where Berlin's complex street semiotics were thoughtfully decoded for the uninitiated.

Topology of the Sex Trade

Altogether, there were eleven or twelve major sex zones in Berlin during the Twenties, none of them "officially" delineated, but each with distinctive attractions and an overall licentious atmosphere. The most conspicuous was called the "Alex," a ten-block slum centered around the Alexanderplatz in Berlin North. Site of the lowest-grade whores in the city (Class Three *Kontroll-Girls*, *Chontes*, and *Gravelstones*) as well as the central police station and a luxurious brothel for straight women, the Alex contained at least 320 houses of ill repute. Only a dozen or so resembled tranquil *maisons de tolérance* of the Parisian variety. The rest were essentially fuck pads, where street prostitutes serviced

The problem, unfortunately, became acute in the Weimar period when prostitute fashion was widely imitated by Berlin's more virtuous females. For instance, one historical badge of shame for *Strich*-violators, short-cropped hair, became the common emblem of the *Tauentziengirl* (a variety of Berlin streetwalker)—at least for a year or two. Then in 1923, the short pageboy coif, or *Bubikopf*, achieved universal popularity as *the* stylish cut for trendy Berlinerinnen.

Prostitutes had to change and update their provocative attire constantly in order to retain a legal means of solicitation. Dress also communicated sex practice. *Boot-Whores* near the Wittenberg Platz, for

Frische Blumen

Above:
Kontroll-Girls
on the
Friedrichstrasse,
1930

once when the madam closed in the early morning; towels and linens sometimes went unchanged for days.

Innocuous storefronts in the alleyways around the Alex and coal cellars also doubled as Transient-Quarters. One celebrated ice cream parlor on Mehnerstrasse transformed into a handjob factory precisely at ten o'clock in the evening. (A jaunty travel writer suggested that the hum from the freezers must have acted as a powerful stimulant for Berlin's hardcore cold fetishists.) The whole operation was finally busted when a local *Kontroll-Girl* complained to a sympathetic *Bull* (vice-officer) that her brood of children was spending far too much idle time at the all-night confectionery.

The Friedrichstadt beckoned with more elevated temptations. A mile-square downtown precinct, compromised of federal ministry buildings, "grand" hotels, state-funded museums, revue-houses, and high-rise compounds for financial and publishing conglomerates, the Friedrichstadt doubled as a tawdry Luna Park when the workday concluded. Between five o'clock tea and three in the morning, this was home to hundreds of *Nepp-Lokals*, strip clubs, gay *Dielen* (bar-lounges), massage parlors, greasy Wurst restaurants, and the Linden-

their clients. The sex was quick and cheap. In an "Hour Hotel," the John paid about one dollar for the use of the room and 35 to 75 cents for the *Kontroll-Girl*. At the 200-plus "Transient-Quarters," or mini-brothels, money (usually in the dollar range) was paid first to the *Kupplerin* (house madam) and then the *Flea* was directed into a bare room for a ten-minute transaction. Hygiene levels were notoriously un-Germanic. The wash basins in a typical Quarter were emptied only

Passage, a dilapidated arcade lane where two to three hundred *Doll-Boys* (underage boy prostitutes) posed before hesitant *Sugar-Lickers* (gay pederasts). Hard-faced *Minettes* applied their psychodramatic skills in top-floor rooms of pensions and tourist hotels.

The Tiergarten, Berlin's dimly-lighted park preserve at the city core, attracted young freelance *Line-Boys* and *Grasshoppers* (female specialists in BJs), who congregated in groups near the park's edge after dark. South of the Tiergarten peered fashionable Berlin West and its elegant midway, the Kurfürstendamm (or the Kudamm). At this nexus of expensive nightclubs, pleasure palaces, lesbian cafés, transvestite cabarets, and American-style bars, high-end call girls, or *Fohses*, by the dozens, positioned themselves between the free-standing display cases set in front of glitzy Kudamm boutiques. ("Shiny merchandise by shiny merchandise" one guidebook ballyhooed.) *Half-Silks* (amateur prostitutes) and *Boot-Whores* respectfully staked out their claims slightly eastward, in the esplanades and street corners by the Kaiser-Wilhelm Memorial Church. Fancy whorehouses and sham fronts for underage sex were tucked away in the quiet neighborhoods abetting the Potsdamer Platz.

The Nolldendorfplatz, an out-of-the-way section in Berlin's proletarian South, featured Erwin Piscator's Communist theatre as its best-known night-time draw. One could also find a surfeit of cocaine and S&M clubs just to the south of Walter Gropius' temple of Red art. Another six blocks further south and east was the clandestine land of black-curtained homosexual lounges and *Racehorse* salons for the delectation of straight sadists.

Above:
Kontroll-Girl

On the Line

Kontroll-Girls crowded Berlin's streetcorners in flush times and bad. They formed the nucleus of the 30,000 round-the-clock itinerant whores. By 1930, nearly 9,000 possessed Kontroll-Books that testified to their fine venereal health. (The others had allowed their medical papers to lapse or ignored the *Pussy-Pressers* altogether.) The *Bulls* categorized the K-Girls into three grades based on appearance, age, and number of clients per day.

The lowest (or Class Three) were known on the street as *Bone Shakers*. Older and most experienced than the others, they looked down upon the undocumented *Grasshoppers* (or *Fresh-Air Girls*), who performed similar duties under the inviting skies of the Tiergarten. Class Two included *Tauentziengirls*, a vivacious streetwalker type, found on the Tauentzienstrasse and characterized by their flapper-style wardrobe and bathing cap-like hats. Curt Moreck, a *Sittengeschichte* chronicler, compared them to swamp lilies and praised them as "an iridescent, demonic perversity." Because of their fresh attitude (*Berliner Schnauze*) and frequent pairing with identically dressed daughters, journalists enjoyed quoting their droll responses to otherwise complex, current-event issues and national trends.

Boot-Whores, although relatively few in number (300 or 350), provided Berlin nightlife with its most ubiquitous local color. Arriving in Berlin during the Inflation, Klaus Mann remembered walking past a group of the outdoor dominatrices, "Some of them looked like fierce Amazons, strutting in high boots made of green, glossy leather. One of them brandished a supple cane and leered at me as I passed by. 'Good evening, Madam,' I said. She whispered into my ear, 'Want to be my slave? Costs only six billions and a cigarette. A bargain. Come along, honey!'" Eight years after Mann's encounter, Moreck reported on the same corner: "One favorite tourist site is located near the Passauer and Ansbacher streetcorners, west of Wittenberg Platz. There, a trio of six-foot tall *Boot-Girls* are garishly cos-

Above:
Tauentziengirl team

tumed in red and black attire like nineteenth-century horsewomen. Snapping a riding crop, the tallest Amazon bellows menacingly, 'Who will be my slave tonight?'"

First-Class *Joy-Girls* were generally the youngest and most desirable of the K-Girl bunch but they faced enormous competition from yet another unique Berlin erotic phenomenon, *Half-Silks*. Mostly fresh-faced secretaries, minor government clerks, department-store

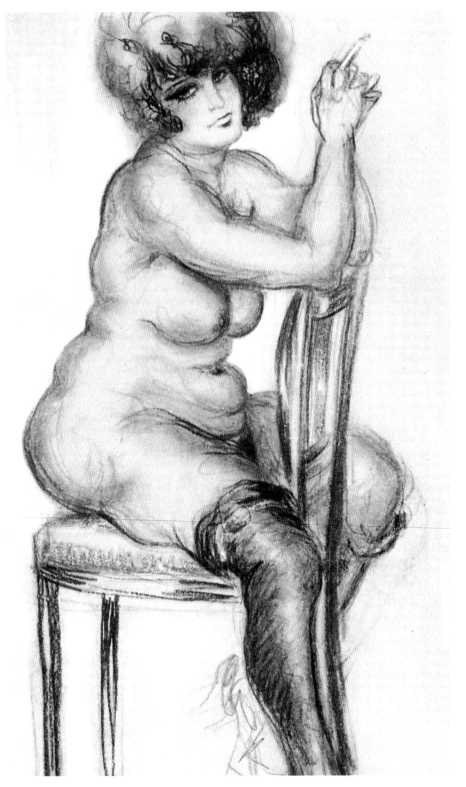

apparel) and, in summer months, teddy bears. It was said that the majority engaged in serious prostitution only during the last third of the month or in the difficult period just before payday.

Nuttes was a term used to describe very young, kittenish flappers. Sometimes it referred to teenaged *Joy-Girls* or coltish *Half-Silks*. Most Berlin sexologists viewed *Nuttes* as a separate prostitute type. Physically they resembled androgynous boys with short hair, flat chests, and long legs, accentuated by extremely short skirts, lustrous silk hosiery, and high heels. Usually rebellious teens from bourgeois families, the *Nuttes*, through their flirtatious demeanor and playful manners, inhabited an enticing middle ground between the brash *Kontroll*-Girls and often fickle *Half-Silks*. A successful Berlin *Alphonse* (pimp) liked to have a handful of Class 3s and one or two *Nuttes* in his intimate stable.

Indoor Varieties

From Renaissance times, Gypsies and Jews were closely identified with white slavery in Central Europe. By 1920, their participation was largely vestigial in Germany. Romany culture became submerged in gooey

employees, and salesgirls by day, these amateur hookers roamed Berlin West by the tens of thousands in the early evening. They were easily recognized by their girlish makeup and unusual accoutrements, like large cloth handbags (where they secreted their daytime

Above:
Posed
photograph
of a *Münzi*

Viennese, Hungarian, Parisian, and Spanish renditions. Gypsies themselves disappeared from German urban life although they were the theme of a vast, mostly invented, erotic literature.

Weimar Berlin had a large Jewish population (around 9% if one includes *Ostjuden* [immigrants from Eastern countries] and thoroughly assimilated/converted/hidden Jews). While they dominated certain cultural fields in pre-Nazi Berlin, especially publishing, law, medicine, theatre, graphic art, cinema, music, architecture, and popular entertainment, relatively few Jews were still involved in common prostitution with the exception of two picturesque types: *Kupplerinnen* (procuresses) and *Chontes*—zaftig whores from southern Poland. In general, *Chonte-Harbors* (Jewish brothels) were not well regarded in Berlin's sex guides but they appeared to attract a sizable working-class and indigenous clientele.

The other varieties of indoor Berlin prostitutes were substantially higher-brow. *Fohses* frequently made their initial contacts in public gatherings, negotiating prices and scenes, but were never considered streetwalkers since their work fell under the (even then) comic rubric of "Massage Therapists." Upscale *Demi-Castors* were

41

Above:
Albert Birkle,
Fohses

peans, captured this Weimar excess best in his farcical recollection of the Alex:

I saw pimps offering anything to anybody, little boys, little girls, robust young men, libidinous women, or (I suppose) animals. (The story went around that a male goose of which one cut the neck at the ecstatic moment would give you the most delicious, economical, and time-saving frisson of all, as it allowed you to enjoy sodomy, bestiality, homosexuality, necrophilia, and sadism at one stroke. Gastronomy too, as one could eat the goose afterward.)

Actually, in Berlin North, *Alphonses* and independent whores organized their perverse attractions in the manner of market-day vendors: like-with-like. Mehnerstrasse (site of the ice cream/masturbation shop) was known as "Old *Mädchen* Street." For those with an itch for mature K-Girls (40- to 60-year-olds but looking considerably older) or a sympathetic motherly touch, there were three infamous Transient-Quarters and a few storefront chambers of the same. On Landwehrstrasse were only beautiful stout *Beinls*. Weighting an average of 220 pounds, these gorgeous street creatures in groups of three and four provided ideal subject matter

essentially the picky *Half-Silks* of the closed-door brothel set. And *Table-Ladies* (Berlin Geishas) applied their exclusive trade in snooty nightclub backrooms and at bachelor pads.

Acquired Tastes

Sophisticated het tourists came to Berlin for erotic "specialties." Luigi Barzini's social memoir, *The Euro-*

for smirking painters of the *Neue Sachlichkeit* ilk.

Other corners near the Alex (like the faraway Tauentzienstrasse) were talking grounds for mother-and-daughter crews. In Berlin North, however, the age difference between the parent and child was striking and even exaggerated. The amusing twin-sister look of the T-Girls faded on Gollnowstrasse into a dark incestuous fantasy. One French journalist, Jean Galtier-Boissiere, described, in sickly pornographic detail, the creeping horror of feeling a nine-year-old's tiny, but proficient, fingers stroking his upper thigh while her broken-toothed mother covered with his face with hot sucking kisses.

Two street types were deemed important enough to be granted a separate nomenclature: *Gravelstones* and *Münzis*. Like Berlin's war-wounded, the *Gravelstones* had their own hideous allure. Outcast prostitutes with grim deformities—acid-scarred faces, hunchbacks, crippled or missing limbs, disfiguring skin conditions—they created their own informal society on Oranienburgstrasse in Berlin North. By the late Twenties, the *Gravelstones* came into their own; men in chauffeured limousines appeared with some frequency to chat with them and if their malformation proved compelling and unusual enough, an all-night arrangement was gamely struck.

Münzis were knocked-up streetwalkers who advertised their condition on Münzstrasse, about seven blocks from *Gravelstone* territory. Conscious of their temporal appeal, the *Münzis* charged triple rates for sessions and organized themselves on the "Münz" ("Coin") according to their stage of pregnancy. Like the *Boot-Whores*, the *Münzis* became a much in-demand tourist sight.

S&M prostitutes publicized their presence in trade newspapers and hotel flyers. *Dominas* were to be found in "Body Culture" clinics and sometimes approached randy foreign couples in lesbian and transvestite nightclubs. More discreet were the *Racehorses*,

Child Prostitution

Child prostitution was a searing social issue long before and after the Inflation era. It involved both female and male children, sex-workers' progeny, runaways, and troublesome adolescents. There seemed to be almost no bottom age for those seeking physical companionship with children. And virtually no end to willing girls and boys.

One unsettling example: In January 1932, a Berlin tabloid exposed a "prostitute ring" of ten-year-old girls who worked independently at the Alex U-Bahn Station. Each girl stood demurely inside a subway entrance foyer, hoping to catch the eye of an impulsive *Cavalier* (heterosexual pederast) on his way to work. Astonishingly, the prepubescent vixens had been whoring unimpeded for months before the story broke.

Of course, all major cities had to confront this pressing and psychologically debilitating civic problem, particularly during hard times. But in Berlin the quandary of kiddy-prostitution was partly resolved by a more cynical, free-market approach: the opening of child brothels.

How many children were actually pressed into sexual service/slavery is unknown. Magnus Hirschfeld reported on one such lucrative operation on Alexandrienstrasse, where a "rapacious harem" of 14-year-old Russian girls "lewdly beguiled" wealthy *Cavaliers* from

young masochistic prostitutes, who were billed as "teachers" at "Institutes for Foreign Language Instruction" or "masseuses" in Berlin South "Beauty Salons." *Minettes*, unlike their French namesakes, enacted standard domination and fetish scenarios (i.e., angry boarding-school mistress; new secretary; enraged customer; Madga Lupesco and King Carol; best friend's mother; industrial spy; blackmailing student; boss' sadistic daughter; old girlfriend) for hefty fees in fashionable hotel suites.

Berlin's industrial elite. The house was, remarkably, shut down by the municipal court after a sensational trial shrouded in political intrigue and late-night government machinations.

Other child dens of iniquity sidestepped the *Bulls* through a ruse of codewords and cheesy disguises. On Bülowbogen in Berlin West, a pederast could enter a storefront "Pharmacy," where he would be asked to enumerate the exact years he suffered from some malady—although the nature of the illness was always left unnamed. The answer had to be in the 12-to-16 range since it signified the age of the child-prostitute he was requesting. The attending "physician" (who had a diploma in hairdressing on the wall) then responded by searching the back cubicles for the properly aged *Medicine*, which was dispensed in hourly "tablets" of

purchase the services of the "child-star," who was whisked in a waiting motor vehicle to his domicile. What would appear to be a rather singular perversion among the Berlin's high society was in fact a favored divertissement. Theatricality, pederasty, star-fucking, and technology all meshed in ways that would have likely startled the wizened flesh-peddlers of Nineveh and Shanghai.

Kietz

The *Kietz*, or underworld life of the Berlin prostitute, was presented in countless ways during the Weimar era. Songs, revues, film melodramas, *faits divers* all doted on the loony spectacle. Police reports and tabloids emphasized the *Kietz'* ugly and dangerous nature. Religious leaders and health officials warned of its spiritual and physical repercussions. And graphic artists naturally recorded the *Kietz'* ironic juxtapositions as a telling panorama on human mendacity and deceit.

Like other workers in debased professions, the people who inhabited the *Kietz* saw it differently. They felt nothing but contempt for outsiders (except for the *Bulls*, who normally treated them with good-natured respect). Most prostitutes claimed their lives were infi-

"blonde, brown, brunette, or Gypsy-black."

More popular (and far more profitable) was the trade in *Telephone-Girls*. Attractive 12-year-old girls and young teens were made up and dressed to resemble adult female celebrities—typically Lya da Putti, Marlene Dietrich, Dolly Haas, or Lilian Harvey. Lonely *Cavaliers* telephoned one of six or seven agencies to

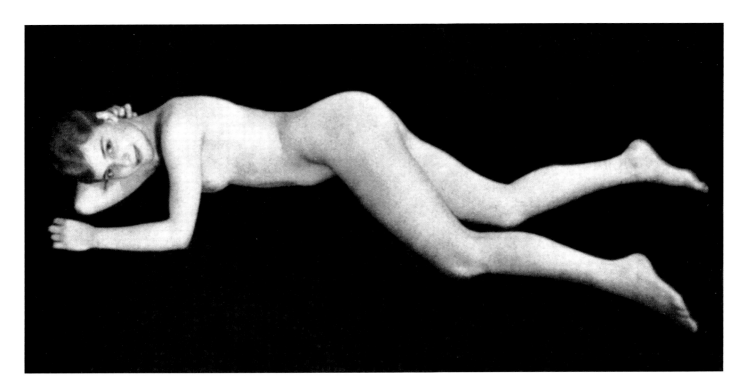

nitely more liberated and interesting than those of their *lumpenprol* sisters. The *Kietz* had its own system of justice, language, familial relationships, annual

customs, sources of satisfaction, entertainments, taboos, and codes of honor. For four years, it even produced its own weekly newspaper, *Der Pranger* ("The Pillory").

And while public servants ranted about infectious venereal disease, for instance, the average *Kupplerin* could cite statistics from League of Nations studies that found Berlin to have rather low rates of syphilis and gonorrhea, compared to, say, London and Paris. "Big and Little Jelly" were occupational hazards but so was mangling a hand in a stamp-press or daydreaming while brushing down a wheat-thresher.

Life in Weimar Berlin could be unpredictable and very unpleasant, but real street violence—a sure cata-lyst for inner-city anxiety and dread—was exceedingly rare, at least until the political situation outside the *Kietz* began to sour. ■

**Opposite
and Above:**
Telephone-Girls

Left:
A *Domina*

Berlin nightlife, my word, the world hasn't seen anything like it! We use to have a first-class army; now we have first class perversions.

Klaus Mann, *The Turning Point,* **1942**

Everyone Once in Berlin!

City of Berlin Tourist Slogan, 1927

GIRL-CULTURE AND THE ALL-NIGHT BUMMEL

Berlin glorified in its image as Europe's showcase of sin. Its own police commissioners often boasted that vice and debauchery were the city's prime industries. (Actually manufacturing, finance, and publishing produced more revenue.) But over 150,000 Berliners made their living in the *Kietz* or were employed in related businesses, notably *Nachtlokals*, seedy hotels, pornographic studios and cinemas, unlicensed casinos and bars, naked boxing and wrestling arenas, private torture dungeons, and like-minded flimflam operations.

On any given weekend in Berlin, six to seven hundred emporiums promised nonpareil sexual pleasures and sights—indulgences unknown even to the orgy-seeking miscreants of ancient Rome and Asia. In each nighttime establishment there was a conspicuous effort to appeal to a specific and novel perversion or erotic taste. Lesbians alone in 1930 could select from 85 same-sex *Dielen*, risqué night-

clubs, and dancehalls. Some of these private concerns barred straights and gay men outright, others welcomed them, and still others restricted their female clientele to circumscribed types or tribadic couplings.

The carnal advantages of class and wealth intensified in Sodom, although they appeared at times to be replaced by more fluid categories of dress, bodily appearance, age, and sexual disposition. Even the standard categories of desire—male/female; gay/straight; normal/abnormal; latent/public—were shaken in such fundamental ways that they astonish even now.

Hidden away in Berlin East, for instance, was a tiny

honky-tonk, the "Monte Casino," where working-class husbands partook in boy sex. While their understanding, prole wives sipped beer and applauded the transvestite revue, the otherwise straight men quietly excused themselves and tramped back to the greenroom cubicles. There they negotiated oral sex with the sweaty, bewigged kid performers. A few Reichsmarks lighter, the lusty stevedores eventually retired to the dining tables of their ever-patient mates. Life was truly a cabaret then.

French journalists, in particular, were impressed by the diverse throngs of harlots and exotic *Strich* trade that the German Gotham featured. But their Descartesian minds boggled at the sporting menu of bizarre classifications and typologies that substituted for natural local color. In the thinking of these fun-loving Frenchmen, wicked Berlin was overly determined and taxonomical, devoid of romantic camouflage, leeringly ironic, intentionally perverse, and far too Germanic. The ancient human exchange between money, sex, and psychic fulfillment had never been so complicated, they claimed; it required a new calculus.

Fortunately there were books for the uninformed. Directories of nocturnal Berlin (in adventurous straight, S&M, gay, lesbian, or nudist versions) could be had at any train station, hotel lobby, or downtown kiosk. Foreigners and provincials alike could plot out, with a thumb-flip, where or where not they were wanted, calculate what to expect and spend, and fantasize how their dream *Bummel* or session might unfold. These lurid Baedekers of the night were indispensable pilots for lost souls.

"Girl-Culture"

Not every Berliner—or tourist—was swept away in the Weimar sex-rush. But the aggregate who participated in some commercial aspect of the *Kietz*,

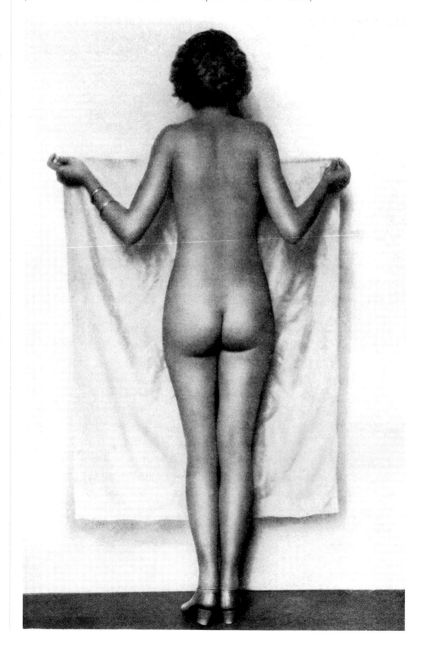

Poisonous fumes or no, the *Sittengeschichten* scholars of the time understood how the whore milieu permeated workaday Berlin. Advertising, music, mass-market periodicals, clothing styles, stage interpretations of Shakespeare and Schiller, high literature, dining arrangements in restaurants, and election propaganda were all indelibly stamped with this new image of female sexuality and the independent woman. In the mid-Twenties, it acquired a name: *Girlkultur*.

An abiding brainstorm of Flo Ziegfeld, the eponymous American producer, "Girl-Culture" redefined the psychology and bodily form of the desirable female. In

especially during the Inflation or the approaching depression, was extraordinarily high. Probably 20 to 25 percent of adult Berlin dabbled in the midnight amusements in the year before Hitler was anointed Reichschancellor. While newcomers thought the erotic madness was, more or less, a function of the uncertain economic times, Berliners themselves jokingly blamed it on their amphetamine-like air (that *Berliner Luft*), which many swore kept their hearts racing at night and then thoroughly revitalized them for the morning commute.

heavily-promoted publicity campaigns and on the stage of his New York Follies, Ziegfeld advanced and constantly reshaped this modern fantasy creature. She was urbane, slim, not much interested in children, socially irreverent, leggy, charmingly vain, and a sexual predator. The Ziegfeld Girl had all the basic physical attractions of the Parisian Flirt, but her gold-digging motivations were refreshingly undisguised and externalized.

The American Flapper persona fit snugly into the unsentimental machine-age *Zeitgeist*. It universalized femme-fatalism. Sex appeal was no longer a mysterious inborn construct but a purchasable commodity, available to the entire female-of-the-species. And seduction could be played out for better rewards than bourgeois marriage—and far longer—when its ultimate goals were money (or diamonds, gold jewelry, furs, penthouses) and emotional dominance.

Berliners, far more than Manhattanites, adapted Ziegfeld's provocative concept to their mentality and lifestyle. It glamorized and extended the war between the sexes. Women and men each possessed something the other passionately desired in the big-city tango. In fact, Berlin's professional *Beinls* were often looked upon as the heartfelt, unadorned subset of the New Woman.

The dazzling sex cards they held were short-lived and not a danger to the gender status quo. The roles of good and bad women in Weimar had become reversed. Any *Bubikopfed* teen was a potential Lulu, or *Nutte*.

Girl-Culture also referred to the precision chorus line, which Ziegfeld's choreographers contrived from a blend of French Can-Can and the American fascination with Taylorist motion economy. Stunning Girl-Groups from Anglo-Saxon countries demonstrated synchronized kick displays that beat the hell out of the prewar *Tangel-Tingel* leg shows. Each angelic dancer, the identical duplicate of the other, resembled an interchangeable machine part or a blank-faced soldier in a Prussian army drill. Here, the New Woman was automated, made trainable, streamlined, remolded into a robotic

doll. Both aspects of Girl-Culture—the Demonic Sex Object and the Rationalized Sex Object—enthralled and animated Berlin.

The pairing or struggle between these modern archetypes largely replaced the old brunette/blonde conflict inside Berlin's venerable theatre prosceniums. Male characters in sex farces and jazzy operettas no longer had to deal with the classic dilemma, the penis versus the heart. The ingenues-in-question were each

beddable hellcats. Which succubi to wed or follow to Paris became the novel contentious denouement.

In Fritz Lang's epic film, *Metropolis* (1927), where Berlin's social and cultural conflicts were projected into a science-fantasy future, the theme of Girl-Culture was handled with recondite humor and a hokey melodramatic touch. One year later, Brecht and Weill bested the movie with their avant-garde musical, *The Three-Penny Opera.* By adding cynical dollops of *Berliner Schnauze* and restituating the Berliner erotic typology to Victorian London, the unlikely modernists perfected the titillating master narrative. Virtually the entire Berlin press corps hailed the brilliant rendering. The Marxist poet Brecht insisted, in his contrarian manner, that the play was a comic, left-wing indictment of capitalism, but the critics knew better. *Three-Penny* was Girl-Culture in song.

What *Berlinerinnen* felt about Girl-Culture is a contentious subject for feminist scholars. Interviews (that I conducted) with women who were teenagers and 20-year-olds in Weimar Berlin and a perusal of popular women's magazines of the period indicate a high degree of personal satisfaction. Suddenly females from Wilhelmian families were accorded social and carnal opportunities that made them the envy of their older sisters. One woman called Girl-Culture sexual suffrage. Female novelists and Berlin's feminists, as was their wont, were considerably more critical of the invented revolution.

Cabaret

Cabaret was, of course, the signature entertainment form of Weimar Berlin. Born in the backhalls and miniature variety-houses of fin-de-siècle Montmartre and Vienna, the cabaret melded lowly amusement genres to Bohemian sensibilities, in the service of a middle-class audience on the slum. In Berlin, the "tenth muse" unraveled, returning to its maverick roots: the brothel and concert-café.

Of the 150 Berlin commercial outlets that advertised cabaret revues, only a dozen or so were traditional

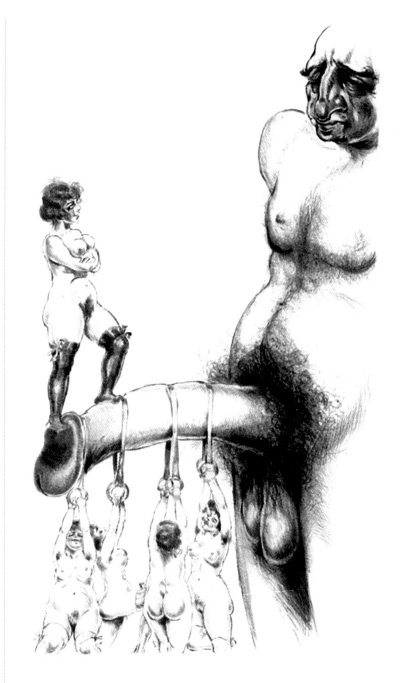

cabarets in the Parisian mode: shows with alternating acts of musical comedy, poetry reading, topical monologues, torch songs, sleight-of-hand routines, dramatic sketches, and the like. In a sense, these were hip Music-Halls presented within an intimate restaurant setting. The evening's mood in these houses shifted expeditiously, from laughter to tears to awe to artistic appreciation and finally back to laughter, with each succeeding act. In the standard Jägerstrasse *Kabarett*,

Above:
Max Liebermann,
Erotic Grotesques,
1920

55

CELLY DE RHEIDT
DANCE TROUPE
IN A TYPICAL EVENING: (1923)

Harry Seveloh, the husband of the lead dancer, delivers a short introduction to the program. He enthuses that Berlin high society has now grown mature enough to enjoy the sights of naked female performers without lewd, sensual stimulation. The spectator's appreciation of the girls' exposed beauty should be of a purely intellectual or aesthetic nature.

Scattered applause from the mature audience. The curtain is drawn, exposing a tiny stage.

however, there were only two moods: the bitterly sardonic and the heart-thumpingly erotic.

Oddly enough, Kander and Ebb got this part right. The literary and political cabarets, because of their high artistic content and celebrity casting, received substantial print coverage, which survived (in bits and drabs) to be analyzed and deconstructed by post-World War II historians. The more popular erotic cabarets hardly merited notice, except in the downtrodden *Galante* monthlies.

One sensational production mounted at the Black Cat Cabaret, "The Dance of Beauty," achieved widespread notoriety due to its novelty during the Inflation and the legal problems that dogged its creators. Described in remarkable detail by Hirschfeld, Paul Markus ("PEM"), and several Berlin newspaper reporters, the performance revealed a relatively early attempt to stitch the naughty cabaret impulse to the protective frame of *Ausdruckstanz* (Expression Dance).

Celly De Rheidt's brazen troupe was forced to disband shortly after this engagement. Her entrepreneurial husband, Seveloh, a former army lieutenant, was penalized 1500 Inflation marks, which he managed to delay paying until the following summer when the fine's actual dollar value approached a near-zero decimal. Celly divorced him, remarried in Vienna, and settled down to be an upstanding Hausfrau, never to heard from again.

Opposite:
Rudolf Koppitz,
1925

Below:
Scene from the
Haller-Revue

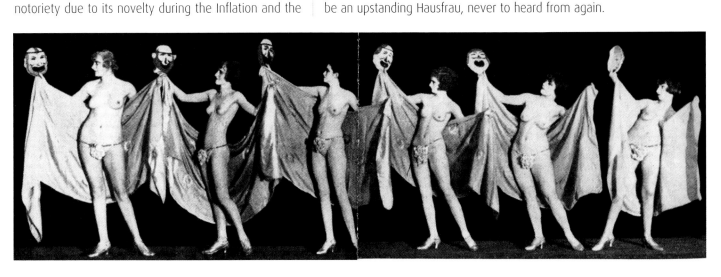

Gypsy violin music slowly ushers in a line of female artistes.

A waltz, danced by Celly de Rheidt and her ballet group, wearing short transparent dance-dresses, commences. A violet light illuminates them as they float across the dance floor, slowly in the beginning, then in a furious pace. Their bodies freeze, silhouetted against the background of the closing curtain.

A short violin interlude. Again the Girls appear and dance a wild bacchanal under a reddish-purple light. They wear transparent dance-dresses that expose one breast. The wild twirls are followed by a brightly illuminated dance scene: a spring serenade with the music of Lecombe, performed by Celly and a young attractive dancer. Each wears a short, fluttering chiffon skirt below a nude torso. The girl suddenly collapses. She is startled out of her dream state and begins to leap rapturously in a flower movement. Her body sways outward, as she lifts her breasts to the warm, life-giving sun.

The stage darkens as a circle of barefoot girls in peasant dresses rush forward to execute a vibrant Hungarian folk dance.

An erotic pantomime, the "Opium Slumber," ensues in quick succession. It begins with the shadow of a Chinaman smoking wanly on an opium pipe. After a few minutes, an evil femme fatale appears and seductively enslaves him to be a victim for her mélange of sadistically lewd games. The club spectators watch this with a special intensity.

This is followed by a carnal "Bullfight," performed to the clicking of castanets. Celly, the female matador, disrobes with exquisite deliberation and uses her diaphanous garb to sexually torment and subjugate the hapless beast. The dance concludes with the defeated bull lying supine next to the high heels of the triumphant—and now naked—matador.

After the Black Cat affair, naturally, no Berlin cabaret was stupid enough to flaunt its fleshy wares as high art in the face of the authorities or, if it did, forget to compensate the local *Polenta* for their impeccable critical faculties.

Foreign tourist guides, true to their calling, championed the *Kabarettwelt*'s indecent rep. Jägerstrasse, the home to 14 or 15 *Nachtlokals*, was publicized as Berlin's hothouse citadel of forbidden sights. Yet, around 1927, a natural downturn occurred. The dark hedonism of the erotic cabaret could be explored in other, more comfortable and accessible surroundings: in ritzy dinner clubs, private *Dielen*, a few showy restaurants, the "Pleasure-Palaces," even on an evening's *Bummel* of the Kudamm.

Most "Golden Age" Berliners patronized the non-literary cabarets for their ineffable atmospheres, the cynical mood (*Berliner Stimmung*) that enveloped the stale, smoky air, and only occasionally for the overpriced intoxicants and nude tableaux. Usually, the cabaret conférenciers, or Masters of Ceremonies, were the chief draw. These tuxedoed wits did not exist anywhere else.

While Friedrichstadt *Lokal* producers experimented with endless sexual and thematic innovations, one outlandish idea succeeded. A malicious conférencier, Erwin Lowinsky, known in the trade as "Elow," rented the for-

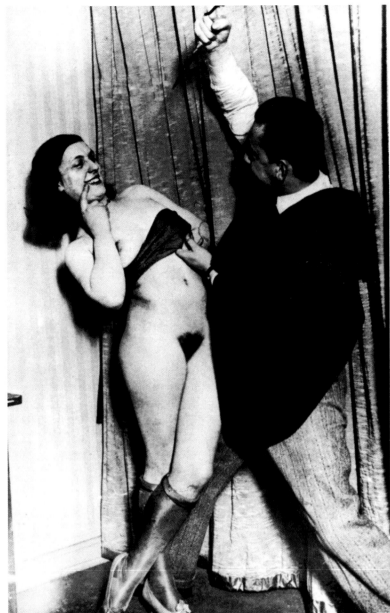

mer *Weisse Maus* cabaret on Jägerstrasse from its new lesbian owners. Running only on Café Monbijou's dark night, Monday, Elow called his enterprise the "Cabaret of the Nameless." Instead of hiring professional entertainers, Elow did just the opposite; his stage was open only to amateur performers, 15 per evening.

Elow chose for his off-night cabaret the most thoroughly talentless types he could possibly find, including—for the greater delight of his demented public—utterly delusional and rapturous sickies. Berlin intellec-

Opposite:
Poster for the Celly de Rheidt *Ballet Beauty Dances*

Above:
Comic "Jack the Ripper" scene in a cabaret, 1926

59

The menacing cadence of an Inca sacrificial ceremony is pounded out by the orchestra. On a mountain plateau, a bevy of pearl-necklaced, naked virgins are forced to participate in the ritual murder of their sisters and then given drugs by a High Priest so they may delight in erotic worship with the nubile corpses.

Finally, a fully orchestrated Spanish mystery play, based on Calderon's *The Nun*, is enacted. A cello solo establishes the somber mood. Then a procession of nuns and monks, led by a bishop, moves through the audience to the stage, which is arranged like the interior of a church and lit in dark purple columns. The procession is accompanied by the sound of harpsichord, violins, and the cello. A trembling young Sister, played by the histrionic Celly, is brought before the altar of the inquisitorial court. The Father declares her unchaste, worthless. Despite her mad pleas, the errant "Daughter of Christ" is mercilessly expelled from her Order. Before a statute of Mary, the distraught teenager rips off her habit and begs for divine intervention. The Holy Virgin magically steps forth, passionately kisses the Nun, fondles each of her breasts with a slow, icy touch, and then presents the Sister with a silver crucifix—all before the eyes of a stunned clergy. Lights out!

tuals compared the milieu of the Nameless to the Roman Coliseum where Christians were savagely martyred, to neighborhood bullfighting rings in Mexico City, and to the execution of criminals by guillotine on Paris' sidestreets.

The majority of Elow's nonprofessionals were cajoled into believing that their appearance would hurl them into cabaret stardom. Generally, they were Berlin's losers: Gogol-like office clerks who believed that their true calling was comic recitation or juggling; frustrated housewives who once trained in Bayreuth; incompetent teenage magicians; tin-eared composer-and-lyricist teams; hypnotists who were banned from the variety circuit because of their chronic inability to bring their volunteer subjects out of deep trance; mad

ber. (A few really schizophrenic or severely incapacitated performers were told by an effusive
Elow that their painfully conceived routine was so
absolutely smashing that they should restart the
whole thing.)

The toxic *Stimmung* at the Nameless was further enhanced by Elow's abusive taunts directed at
the hard-drinking spectators, who often responded
with hearty anti-Semitic invective. The Cabaret of
the Nameless played to full houses almost into the
Nazi period. Elow, the peripatetic imp, ended up in
Hollywood, where he vanished into American
show-biz obscurity, leaving behind just an archive
of his Berlin press clippings.

Opposite:
James-Klein
Revue,
*The World
Unveiled,*
1924

Left:
"Indian Goddess"
in revue sketch

Below:
Grit and Ina
van Elben's
dancing-machine
at the Tingel-
Tangel, 1931

Napoleonic-posturing poets; and psychologically impaired dilettantes who assumed
their renditions and imitations of Winter-
garten headliners were superior to the
originals.

At the low point in each act—and
Berlin's journalists reported many such
moments—Elow jumped on the stage and
mockingly polled the audience whether or
not to allow the "artiste" to continue. Only
the most pathetic and hopeless creatures
were encouraged to complete their num-

extravagant choreographic and musical displays. In the revue, however, an underlying aesthetic and dramatic thesis held the evening together. A single team of creators assembled and molded the production. Foreign dance troupes or renowned starlets could be dropped into the show at any time, but their independent routines had to further the revue's "plot."

Although conceived in Paris and New York, the erotic revue blossomed in sensation-hungry Berlin. It was mammoth, hectically paced, thoroughly cosmopolitan, and oozed Girl-Culture sex. Berliners flocked to the revue-palaces, bought the Tin Pan Alleyish recordings, marveled at the chorus girls' legs (which became iconic images in

Right:
The Tiller Girls

The Erotic Revue

In the mid-Twenties, erotic revue, another Ziegfeld invention, supplanted cabaret as Berlin's stylish Jazz Age destination. It combined the lavish features of operetta and Music Hall in the old cabaret format. Like the variety show, its principal competitor, the program of the revue unfolded in episodic set pieces. Olio acts followed spectacle numbers; comic interludes punctuated the space between

the pictorial monthlies). Revues were a testament to Berlin sophistication—what other city had its own *Gesamt-kunstwerk* erotica? But the revue structure also spoke, in a subterranean way, to the Germanic need to control desire through objectification and derision.

Each of the eight major revue-theatres had its own distinct appeal and style of presentation. One was noted for its exquisite dance numbers and kaleidoscopic scenery; one hired better composers and *Schnauzer* lyricists; another veered to the experimental or hot topical issues; still another was famed for using only glamorous Girl-Groups from aboard. But no revue-producer was more detested by his colleagues or more beloved by the voyeuristic public than James Klein, who excelled in mounting season after season of hit shows blanketed with excessive amounts of gratuitous female nudity.

A typical James Klein Revue began with a simple dramatic premise: an obese Oriental prince learns that he will be disinherited in five years if he does not marry and produce male heirs. (Big naked harem number.) The chubby, disgruntled simp immediately enlists his lackey Cohen (incidentally all the revue directors were Jewish) to find the finest specimen of raw feminine beauty on the entire planet. Cohen then subcontracts the onerous task to two Berlin playboys, who obediently traverse the world's fleshpots in order to win the million (post-inflationary) mark reward. Their journey takes them to every

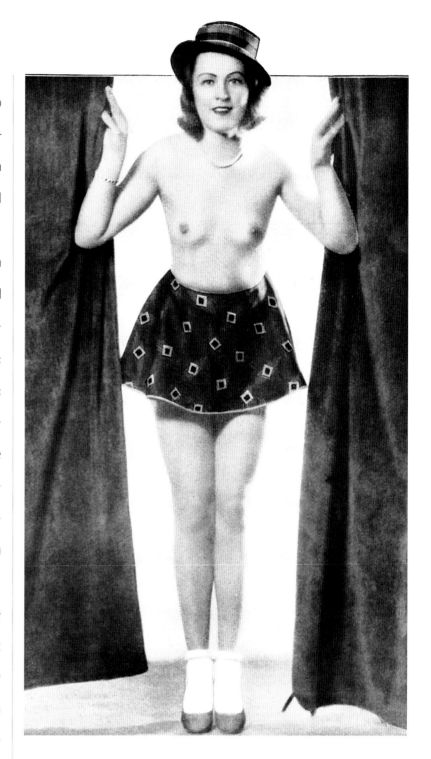

continent, although the nude aboriginals are always milky-white and look suspiciously French, with stopovers in Berlin's *Kietz* and a heavenly apparition of 74 perky, rouged breasts. (Count 'em!)

The 1929 depression brought down the curtains on Klein's erotic dreamscapes. His last show was titled

Above:
Scala
Revue
Girl

Above:
Futuristic
fashions
from Klein's
*Everyone
Naked*, 1927

Goddamnit! 1,000 Naked Women!, which might have been a tad ambitious. Klein remained in Berlin in the Thirties, contented that he avoided his creditors and bankruptcy proceedings. Nothing is known about his fate afterwards. It was assumed that he fell victim to the Nazi genocide.

Klein's fellow revue-directors lost their theatres as well during the economic tailspin. Yet the hard-partying denizens of Berlin were unfazed. They discovered a new venue for their pursuit of the extraordinary: environmental restaurants and Gargantuan nightclub retreats.

Theme Restaurants
and Pleasure Palaces

In 1932, the city of Berlin approved licenses for 119 "luxury-class" nightclubs, 400 bars or *Dielen*, and 20,000 restaurants. This meant Weimar Berlin had one dining establishment for every 280 residents (the ratio

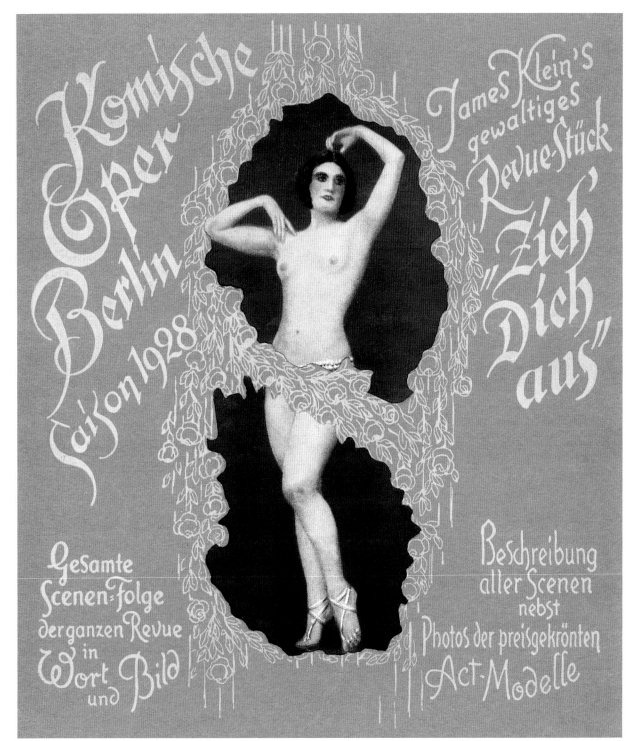

in New York City in that year was 1 to 433). For the most part, the food in Berlin was not of great interest to the non-German tourists; Paris, Vienna, and Rome satisfied that craving in spades. Instead, Berlin had dozens of "theme" and "event" restaurants. They rivaled the cabarets and revue-houses in popularity.

One unusual joint was the "Hackepeter," north of the Alex. Named after the Rheinish specialty (chopped raw pork and minced onion drizzled in hot, bubbling lard), the restaurant featured a "Hunger Artist." Encased in a sealed glass booth, Jolly sat in his underwear and chain-smoked cigarettes. Two funeral-attired "observers" alternated

LUSTIGE BLÄTTER

Nr. 40 / 42. Jahrgang / Preis 50 Pf.
Berlin, den 2. Oktober 1927

Angeschmiert

Nuttes came to the Hackepeter just to marvel at their unshaven prince-in-a-cage. (Male columnists thought he looked more like a frozen lizard than a hunk.) Among the worshipping female hordes was the young American heiress, Evelyn Rockefeller. In a lovesick plea leaked to the press, Evelyn proposed immediate marriage, a Monte Carlo honeymoon, and eventual retirement on her New York estate.

In March 1926, Jolly completed a 44-day fast, surpassing all known records. To celebrate, Lotte Schulze, the Hackepeter's owner and a war widow, invited the entire corps of city-desk editors to a sumptuous banquet of Rheinish delicacies. Jolly's observers and the midget joined in the festivities but the champion hunger artist absented himself. He was with Evelyn.

during the 24-hour proceedings, ensuring no food ever graced the hunger artist's lips. During dining hours, a midget announced the number of days and hours that Jolly fasted in his binge of voluntary starvation. Usually the Hackepeter regulars showed their appreciation by tapping against beer steins with their greasy utensils.

Besides being an object of carnival-like fascination, Jolly was also considered a romantic idol. Starry-eyed

At the end of the month, Jolly rejoined his place at the Hackepeter and issued a public statement, rejecting the millionairess' marital offer. Jolly maintained that he had fallen into a deep "spiritual depression" after his 44-day ordeal, which was why he foolishly agreed to the engagement in the first place. Jolly since realized that no hunger artist can both wed and be true to his calling.

The Berlin journalist Adolf Stein (**a.k.a.** Rumpel-

Above:
Jolly on display

Rockefeller dynasty's family tree (as far as I can tell) or in the New York Social Registry of the period.

The theatricalization (or eroticization) of Berlin restaurants took many peculiar forms. "Heaven and Hell" dropped the two afterlife locales side by side, like movie-sets, within a single restaurant-nightclub, supplying separate menus and styles of service. "Café Braun" masqueraded its help as world leaders and show-business personalities. The "Quick Bar" brought a bit of

stilzchen) thought Jolly changed his mind once more, years later, and followed Evelyn to her Long Island mansion. Where Jolly—and Evelyn—really wound up is unclear, since Evelyn's name does not show up in the

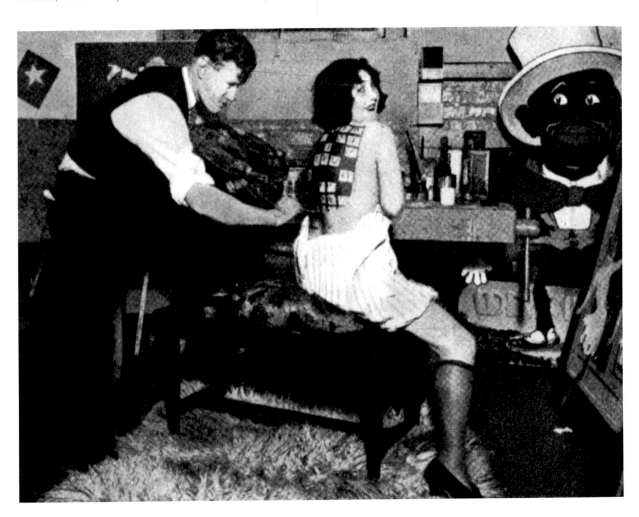

Reigen

Heft 1, 1926 – M. 1.50

Wilhelm Borngräber Verlag

The Game of Love

or

MAX, PIETZSCH, AND THE GIRL
A Game for Adults

Max, Pietzsch, and the Girl is ideal for whiling away the hours. Ideal for groups of dance partners, for flirting at health resorts, for Sunday afternoon outings, in short, for all of those moments when one would like to—but wouldn't dare say so. The players are Max, Pietzsch, and the The Girl. Success will follow. The game affords opportunity for appropriate and also inappropriate remarks. You should expect the game to last several years.

Basic Rules:
The game is played with a die. Players should choose appropriate objects to serve as game pieces. For men: collar buttons, trouser buttons, etc. For women: thimbles, small hair clips, stocking fasteners, or pralines.

Main Rules:
If a player lands on a square which is already occupied, he forms a couple with that player. Each player rolls for himself, but brings his partner along when advancing by regular rolls. When a player lands on a colored square, he alone may make an advance, and the couple separates. As usual. The author cannot prevent that, in this game, two men may also form a couple.

The first player to reach the goal receives two-thirds of the pot, and the second receives the last third. If a couple takes first place, it receives the entire sum. It is the responsibility of the man in the couple to pocket or fritter away his half, or to pass on the amount to the The Girl. Which we certainly hope he will do.

Starting the Game:
Each player pays ten items into the "Bank." (Items may include: pfennigs, thalers, kisses, chocolate cookies, cigarettes.) The Bank should be held by the Marriage Licensing Bureau. Payments and withdrawals are made at the Bank throughout the course of the game. Filching from the pot is strictly forbidden.

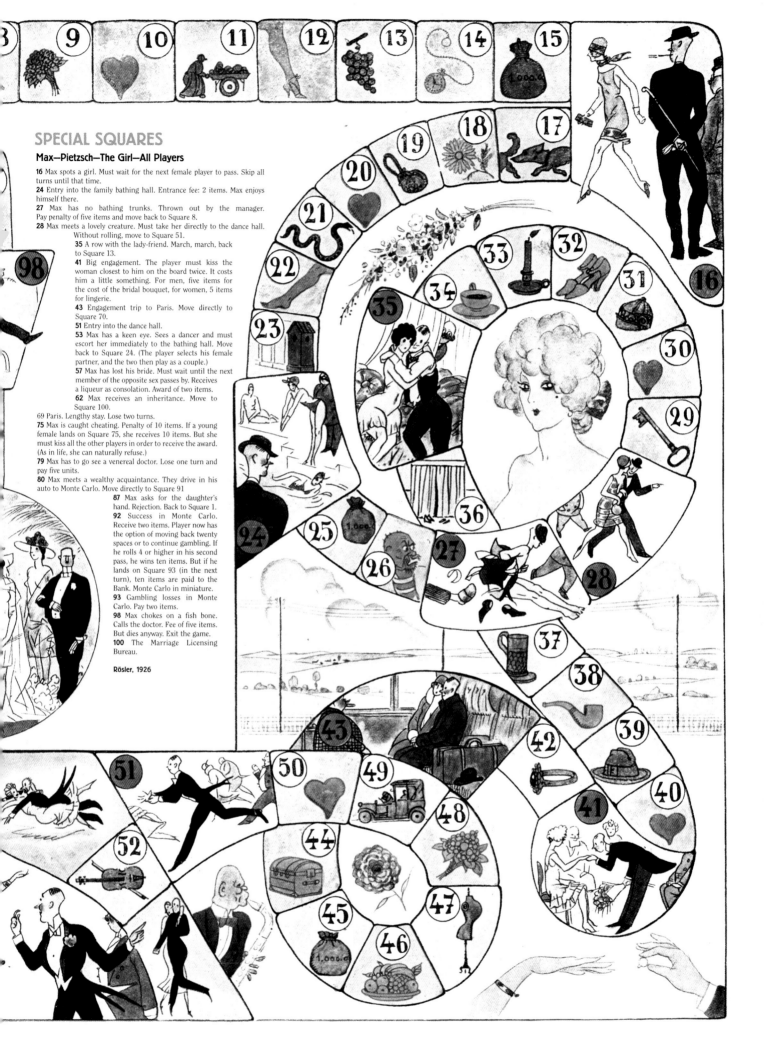

SPECIAL SQUARES

Max—Pietzsch—The Girl—All Players

16 Max spots a girl. Must wait for the next female player to pass. Skip all turns until that time.

24 Entry into the family bathing hall. Entrance fee: 2 items. Max enjoys himself there.

27 Max has no bathing trunks. Thrown out by the manager. Pay penalty of five items and move back to Square 8.

28 Max meets a lovely creature. Must take her directly to the dance hall. Without rolling, move to Square 51.

35 A row with the lady-friend. March, march, back to Square 13.

41 Big engagement. The player must kiss the woman closest to him on the board twice. It costs him a little something. For men, five items for the cost of the bridal bouquet, for women, 5 items for lingerie.

43 Engagement trip to Paris. Move directly to Square 70.

51 Entry into the dance hall.

53 Max has a keen eye. Sees a dancer and must escort her immediately to the bathing hall. Move back to Square 24. (The player selects his female partner, and the two then play as a couple.)

57 Max has lost his bride. Must wait until the next member of the opposite sex passes by. Receives a liqueur as consolation. Award of two items.

62 Max receives an inheritance. Move to Square 100.

69 Paris. Lengthy stay. Lose two turns.

75 Max is caught cheating. Penalty of 10 items. If a young female lands on Square 75, she receives 10 items. But she must kiss all the other players in order to receive the award. (As in life, she can naturally refuse.)

79 Max has to go see a venereal doctor. Lose one turn and pay five units.

80 Max meets a wealthy acquaintance. They drive in his auto to Monte Carlo. Move directly to Square 91.

87 Max asks for the daughter's hand. Rejection. Back to Square 1.

92 Success in Monte Carlo. Receive two items. Player now has the option of moving back twenty spaces or to continue gambling. If he rolls 4 or higher in his second pass, he wins ten items. But if he lands on Square 93 (in the next turn), ten items are paid to the Bank. Monte Carlo in miniature.

93 Gambling losses in Monte Carlo. Pay two items.

98 Max chokes on a fish bone. Calls the doctor. Fee of five items. But dies anyway. Exit the game.

100 The Marriage Licensing Bureau.

Rösler, 1926

exotic Americana to European shores. At its oval counter, one could order just milkshakes or Martinis from a toothy, white-capped soda-jerk. In the Quick dining hall, breathtaking beauties, incongruously dressed in Puritan-Shaker outfits, took orders for dubious Blue Plate Specials.

Theme-restaurants, nightclubs, and dance halls began to overlap in the Twenties to form the newest enclaves of Berlin's nonstop action. But among the fortresses of Girl-Culture, still anoaher modern concept was added to the glamorous melange, the department store. Instead of cabbing from *Diele* to restaurant to nightclub, one could experience everything in a single, multi-leveled building. Two of these Pleasure-Palaces became world-renowned, "Haus Vaterland" and the "Resi."

Occupying an entire city block, Haus Vaterland radiated modernism. Like a still from *Metropolis*, the domed roof of Vaterland was crowned with a Futuristic ring of neon bands. The arresting sight was said to resemble the head of a giant phallus. Inside its five floors were twelve restaurant-"environments" and a separate variety house. The Vaterland issued its own magazine, *The Berolina*, and could accommodate 6,000 patrons at any given hour.

The twelve dining arenas were devoted to international and provincial cultures—mostly fabricated—and appropriate culinary spreads. One could select from Turkish, Bavarian, Spanish, Viennese, Baden, Rheinish, Japanese, North German, Italian, Hungarian, Prussian, or American cuisines. And the amusements were site-specific too. The glittering motto of the Vaterland illuminated the Potsdamer Platz entrance, "Every Nation Under One Roof!"

Opposite:
Manassé,
*The Unconscious
in the Mirror*

Above:
Lutz Ehrenberger,
*At the Nightclub
Heaven and Hell*

The theatricalization in Haus Vaterland was extreme. For instance, in the Rhineland Wine Terrace, an artificial river flowed at the edges of a 70-foot panorama of the Rheinish countryside and a castle ruins. Stationed inside the mock fortification stood a student *a cappella* group, the "Cologne Boys." For 55 minutes of each hour, the Terrace was bathed in sweet synthetic sunshine; suddenly, on the hour, the music stopped and "the Storm on the Rhine," a five-minute environmental "event," started up. First, an ominous cloud-cover darkened the entire room—so dark that partygoers couldn't even locate the sauerkraut on their plates. Charges of simulated lightning and a huge clap of thunder resounded. Then a mechanically operated rain shower swept across the entire vine-garlanded enclosure. The "Storm" con-

cluded with a blinding sunburst from a battery of electric apparatuses and a cheery rainbow. These five minutes were said to be the best theatre in Berlin.

The Resi offered another kind of diversion. It was an interactive pickup bar-*cum*-wired nightclub. Designed in another monstrous Baroque style, Montmartre Music Hall crossed with UFA spaceship, the Resi sported several tiers of dining, dancing, and infantile play. One of its many ceilings was a motorized glass dome, painted with images of squawking birds and exotic flora. Mechanical geysers erupted with three-foot streams of sparkling, dyed water and 100 mir-

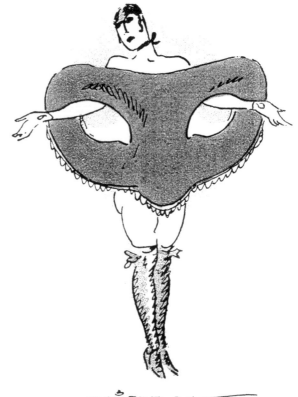

**This Page
and Opposite:**
Images of
the Resi

rored-balls continuously revolved and then split open, like welcoming orchids, when the overhead lights went down. There was a downstairs private rendezvous wine-room, competing bands and bar counters, a parquet dance floor for one thousand box-steppers, even a gigantic "Carousel and Shooting Gallery" for drunken revelers, attempting to relive adolescent Luna Park memories.

Mostly patrons came to the Resi for its promiscuous atmosphere and helpful technology. On 150 tables and 50 balcony stations, numbered telephones allowed celebrants to dial up complete strangers from across the palace and converse in naughty word-play or whisper instructions which bar to meet at. Additionally, an ingenious pneumatic system, built into the Resi handrailings, allowed guests to send small goodies to potential comrades-of-the-evening. On request, waiters brought gift-menus. Lovestruck customers selected from a list of 135 pocket-sized presents, like a bottle of perfume, cigar-cutter, or travel plan for a secret weekend (encased in leather). The luxury item was then placed in a sealed container, rocketed through hidden pneumatic tubes, and finally landed with a dramatic whoosh in a basket at the edge of the intended's table.

Resi flyers assured the nocturnal public that this was "Berlin at its most beautiful." The institution outlasted Weimar and became a favorite attraction during the 1936 Nazi Olympics. Allied bombers smothered its randy charms in a devastating nighttime raid in 1944. The last Pleasure-Palace of Berlin finally imploded. ■

Along the entire Kurfürstendamm powdered and rouged young men sauntered and they were not all professionals; every high school boy wanted to earn some money and in the dimly lit bars one might see government officials and men of the world of finance tenderly courting sailors without any shame.

Stefan Zweig, *The World of Yesterday*, 1943

Berlin has become the paradise of international homosexuals.

Ilya Ehrenburg, 1931

BERLIN MEANS BOYS

A Prussian military garrison for most of its history, Berlin had long been identified with soldierly "sex inversion" and homosexual prostitution. The "shame of Berlin" and its "ever increasing vice"—a subject that caused Lutheran ministers to contort in apoplectic rage— referred explicitly to uranic (or homosexual) activity, not to the more prevalent sight of *Beinls* carousing in *Strichless* taverns. 180 years before Christopher Isherwood bade bittersweet farewell to the city of smooth-skinned *Line-Boys*, Berlin had already been tagged a "bugger's daydream."

In the 1750s, Friedrich the Great, the father of modern Prussia, decreed that his Praetorian Guard must forgo the august rites of marriage. German women, he proclaimed, weakened the fighting skills of his Spartan-trained regiment. Following the example of their chivalrous leader and his effeminate brother, Prince Heinrich, the Guardsmen

BERLIN GAY TYPES

—Highly refined male homosexuals with distinct feminine features. Often recognized by their plucked eyebrows, "Belladonna" eyes, face powder, lipstick, and heavy use of perfume. They sported sleek *Bubikopf* or Eton haircuts and modeled themselves after Rudolf Valentino and Conrad Veidt.

—Older, large-framed gay men. Usually cross-dressers attired in oversized dressing gowns. [Variant pejorative names: ████████, ████████, ████████, or ████████.]

—Mostly 20-year-olds who traveled in packs of six to eight. Often costumed in garish, leather fetish outfits. On weekends, they moved from *Diele* to *Diele*, carrying their own stimulants.

—Handsome, well-built, working-class men. Typically open-faced and cheery. [Variant names: ████████ or ████████.]

—Men with large penises. [After the German city.]

—Top men. [Also known as ████████, ████████, or ████████.]

—[Originally from the Hindi, referring to a low-working caste.] Older Gymnasium or university students who hired ████████. Frequently claimed to be straight.

—Youngest gay hustlers, from nine years old to 13. Virtually penniless, most worked solely for food, cigarettes, or lodging. Favorite hangout was the Anatomical Museum in the Linden Passage. Estimated numbers in 1930: 2,000–3,000.

—Bottom men. [Also known as ████████.]

—Male transvestites. [Variant name: ████████.]

—[Sometimes translated in British guidebooks as "Avenue-Boys," "Trick-Boys," and "Game-Boys."] Teenage male prostitutes, from 15 to 19. Seen everywhere in Berlin, most conspicuously in gangs of four or five in fancy hotel lobbies, gay *Dielen* and bars near the Alex, and in the Tiergarten. [Also known as ████████ and ████████.] Estimated numbers: 20,000–25,000.

—Predatory Line-Boy pimps.

—Generic slang term for all overtly gay men. [Variant names: ████████, ████████, ████████ (after the infamous paragraph of the German Penal Code), and ████████.]

turned to boys for their sexual pleasure—as did much of the Prussian Officer Corps and the elite cadets from Gross Lichterfeld, who could wed without dishonor.

Homosexual attachments were freely acknowledged and officially tolerated at Berlin's military academies. It was rumored that half the Potsdam militia could be found in the arms of boy prostitutes in the Tiergarten on any Saturday night. Prussian penal codes formally forbade sodomy, calling it "purposeless and obsolete," but its effect on barracks' couplings or anonymous street encounters was nil.

Throughout the nineteenth century, Berlin acted as a magnet for pretty German boys from the countryside, bisexuals, and cross-dressers. The city's jumbled record on *Strich* regulation and its proximity to the garrison encouraged a growing traffic in *Line-Boys* and the slow establishment of a homosexual subculture.

Previous Left:
Manassé,
Das Magazin,
1931

Previous Right:
A *Line-Boy*,
Der Eigene,
1924

Opposite:
In the Bathroom,
1925

Left:
All males
at the
Marienkasino

Below:
Otto Schoff, *Boys'
Love*, 1925

By the end of the Wilhelmian era, it was impossible to ignore Berlin's distinctive queer nightlife, which suddenly flaunted its size and diversity. Socialists, advisors to the Kaiser, schoolboys, federal judges, and

pickpockets all participated in it. (Some to their public disgrace and sorrow.) In the Friedrichstadt and adjacent neighborhoods alone, one could count 38 *Dielen* and cabarets that were devoted to a same-sex male clientele. (After the Collapse, these numbers tripled.) Every dreaded vision that the village preachers had predicted came frightfully true and then some; German-speaking faggots had found a home and an arena for experimentation.

The "Homosexual Question"

During the 1860s and 1870s, when the old Napoleonic and local ordinances were being revised, German doctors and jurists began to grapple with the physiological and social issues of "man-to-man love." The questions they raised were remarkably prescient

SOCIETY MEN—Outdoorsy and heavily-bearded men. Mature, over-50-year-olds. Elaborate facial hair. Bears.

SUGAR-LICKERS—Nighttime gay pederasts.

TREE-STUMPS—Middle-aged homosexual clients in working-class gay *Dielen* who passively observed the preening boy trade.

WILD BOYS—Homeless, 12-to-18-year-old gang members. Lived and traveled in small groups on the outskirts of Berlin. Traded sexual favors for cigarettes and meals in low-class *Dielen*. Estimated numbers in 1929: 1,500–2,500.

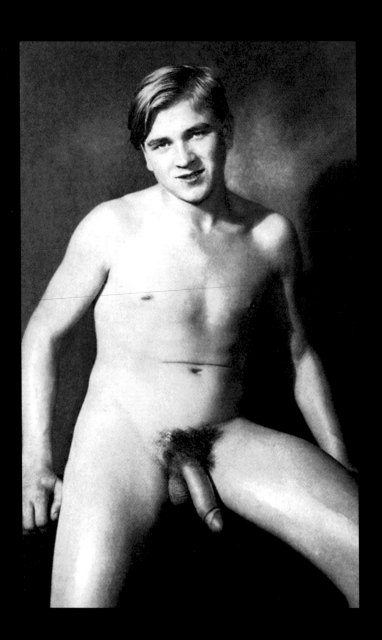

and crucial to the overall development of German sexology and organized gay life in Berlin.

First, the medical and psychological inquires: Was homosexual lust an inborn or inherited condition? Were there "constitutional" portents of the pederast character? (Many physicians believed then that an unusually tapered penis or an anus with a funnel-shaped cavity were clear biological indications of the uranic personality.) Did an "unhealthy" family dynamic arouse male-bonding and a physical rejection of female sexuality? Could a lifetime of same-sex attraction be acquired through brief exposure to an all-male environment, say, during camping or military school?

Then the legal issues: Under which circumstances should sodomy be considered a criminal offense? Only

Berlin raté
13 i 33

Opposite Left:
Photograph from
Die Insel, 1931

Opposite Right:
Christian Schad,
On the Corner,
1929

Left:
Sergei Eisenstein,
Spoiled Berlin,
1933

when it involved children? Could homosexual desire be reversed through medication, behavioral reconditioning, hypnotic suggestion, or penal threats? And if male seduction was a premeditated transgression—and not the product of biological orientation—what punishments were appropriate and effective?

In 1871, the judicial aspect of homosexuality was finally resolved in the new Federal Criminal Code. Germany had consolidated into a single Wilhelmian state, the Second Reich, and immediately formalized its statutes and regulations according to the dictates of the Kaiser's Assembly.

Paragraph 175 covered homosexual relationships: "paracoital" activities between males subjected them

or the "habitual seducer" to imprisonment and fines. (Female-to-female sex was utterly ignored in the Code.) Unfortunately for the puritanical German magistrates, the precise meaning of "paracoital" was left undefined. In the Weimar era, it was understood to be just anal penetration and "intercrucal intercourse" (leg and thigh humping). Street-smart Nazi legislators immediately added oral sex, mutual masturbation, and other forms of gay sexual contact, including flirtatious glances, to the Paragraph in 1935. They also considerably augmented the punishments for second-time offenders.

GERMAN GAY MAGAZINES

—("Journal for Human Rights"), "Official Paper of the League of Human Rights, 'the Organization of 12,000.'" Motto: "For Truth and Justice." Weekly edited by Friedrich Radszuweit, head of the "German Friendship Union." Serious publication with united goals for gay, lesbians, and transvestites. Alternated between Third-Sex and Libertarian philosophies. [1922–1929]

—("The Third Sex, the Transvestites"), a periodical for "ordinary" transvestites. Lots of fashion tips. Published by Radszuweit. [1929]

—("The Unmarried"), unidentified gay monthly. [1927]

—("The Exceptional"), "the Journal for Male Culture," later "the Newspaper of Friendship and Freedom." "A Book for Art and Manly Culture." First homosexual periodical in the world. Small intellectual, but highly influential, periodical edited by Adolf Brand and Konrad Linke. It contained color drawings, philosophical essays, photos of nude boys, adventure stories, and manifestos. Circulation 3,000 to 6,000. Affiliated with the "Society of the Eigene." [Intermittently published from 1899 to 1929.]

—An artistic journal devoted to boy-love. Poetry, short stories, and uncommonly hardcore drawings. Probably influenced in style by *Die Schönheit.* [circa 1919]

—"Magazine for Friendship and Freedom, Love and Life-Art." A gay pictorial edited by Brand. Militant Homosexualist competitor to *Der Insel*—[1930–1932]

—A continuation of Brand's *Der Eigene.* [1929–1931]

—"The Official Organ of the Cultural Cartel." Motto: "For a Liberated Humanity." A stylish one-man effort opposed to the "League of Human Rights." Gay monthly edited by Curt Neuburger. [1924–1926]

—("The Friend") A decoy gay publication of *Der Freundschaft* during a brief period of censorship. [1924–1925]

—("The Friendship") Motto: "For the Liberation of Differently-Inclined Men and Women." First Weimar paper with nude photographs, openly gay personals, and advertising. Between 1923–1926, it functioned as a weekly info sheet for Magnus Hirschfeld's Scientific-Humanitarian Committee. Edited by Karl Schultz. Later a popular monthly. [1919–1933]

German Gay Responses

Paragraph 175 provoked many political and scientific responses among German intellectuals and ultimately galvanized homosexuals in Central Europe to organize for the protection of their legal rights and communal lifestyle. (This was two generations before the Stonewall Revolution in New York.) "One-Seven-Five" gave urgency, new definition, and a common goal to Germany's estimated two million gay men, who otherwise lived in civic isolation from one another.

From the start, however, bickering over the "psychogenesis" of their orientation, public persona, strategic style, political alignment, use of language, attitude toward women, and sexual tastes divided German queer leadership. Essentially, three schools of thought emerged: the Militant Homosexualists, the Third Sexers, and the Libertarians. Each grouping had its own organizations (which seemed to change names every half-decade), periodicals, notion of fair play, artistic sense, and theoreticians.

Led by Adolf Brand, the indefatigable editor of *Der Eigene*, the Homosexualists envisioned a new Nietzschean hierarchy, along an imagined, antiquitous Greek classification. Wise and muscular Aryan pederasts with their admiring boys headed the Homosexualists' proposed social order, followed by grades of straight men, based on physiognomy, racial purity, and intelligence; then women. (These lessers were necessary for replenishing the race.) At the very bottom were effeminate men—the sexually enfeebled, the sissies and cross-dressers, all those who gave sodomy its reviled façade of weakness, narcissism, and emotional hysteria.

The Third Sexers attempted to explain homosexuality as a normal genetic phenomenon. Men with "female souls"—and women with male sexual dispositions—were normal "miscues" in the process of natural selection. Rather than pathological beings, homosexuals formed a "Third Sex," neither "full man nor full woman." According to Magnus Hirschfeld, Berlin's renowned sexologist and human rights leader, gay men and women inhabited an "intermediary" zone on the wide

FR. RADSZUWEIT

MÄNNER ZU VERKAUFEN

LIPSIA-VERLAG LEIPZIG

Renée Sintenis
(Radierung)

spectrum of human sexuality. In the radical ideology of the Third Sexers, all sexual behavior (which involved consenting adults) was worthy of individual respect and state protection.

The Libertarians, the vast majority of Germany's gay men and women, followed neither the Nationalist nor International-Socialist rhetoric of Brand and Hirschfeld. Represented by Friedrich Radszuweit, an organizer from Hamburg and Al Goldstein-like publisher, they pursued their same-sex endeavors through social ties and apolitical means. Other than working for the abolition of Paragraph 175 and related censorship laws, the Libertarians eschewed the superheated cauldron of Weimar politics. Relatively few dabbled in reactionary or progressive causes and then only as German voters who happened to love members of their own sex.

"Origins" of Homosexuality

While Brand, Hirschfeld, and Radszuweit conducted a battle royale for the allegiance and support of Germany's gay community and its many sympathizers, straight psychologists in Berlin promulgated their own theories which they thought explained the baffling origins of adult male-to-male desire. Strict Freudians acknowledged the innate bisexual nature of the human organism; homosexual feeling was a normal and short phase in a healthy boy's development. For those who never outgrew the emotional stage, the Freudians subscribed to a flipped formulation of the master's prized Oedipus complex: Growing up in the household of a domineering mother, the budding homosexual over-

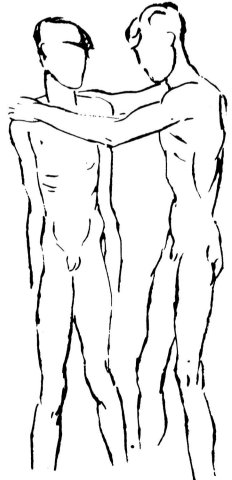

Above:
Marcel Vertès,
*Parisian Night
at the Lokal*

**Opposite
and Below:**
Renée Sintenis,
Boys, 1923

—("The Island") Libertarian monthly published by Radszuweit. Featured provocative photos, gay fiction and news, and ads for gay books and "massage services," personals, and *Dielen*. Largest queer periodical with a print run of 150,000. Originally "Island of the Lonely" section from the *Blätter für Menschenrecht*. Brother zine to the lesbian *Die Freundin*. [1925–1932]

—("The Circle") Swiss gay intellectual journal, which outlasted the Weimar and Nazi eras. Good source for exile queer literature and postwar ideology. [First year 1932]

—("The Mercury") Literary gay monthly. [1922]

—("Bulletin of the S-H C") News periodical of Hirschfeld's Scientific-Humanitarian Committee. [1926–1933]

—("New Friendship") "Weekly for Friendship, Pictures and Enlightenment." "Organ of the German Friendship League." Edited by Max H. Danielsen, a former editor of *Der Freundschaft*. [1928]

—Gay pictorial magazine from the Phoebus Verlag. Edited by Kurt Eitelbuss. [1927–1929]

—("Round Letter") Homosexual literary journal. [1932]

—("The Sun") Queer monthly from Hamburg. [1920–1921]

—("The Stream") Politically-radical gay monthly. [1920]

—("The Auntie") An offprint of *Der Eigene*. For *Aunties*. Filled with anti-Hirschfeld invective. [1924--1925]

—Literary gay journal edited by René Stelter. Later merged with *Der Freundschaft*. [1922–1927]

—

("Weekly Paper for the Enlightenment and Contemporary Improvement of Ideal Friendship"), gay newspaper with Third-Sex orientation. Edited by Schultz. [1919–1922]

identifies with his emasculated or absent father. After puberty, the boy projects his own image onto his male consort as he unconsciously performs the double role of a sexually caring mother.

Disciples of Wilhelm Stekel took a more primitive psychoanalytic approach. Homosexuality was quite simply the penultimate rejection of women, a reaction formation against oedipal cravings and traumatic memories of a parent's coital activity. Adlerians, of course, saw same-sex love as an advanced tactic to attain power and status. In their analysis, the physically weak boy discovers that his self-ideal of superiority cannot be based on normal feelings of masculinity and aggression. He learns to assert himself sexually by exciting and controlling other homosexuals.

Wilhelm Reich, who arrived in Berlin in 1930, advanced an even more hostile psychogenetic theory. The Passive-Feminine Homosexual ("Subject Homosexual") reacts to the hysteria of his mother through passivity and an identification with female sexuality. Contaminated by an emotionally-inert emotional core, he deals badly in daily interaction, which typically manifests itself in a pronounced weakness of body movement (especially in the shoulders and arms). The Aristocratic Homosexual ("Object Homosexual") develops a different character armoring—corporal rigidity and hyper-aggressive behavior. Each struggles with the hidden fear that his father will one day savagely punish him for his inadequate heterosexual longings.

Even Carl Jung, working in faraway Switzerland, saw homosexuality in a negative light as well. He believed that the perverse attitude began with an over-protective mother ("the Female Shadow") who sexually tied her image to a confused and desperately insecure infant son. The boy would be condemned to discover that true fidelity to his mother meant sexual avoidance of all other females later in life and sexual congress only with men.

Interestingly, the psychoanalytic and related psychogenetic theories—largely because of their straight

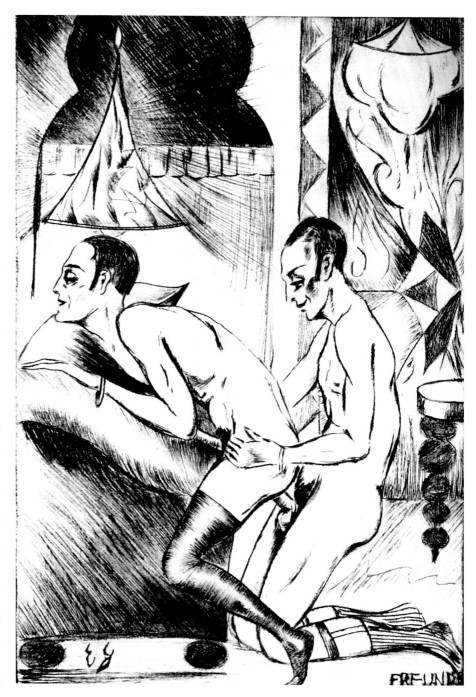

Opposite:
Hildebrand, *The Inspection*

Above:
Ernst Gerhard, *Friends*, 1925

89

Homosexual Life
in Weimar Berlin

The idyllic gay portrait of dapper German Army officers in capes and peaked caps transfixed by demure Line-Boys on the Tiergarten benches disappeared from view in 1919. It was beggars who retained the combat dress of the defeated army. Berlin's gay community at the beginning of Weimar adopted a different wardrobe, the sailor's blouse and cap (alongside the tailored morning-coat of the perfumed dandy). In homosexual *Dielen*, middle-aged *Sugar-Lickers*, *Coolies*, *Doll-Boys*, even crotchety waiters wore the crisp blue-and-white insignia of jaunty marines on shore leave. The change of uniform had various meanings. Partly, it was matter of identification—straights didn't wear them—and they were a Wilhelmian echo of adolescent androgyny. More significantly, Berlin's core homosexual community had expended far beyond the units of the Potsdam garrison.

In 1922, one of Berlin's police commissioners estimated the total number of gay men to be in excess of 100,000 and teenage male prostitutes (whom he did not consider to be truly queer) around 25,000. Over the

Above:
Hildebrand,
The Dinner

and Jewish associations—were ignored by Berlin's queers, who appeared content with their orientation. Only anxious bisexual men and fellow social scientists showed obvious interest.

next eight years, the numbers of resident queers sky-rocketed. Partly because of more sophisticated polling methods and real growth, the homosexual populace was determined to be over 350,000 by 1930.

Unlike Berlin's lesbians, the gay community was noticeably invisible during daytime hours. At various times, homosexual men supported a gay-themed play-house, "The Theatre of Eros," a bowling league, stamp-collecting society, poetry readings, and a handful of other artistic enterprises, but mostly closed-door, nighttime venues, like winter-balls, cabarets, dance halls and *Dielen* were their traditional haunts. Berlin queers lacked a resolute sense of political and social cohesion, despite the intensive efforts by the

Homosexualist and Third-Sex organizers. (Probably less than ten percent belonged to all-male clubs.) Fear of public exposure and unadorned hedonistic concerns guided the majority of deviant lifestyles.

A former *Line-Boy*, only identified as "Erich" in an interview conducted in 1978 (and later transcribed in *Gay Voices from East Germany*), recalled the closeted, if exhilarating, times:

Above:
Hildebrand,
On the Town

Left:
Schad,
Zauberflote,
1930

91

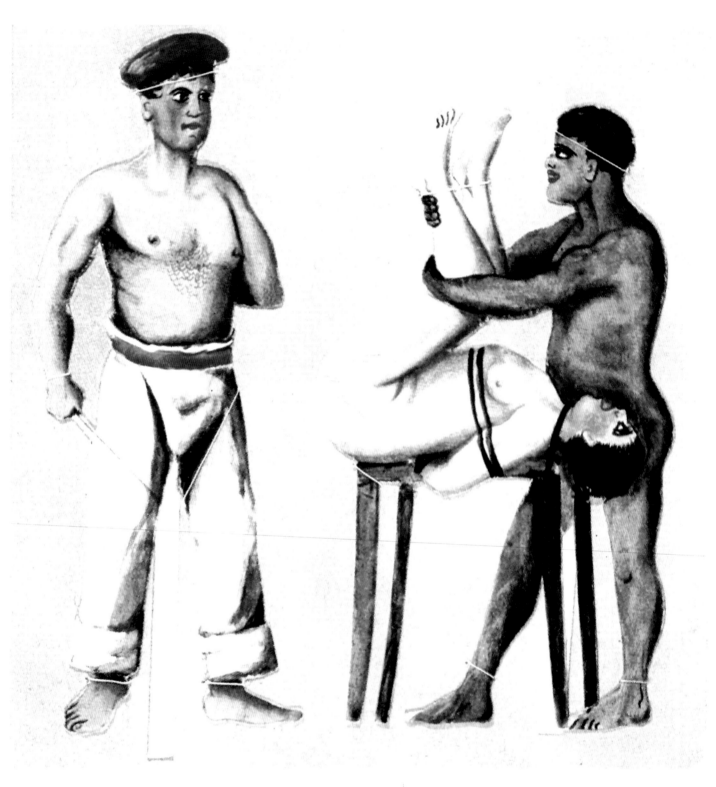

Above:
Amateur
fantasy
drawing

In the Twenties there was scarcely an occupational group that was not represented at the famous
drag balls in the big Berlin ballrooms. We "simple
lads" came dressed as Asta Nielsen or Henny Porten
[European film stars] and let ourselves be served
champagne by coarse, cursing taxi drivers or man-

servants. It was part of the craziness of the setting
that these tough servants and taxi drivers exchanged
their gear next morning for the judge's robe or the
doctor's white coat. It even happened that an "Asta"
would be sent to the clink for shoplifting a week
later by her "manservant."

PANOPTICUM
PASSAGE THEATER
Panopticum

The Friedrichstrasse, Berlin, Germany.

Above:
The Linden-Passage at Friedrichstrasse corner

Erich likened Weimar to a mad carousel ride, where centrifugal forces blew some youthful participants into the gutter, while other teenage daredevils leaped on the treacherous merry-go-round to replace them.

Still, the sexcapades of homosexuals more than rivaled the piquant Bummels of the het Girl-Culture. For some straight Berliners, queer promiscuity and sexual bravado was a cause for envy and erotic introspection. Curt Riess captured this covetous relationship sardonically in his Berlin memoirs. Two distinguished-looking men at a table in the *Nachtlokal* "Schwannecke":

Walter Steinthal (editor of the 12-Uhr Blatt *and a famous womanizer), "I could see myself fucking a boy. But he'd have to be young. Fourteen or fifteen."*

Hans Heinrich von Twardowsky (a flamboyant gay actor), "Why not?"

Steinthal: "He would have to be a natural blonde."

Von Twardowsky: "Why not?"

Steinthal: "And he couldn't have too much hair on his body."

Von Twardowsky (staring at Steinthal in icy disgust before making a fast exit): "Goddamnit, man, you might as well fuck a woman!"

Wandervogel and the Wild-Boys

Implied and overt forms of male homosexuality, of course, had other public outlets in Berlin. The military, the elite Gymnasiums and academies, the Life Reform (or *Nacktkultur*) movement were all embroiled in florid accusations of male pederasty and sex scandal throughout the Wilhelmian era. But one mass association in particular was thought to be rife with man-boy love: the unique German Youth Movement known as the *Wandervogel* ("Wandering Bird").

93

Right:
Winnetou,
Wild-Boy
Chieftain of
the Wild and
Free gang,
1932

back-to-nature doctrine, railing against deleterious urban lifestyles and the consumption of alcohol and meat. Forty-kilometer hikes over mountainous paths, the robust singing of German folk ballads, countryside overnights, and frolicking male camaraderie were the signature activities of the Wandervogel. Curiously, the steadfast movement eschewed politics. But its appeal just before the Great War struck a deep patriotic chord. Nationalist, Catholic, and Socialist leaders fielded their own *Wandervogels* with separate flags, anthems, and uniforms. Five years into the Weimar period, Nazi, Red Front, and German Zionist organizations also created corresponding versions of bronzed warrior-youths, marching in place. These ideologically opposed squadrons of husky German teenagers often crossed paths in desolate terrains and pitched camp within bonfire sight of one another.

Despite its wholesome image, the *Wandervogel* movement could not avoid the stigma of male-to-male sex and gay seduction. In fact, the original organization nearly expired when one of its adult chaperones was accused of being a supporter of *Der Eigene*'s Militant Homosexualist philosophy. The counselor quickly

Although it resembled the Anglo-Saxon Boy Scouts in popularity and appearance, the *Wandervogel*, astonishingly, evolved in a strange Pied Piper fashion. This was an overnight phenomenon, created by male teens for male teens. Its institutional founding took place in the Berlin suburb of Steglitz in 1896 and grew exponentially across the nation for the next 35 years.

A product of Pan-German and Naturalist sentiments, the *Wandervogels* proselytized a Romantic

resigned and some all-female units of *Wandervogel* were hastily assembled but neither action really cooled the sexually-charged atmosphere. The entire *Wander-vogel* experience, according to the autobiographies of its precocious founders, was shot through with homo-erotic tension.

Even more obviously gay were the *Wild-Boys*, teen-aged members of anti-social gangs that lived in the outlying districts of Berlin. Working in groups of six or eight, these 14- to 18-year-old runaways established Peter Pan-like encampments in park sites, warehouses, and abandoned apartments. Led by punkish-dressed chieftains called "Bulls," each *Wild-Boy* association had its own elaborate blood-oaths and ceremonies of ritualized sex.

Typically, a young initiate would forced to box (or knife-fight) with the toughest member of the crew, be gang-raped while bound and gagged, ordered to masturbate publicly and then ejaculate on command, or act as a living commode for his drunken associates. Some newly-inducted boys were chosen by the *Bulls* as their "queens" or designated shared "girl-friends" for the pack. Most *Wild-Boys* sported pirate-style earrings and garish tattoos. While the majority of gangs flaunted their ragtag, hobo garb, others paraded around in distinctive

group costumes, like top hats and shabby tuxedoes, American trapper outfits, college graduates in mortar-boards, or paper buffalo heads. The gang names alone testified to the influence of Karl May's North American frontier novels and other staples of German pulp fiction: "Fear No Death," "Indian Blood," "The Forest Pirates," "Wild West," "Girl-Shy," "Santa Fe," "Gypsy Love," "The Dirty Boys," "Red Apaches."

Left:
Winnetou's
Queen

Above:
Wild and
Free's
Test of
Strength,
1932

The *Wild-Boys* subsisted through a host of criminal enterprises, mostly cat burglary, smash-and-grab robberies, car theft, and unglamorous forms of boy prostitution. *Boosts* (unscrupulous proprietors of low dives) procured the services of the prettiest and youngest of gangs for *Sucker-Lickers* seeking passive *Kitty-Receivers*. Other 14- and 15-year-olds were sent out independently by the Bulls for a *Bummel* on the Alex *Kietz*. Although sometimes confused with eccentric *Wandervogel* groups by the *Polenta*, the authentic *Wild-Boys*—200 crews in Berlin North alone—fell seamlessly into the city's notorious gay demi-monde.

Daniel Guérin, a French gay anarchist, visited a *Wild-Boy* outing near Berlin's Lake Lehnitz in September 1932. There he interviewed Winnetou, the group's Bull, and recorded Wild-Free's campfire pastimes and initiation rites (*Vu*, "A Return to Barbarism," March 8, 1933). Winnetou gamely explained to the foreign journalist his sado-sexual ethos: occasionally, naked newcomers were tied to the tops of trees and violated with phallic-looking sticks; other times the would-be nomads were gangbanged on *Stoszsofas*, or fuck couches.

Remarkably, the sociopathic Winnetou showed up on a Berlin thoroughfare one year after the *Vu* tête-à-

tête. Then he had the familiar bearings of a menacing Nazi tough. Winnetou, however, recognized one of Guérin's left-wing colleagues and greeted her warmly as his old happy-go-lucky, *Wild-Boy* self.

Male Prostitution

The enormous volume of sex-traffic in boys and very young men differentiated Berlin from all previous centers of debauchery and "decadent" tourism. Nearly every Western metropolis in the interwar period, naturally, had a substantial number of clandestine homosexual bars and backstreet arenas where gay men could secure the ministrations of male prostitutes. Hamburg, in 1930 for example, claimed the second greatest concentration of *Line-Boys* in Europe at 5,000 strong and growing. But

Berlin, the acknowledged leader then, had at least seven times that many; a figure which, according to the calculations of its vice commissioners, was also growing by the month.

Christopher Isherwood wasn't exaggerating when he wrote, "Berlin meant boys."

Above and Below: *Wild-Boy* sexual initiation

DAS LUSTHAUS DER KNABEN

familial arguments. Male prostitution in Berlin continued to swell for a simpler market reason: the demand for it increased.

Beginning at nine in the morning, hundreds of *Line-Boys* were already on the *Strich* as they waited in and around the public lavatories of the city's luxury hotels. British businessmen were the early morning targets; shy American tourists in the afternoon, followed by stingy German provincials before evening hours. By dark, Berlin's homosexual *Kietz* was in full swing. The

Above:
Guy de Laurence, *The Lust House of Boys,* 1922

Right:
Schoff, *Boy's Love*

Opposite:
Amateur photo, *The White Linen Shorts*

Most foreigners attributed the spread of male prostitution to the Republic's fiscal malaise and political failure to stem the plummeting employment rate among Germany's unskilled laborers. The congested corners of rowdy *Wild-Boys*, *Bubes* (or "Butchers"), *Line-Boys*, and *Doll-Boys* in the Friedrichstadt, to them, was only one appalling symptom of the national moral collapse. Others saw a link to Berlin's female prostitution problem: young whores were constantly introducing their junior male siblings into the lurid profession. While both theories contained a bit of dismal truth, municipal statistics, in general, supported neither the economic nor the corrupt

Tiergarten, the Alex, and the Linden-Passage were first destinations of Suitors seeking *Doll-Boys* (under 14) or run-of-the-mill *Line-Boys*. In Berlin South, slightly more mature *Wild-Boys* and *Bubes* were available at gay pick-up *Dielen*.

The only quarter identified with adult homosexual trade was in the West. There, an unknown number of "Massage Parlors"—around two dozen repeatedly advertised in gay publications—featured erotic special-ties. Like their sister straight houses to the east and south, the queer Parlors offered sessions in B&D, flagel-lation, and costumed roleplay but with a much greater emphasis on scatological scenes. While adding variety to the local color, they certainly never amounted to more than five or ten percent of Berlin's wholesale traf-ficking in male flesh.

Gay *Dielen* and Entertainment

The heart of Berlin's indigenous gay life was its *Dielen* and bars. The exact number of these varied from guidebook to guidebook. The commonly cited figure was 65 or 80. But if one included restaurant backrooms, unlicensed *Kaschemmen* (criminal dives), and lounges that accommodated separate gay, lesbian, straight, and/or transvestite patrons, the sum easily doubled.

Many of the *Dielen* shocked outsiders due to the casual, unsalacious atmosphere. They were just bare

bones pick-up bars—dimly lighted joints for queers with beers. More gratifying to tourist tastes, of course, were lounges that featured human displays of Berlin exotica; "Café Monbijou" and the "Dé Dé" both adorned their cabaret platforms with naked hermaphrodites, who did nothing more than nonchalantly smoke and smile wanly from their elevated chairs. The "Lion Cub" *Diele*, which was decked out as a Wild West saloon, offered interactive delights. The pumped-up waiters, or "cubs," were attired in sailor or butcher-boy dress. On the menu was a extensive list of international beers and the names of the service staff. For just a few pfennig more, one could cop a sensuous feel from the biceps or hairless chest of a lusty *Bube*.

Other gay amusement sites restricted their paying guests to an identifiable clientele or ones adhering to a special dress code, like elderly, fat men who dressed in schoolboy's knickers or tight-fitting sailor suits. The "Nürenberger Diele" and the "Kantdiele" catered exclusively to balding stockbrokers, who spent their picturesque evenings dancing with "elegant pansies." At the swanky "Hollandaise" nightclub, homosexual couples appeared, at first, to be straight fashion-horses; the men in tuxes, their mates in understated velvet and pearls. Only at close listening range could an inexperienced observer unscramble the daunting gender puzzle.

Each *Diele* and ballroom had its little quirks and protocols. Isherwood immortalized one of them, the "Cosy Corner," in his series of "Berlin Stories" and increasingly confessional memoirs. Between 1929 and 1933, the expatriate Isherwood became obsessed with the bar and its denizens. He talked about it in London and Paris, wrote about it, and made it the first point of interest for his queer colleagues touring Berlin. Even the incorrigible bisexual occultist Aleister Crowley was dragged there by Isherwood. Within a moment of entering the Cosy Corner, the "wickedest man in the world" walked up to one of the open-shirted *Bubes* and clawed the boy's chest with his razor-sharp talons. A horrified Isherwood immediately persuaded Crowley to offer the tough some money before they made a fast getaway. On the street, both were relieved; Isherwood because his quick thinking prevented a retaliatory assault, and Crowley because he made his indelible mark on the "City of Satan." ■

Lesbian emotional needs are truly inordinate. They build a world of their own—in their houses, in their lounges, in their literature, and especially in their love practices. Lesbian desires reel over stars, aromas, sounds, and luminous colors. Caresses of soft and pliant hands, nail and tooth, soft bites and pulling of hair, and finally, after great tension, an utter free-fall and drowning until their own egos are dissolved into a moment of measureless bliss.

Ruth Roellig, *Lesbians and Female Transvestites*, 1929

"We are the New Spirit.
We do it with Brazenness."

Sign above the ladies room in the Toppkeller, 1930

HOT SISTERS

Before the First World War, a rigid classification of lesbian types was already well established in the Central European mind. Frumpy, sexless aunts, monstrously ugly town gossips, and man-hating adventuresses—each understood to be a tribadic archetypal figure—appeared with some frequency in the popular fiction and stage melodrama of Berlin and Vienna. These images of unmarried females were repeated, with shocking naiveté, in widely-published psychological portraits that examined urban dementia and female criminology. Even among the new breed of sexologists, the spectrum of lesbian behavior was grossly delimited to the freakish, the misguided, and the intentionally perverse.

The characterology of non-heterosexual women followed a common delineation, beginning with the Constitutional Lesbian. A hormonally unbalanced matron, the Constitutional Lesbian was immediately recognized by her shapeless contours and unflattering mixed-gendered

BERLIN LESBIAN TYPES

—Masculine, or butch women. Often wore male clothing, especially fedoras and leather ties. Recognized by their long leather coats in winter and ubiquitous cigars. Some *Bubis* sported delicately drawn "mustaches" (imitating Spanish aristocratic women). Reputed to be the best automobile drivers in Berlin. Attracted to *Mädis*, who referred to them as *Daddies*.

—Tuxedoed, sophisticated power women. Identified by their immaculately coiffed dark, curly hair, which hung loose, Gypsy style (called *Titus-kopfs*). Their faces powdered ivory-white, they often wore horn-rimmed eyeglasses or monocles. Serious and ironic. Attracted to *Garçonnes*.

—Pert, saucy femmes. Usually attired in exaggerated French street urchin clothing when clubbing.

—Young women with *Bubikopf* haircuts and shaved, penciled-in eyebrows. Stylishly dressed in French male fashions. Had their own weekly magazine, *Garçonne*; motto: "For Friendship, Love, and Sexual Enlightenment." [Also known as   or   .]

—Generic name for homosexual women. [Variants: .]

—[From French underworld argot] Expensive lesbian callgirls, who appealed to both genders. Found in many lesbian clubs and fancy tourist hotels in the Friedrichstadt.

—Heavily made-up professional prostitutes who serviced only female clients. Frequently seen on barstools in lesbian lounges, facing the dance floor with a vacant stare and long cigarette-holders in their hands. [Variant name: .]

—Ultrafemmes. [Variants: ,   , or   .]

—Sexually aggressive but refined and socially well-positioned *Bubis*. Characterized by their androgynous "Diana" features. Exhibited a perverse taste for confused, working-class *Mädis*. A staple of lesbian romantic fiction. [Known as   in the Wilhelmian and Inflation periods.]

—Unattractive, career *Bubis*. Defined by their shapeless exteriors, mannish attire, and facial hair. Tadpole sexuality was often sublimated into progressive social causes and artistic pursuits.

apparel. Depending on the grotesqueness of her body and degree of sexual inertia, she could be a harmless "Old Maid" or the trouble-making *Tadpole*, an embittered mannish concoction with facial hair and a destructive revolutionary disposition.

A second variety, the Situational Lesbian, provided more hope for social redemption and visual appeal. This included young bourgeois women who, during their wayward adolescence, were cloistered away from nor-

mal social interaction with virile males. Those extended periods of female isolation (particularly in all-girl boarding schools or sinister nunneries) and exposure to the teachings of predatory lesbians were thought to pervert the girls' natural inclination for heterosexual courtship and marital happiness. Petty female criminals and prostitutes as well were prey to sexual inversion due to long-term male mistreatment and a learned contempt for societal mores. (At least, these types could be saved with sympathetic instruction and the adornment of proper female attire.)

Finally, there was the *Scorpion*—a hopelessly evil femme fatale who took sick delight in the corruption of unworldly, ego-shattered girls. The

menacing *Scorpion* was a made-up vampire who not only enjoyed the taste of virgin blood but the creation of man-hating progeny—"When she walked into the room, all the young women knew they were in abject moral danger!" The *Scorpion* was more than a defiling agent, a succubus who castrated men without their knowledge or physical presence, she was the living

symbol of a new social order without erotic boundaries or familial conventions. Now heterosexual men had an additional day-to-day worry: sexual competition from females—especially from haughty aristocrats (particularly those with mixed Spanish or French lineage), vengeful widows recently returned from Paris or Budapest, and overly attentive Bohemian artistes.

Previous Left:
Margit Toth,
Hot Sisters

Previous Right:
A *Garçonne*, 1928

Left:
A *Gougnette*,
1926

Above:
A 17-year-old
Mädi, 1931

illating) insight into another form of female sexuality. It was as if the lush German South Seas colonies—already lost in the war, together with their dusky, bare-breasted maidens—had come home to Berlin, an emotionally unsettled city, waiting for new voyeurist sensations.

Female secretaries, clerks, and daughters of shop-keepers, most of whom never even heard the word "Sapphic" before, started to spend sisterly time with one another, especially at night. An erotic community, independent of and unconcerned with men's desires, was coalescing in the center of Europe. Interestingly, after the Armistice, foreign journalists remarked that post-Wilhelmian Berlin seemed different, that whole sections of the city, especially in the West and South,

Above:
The artist
Renée Sintenis
and a *Hot Sister*

Far Right:
Kamm,
The Sharper

A German-Speaking Lesbos

Around 1917, in the third year of the Great War, the iconography of lesbian life in Berlin underwent a sea change; suddenly, male graphic artists and writers presented women with same-sex cravings as desirable and darkly exotic. What was once universally considered sexual-ly repulsive or threatening now provided an erotic jolt for heterosexuals, an amusing if mysterious (and therefore tit-

appeared to be devoid of sexually potent males, if one excluded pimps and other criminal riff-raff.

Paris and Berlin

Long before Berlin's lesbian heyday, turn-of-the-century Paris had infamous same-sex female bars and clubs, mostly tucked away in the Montmartre distinct, and chic balls where top-hatted women flaunted their tribadic lifestyles with shocking nonchalance. In fact, before the Collapse, Berlin lesbians looked to Paris as a cultural Mecca, a mythic capital of elegant liberation and delicious sexual ambiguity. French idioms, often mixed with Apache argot, haute street-urchin fashion, and teasing representations of Parisian female beauty percolated through the German queer

nightlife in the early Twenties. But, by 1924, everything became reversed: it was the Parisian lesbians who longed for the freedom and sexual chaos of Berlin. The international center of female homosexuality slid eastward and changed languages.

Trends in sexual behavior sometimes evolve in half-year cycles but the topography of lust rarely budges in

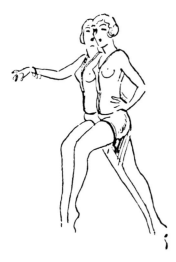

any one decade. So the transformation from Paris to Berlin as the playground for women seeking the love of other women can only be described as extraordinary and unprecedented. Of course, Berlin's growing status as a *Hauptstadt* of commercial sex had a part in it. Yet other factors should be considered.

Berlin, the Lesbian Eldorado

Like its male counterpart, Berlin's lesbian population was said to be enormous, large enough to support several dozen social clubs, two ice-skating leagues, a nudist retreat and three outdoor sports associations, six journals, and (as the guide books in the tourist hotels proudly announced) 85 nightclubs and lounges. But exactly how many women actively participated in

Berlin's lesbian subculture is difficult to assess. Magnus Hirschfeld estimated in 1930 that Berlin was home to some 400,000 lesbians, but that figure appears to be grossly inflated if we adhere to current definitions of sexual orientation. (Today not every female who engages in a short-term, same-sex relationship would accept the lesbian tag.)

Based on other criteria, like club memberships and magazine subscriptions, the number of *Hot Sisters* in Berlin (excluding *Kontroll-Girls* and *Chontes*) was closer to 85,000. Paris, in the same years, could never tally more than 5,000 lesbians—again if one discounts female street prostitutes, of whom 25% were said to be constitutionally (or situationally) homosexual.

Nearly every social class and profession that allowed women was represented in the Berlin all-girl queer subculture. While most lesbians were employed in typically straight industries like government, publishing, entertainment, manufacturing, fashion, advertising, low-level commerce, and education, many worked

exclusively in establishments that catered only to their own community. In other European cities, lesbianism was a choice allotted to just the very wealthy, glamorous, or patently avant-garde; in Berlin, any woman could pursue a same-sex lifestyle and find thousands of like-minded partners. Never in European history had women seeking the companionship of other women been so open and adventurous.

The German penchant for classification and uniforms further differentiated the Berlin lesbian milieu. *Bubis,* *Dodos, Gamines, Garçonnes, Gougnettes, Hot Whores, Mädis,* and *Sharpers* were the expressive orders that

LESBIAN
SOCIAL CLUBS

—An organization of six hundred *Garçonnes*. Its headquarters was MALI AND INGEL, which they attended on weekdays. [For one-year the Monbijou Westies met at the HOHENZOLLERN LOUNGE.] Only chi-chi fashion-conscious *Garçonnes* were eligible for membership status. Tickets for the Monbijou West's two annual winter balls at the Scala Variety theatre were said to be the most sought-after items on the Berlin lesbian social calendar.

—Small auxiliary lesbian faction of "Association of Human Rights," the powerful male homosexual Berlin organization. "Girl-Friends" coordinated many cultural projects, including lesbian sporting activities, outdoor health weekends, Sunday book-club readings, informative lectures, and a score of private educational classes. Its members contributed to the influential gay newspaper, *Blätter für Menschenrecht*. Less successful were its social events and winter-time celebrations.

Divided into two sections, a "Southwest" club, which held Wednesday dances at the ZAUBERFLÖTE, and a sister "Northeast" unit that met at the ALEXANDER-PALAST and KÖHLER'S DANCE HALL twice a week. Partly because of their over-developed intellectual nature, *Girl-Friends'* planning of costume parties suffered from vastly overhyped advertising, weak leadership, and a general "North German" stiffness. Highpoint of the balls was always the Tyrolian "Choo-Choo" dance, in which the dancers assembled in a long line, and the "Wash Waltz," where participants mimed scrubbing down their partners with imaginary brushes.

—An exclusive Jewish club of *Gamines*, which met on Monday afternoon at the ZAUBERFLÖTE. It was also an affiliate of the "Association of Human Rights." At their annual September ball and dinner, the "Ladies' Pearl Festival," each Erato member received a pearl-necklace. Headed by feminist writer Selli Engler, the editor of the monthly *BIF*, the Journal of Ideal Female Friendship.

one was supposed to inhabit by reason of sexual outlook and sexual affect. And even those types contained distinctive categories based on class status, political affiliation, perceived affluence, romantic interest, and appearance. The lesbian *Dielen* and associations, for the most part, appealed to specific couplings, for instance, only *Dodos* and *Garçonnes*, *Sharpers* and underclass *Mädis*, or like-minded *Gamines*.

Also a vitalistic philosophy of lesbian superiority animated both the separatist and apolitical associations. Ruth Roellig, a highly regarded journalist and colleague of Hirschfeld, wrote in 1929, "Lesbian love arises from the refinement and depth of emotional experience where all the forces of body and soul become fused, and then unfolded. Not to perform sexually when God has blessed one with an ideal love-soul would be to

"LADIES CLUB MONBIJOU"—A member of the "German Friendship Association," the Monbijou encouraged *Garçonne* cultural activity, especially the reading of private poetry and contemporary erotic literature. Met weekly at the CAFÉ DORIAN GRAY and was long associated with the lesbian news publications *Frauenliebe* (after 1928 called *Garçonne*) and *Neue Freundschaft*.

"LADIES CLUB PYRAMID"—A loosely-organized society of *Garçonnes*, the Pyramid officials created exciting social gatherings every Monday evening at the TOPPKELLER but without the heterosexual prostitutes, men, and other gawkers. Ongoing lovers' quarrels, especially those between club members who were working-class *Garçonnes* and artistic types (including actresses from Erwin Piscator's theatre collective) erupted through the night and were generally settled in the Topp courtyard with "heartfelt apologies, tender embraces, and impassioned kissing."

"LADIES CLUB SCORPION"—Organized by the charming *Bubi-meister* Walterchen, the Scorpion held relatively sedate dances at the downbeat TAVERNE on Thursday, Saturday, and Sunday evenings. Thought to be named after the best-selling German lesbian novel, *The Scorpion* by Anna Weinauch, the prewar generic name for lesbian temptresses, or Walterchen's astrological sign. (Or all three.) A place for not so elegant *Bubis* and *Mädis*.

"LADIES CLUB VIOLETTA"—A militant lesbian organization of 400 working-class women, female transvestites, and their supporters. Established by super-*Bubi* Lotte Hahn, a legendary fighter for lesbian legal rights, the Violetta contemptuously looked down its nose at the social rostrum of more insular associations. It was critical of the emphasis on physical appearance ("Sex-Appeal") and the cult of stardom that many Berlin lesbian clubs consciously promoted. To counter that exclusionary world view, Hahn threw frequent Sunday picnics in the Tiergarten and organized "beach party" outings in the summer. Violetta also supported a feminist Body Culture regimen for indoor workers. More than any other Berlin society, the Violetta dealt with the problems and needs of full-time female transvestites.

Heavily advertised as an ideal meeting-place for lesbian singles, the Violetta organized its own dances three times a week at the RHEINISCHER HOF,

„MONOKEL"
dle Bar der Frau
(früher K Ü KA)   Budapeeter Straße 14

◆

Das
Tanz-
Kabarett
der
mondänen
Welt

◆

Eintritt frei!
Gepflegte Biere

deprive oneself and others of a great pleasure. Among lesbians, there may exist love affinities which no longer vacillate desperately between angel and brute, but in a love that is sacred, pure, and beautiful in itself."

Artistic types, like the lesbian Body Culture enthusiasts Hedwig Hagemann and Dora Menzler, claimed that women's sexuality was much more complicated and dense with erotic possibilities than that of men; therefore, at their semi-mystical demonstrations of young naked female dancers, male spectators, with very rare exceptions, were prohibited. Although there was some tactical individual empathy with gay men and male transvestites, most lesbians in Berlin lived in a utopic environment separate from and independent of men.

Lesbian Nightlife

Like other Berliners, lesbians were internationally esteemed for their unusual nightlife. "Married" or single, the *Girl-Friends* played out their vivacious lifestyle in seemingly promiscuous capers and taunting public displays of affection. Sexy personal columns and highly detailed stories of brief romantic affairs were the basic fillers of all lesbian publications. And nearly every lesbian organization, especially ones with serious political agendas, advertised late-night, hard-drinking weekly parties and exclusive masked balls from late December to February.

These spirited affairs were restricted to dues-paying members, but a half-dozen lesbian clubs also

welcomed a curious tourist trade. In fact, the English Cook Travel Agency featured such tours after 1928. Precisely at midnight, special coach buses picked up kinky sightseers at each of the major Berlin hotels and delivered them to the "Toppkeller" and other late-night sapphic emporiums in the Berlin West, near Bülowstrasse. For straight British couples, in particular, these anthropological excursions were the memorable high point of their Continental revelry.

Above:
Von Perckhammer,
Ecstasy

Left:
Mammen,
The Siesta,
1931

113

The Toppkeller opened its arms to sensation-hungry outsiders and "only-in-Berlin"-quoting journalists. Visually the nightclub bristled with intriguing contrasts and its entertainment atmosphere radiated high deviance, even by the proudly wacked-out standards of the city. Rumpelstilzchen, who was accorded carte blanche privilege there, noted that his fellow newspapermen affectionately referred to the three-storied funhouse as the "Les-Botanical Gardens."

The Topp was hidden away from the street. Customers had to cross a dark courtyard and three gates (the first bearing a symbol of a toilet) and then negotiate a narrow stairwell before they reached the club's ante-chamber. In the foyer, each guest was inspected by two enormous,

MANUELA, NATIONHOF, or ZAUBERFLÖTE halls. Particularly well received were its "Sailor Parties," "Transvestite Parties" (cross-dressing was mandatory for admittance), and "Fun Evenings," where each Violetta member had to fill out a card indicating her wildest sexual fantasy. The violet and the popular lesbian "Lilac Song" were the club's emblem and signature theme. Always championed in the oldest German lesbian newspaper, *Die Freundin*, a biweekly much respected in straight leftist circles.

_____ —A little-talked about organization of *Sharpers*, Lametier members met socially at the SCHUBERT HALL in Berlin West on Sunday evenings.

cigar-smoking *Bubis*, holding court at a ticket table. Once approved, female customers were expected to bend forward (depending on their state of dress) in order to receive a complimentary kiss from one of the *Bubis*. Men, after paying admission, were merely waved through.

Inside, the Topp shook with libertine excess. The place swarmed with pouty glam dolls, club girls, whores of every stripe, foreign dignitaries, star-struck *Nuttes*, and in-the-know pervs. "Beauty" contests (where patrons voted on the shapeliest body parts of otherwise cloaked volunteers) opened the evening. Lesbian reel-dances and spin-the-bottle type party-games filled the dance floor until midnight. Then under the conductorship of a statuesque *Domina* named Napoleon, dizzy *Hot Sisters* warbled their way though the "Lilac Song," Berlin's unofficial lesbian anthem.

The proprietor of the Topp was the gorgeous blonde, "Gypsy-Lotte." A dynamic *Sharper*, she was said to know the exact erotic preferences and favorite drinks of her *Diele* regulars. Lotte's liberating wit and scintillating personality drew together the Topp's broad and variegated audience. And whenever the carnal atmosphere began to dim, Lotte scolded the clubgoers with her much-remembered

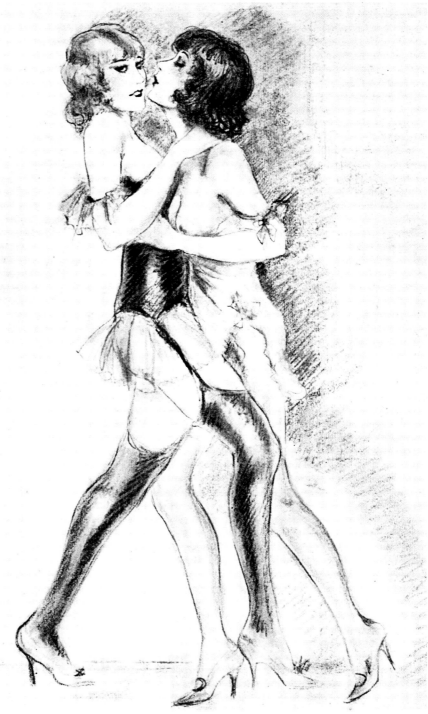

catchphrase: "Mood, mood, children!" On "Elite-Women's Night," a monthly feature, Lotte donned a fortuneteller's costume and transformed into her alter-ego character, "Princess Nana Hama," a man-crazed, Gypsy clairvoyant. Lotte's parodies of sexually fiendish straight women especially delighted her many doting lesbian fans.

Opposite:
Schlichter,
Women's Club
(The Topkeller),
1925

Above:
Vala Moro,
*Young
Newlyweds*

Lesbian Social Clubs

More typical of Berlin's *Girlfriend* nightlife was its unique institution of lesbian social clubs. There were at least three dozen of these and they ranged in size from 600 to less than ten. The smallest clubs functioned more like extended families than determined political cells or narrowly-focused women's associations. The club members socialized on a regular basis, took holidays together, often pooled their money, and made a conscious attempt to forge a group identity. The activities of the lesbian social clubs were relatively easy to track because of their openness and the lesbian press' coverage of them. A good example was "The Whistle Club," a hard-partying crew, consisting of seven to twelve *Gamines*.

Beginning in 1928, the Whistle Club met every Thursday at the "Princess Café," a Berlin West nightspot and *gemütlich* restaurant. Mostly secretaries and fed-

Right and Opposite: *Gamine* club on an outing

116

eral clerks during the day, the Whistlers banded together to open a joint savings account, shared a wacky lottery-betting scheme, and, in winter, registered as a skating society. Their madcap activities at the café included out-of-key sing-alongs with the conférencier Erich Fuchs, line dancing, and constant erotic funhousing with all-work barmaid Liselotte.

Each Whistle Club member transformed into an erotic play-character at night, and none more so than the entertaining Irma, a tiny flirtatious boy-girl with striking Slavic features and a brown *Bubikopf.* Always dressed in an

adorable sailor suit, Irma was known for her favorite pastime, "rag-doll." She sprang from chair to chair, allowing her clubmates to fondle her flagrantly and play with her body as if she were a mechanical, wind-up toy soldier or lifeless (if spectacularly sexy) puppet.

Another public amusement involved the meticulously groomed, blonde Liselotte. She was actually a fastidious and highly secretive male transvestite. Her gender dysphoria was the target of practical jokes and smutty teasing from the lesbian regulars and a source of confusion for the casual straight drop-ins. Broken-toothed Grete Nissen, the proprietor of the Princess Café, often accompanied the Whistle Clubbers in their choral performances and actively encouraged their sexual torment of Liselotte, apparently her son. ■

Those who study the problem of transvestitism more closely and have the opportunity of meeting many transvestites, are surprised again and again at the extent and intensity of this peculiar phenomenon.

Magnus Hirschfeld, *Sex Knowledge,* **1928**

I was told that some of those [prostitutes] who looked most handsome and elegant were actually boys in disguise. It seemed incredible, considering the sovereign grace with which they displayed their saucy coats and hats. I wondered if they might be wearing little silks, under their exquisite gowns. Must look kind of funny I thought—a boy's body with a pink, lace-trimmed shirt. Not very pleasant, though. Were there Russian princes among those picturesque, if somewhat revolting hermaphrodites? Or sons of Prussian generals, who, in such a bizarre mode, protested against the rigid principles of their fathers?

Klaus Mann, 1942

CROSSED BOUNDARIES

Rouged *Line-Boys* in female garb plying their trade near the Passage, *Aunties* in long gowns quietly sharing a beer in darkened lounges, and raucous transvestite nightclubs in the Berlin West were among the most common representations of Berlin decadence. German provincials, foreign sightseers, and gossip columnists alike gravitated to these baroque displays of gender mystification. Both sexual freak show and a high-class amusement, public drag scenes provided a comic relief from the more threatening forms of erotic behaviors on Berlin's ever-widening spectrum. Most Berliners and fellow tourists, straight or gay, could share a judgment on this one resplendent perversion: cross-dressed men and women were ridiculous, pathetic, harmless creators—contemptible, beyond the pale of serious sexuality. They were truly queer.

There were political implications as well: for the National Socialist Movement and the growing reaction in the early Thirties, male transvestism was the most ubiquitous sign of a weakening morality and sexual degeneracy of the Republic under democratic rule. Mustached *Aunties* were comical figures but also disturbing and concrete symbols of Germany's psychological evisceration.

OUR EXCURSION TO "EL DORADO"
by Bernard Zimmer

While we check our overcoats, a pretty young woman makes her charming entrance in front of us. She removes her hat, slides out of a big sable coat, applies red polish to her lips, and flirtatiously brushes back her platinum-blonde bangs.

"What an entrancing mademoiselle," I remark.

We enter after her. The Eldorado reminds us of little bar-restaurants from the French countryside: a bit of theatre, a bit of dancing. We catch sight of our ravishing blonde friend, who sits down at a nearby table. It is filled with a dozen strangely dressed companions.

"You know," our waiter points out," all those pretty girls sitting at the table over there are really men!"

That is the attraction of the house.

These false ladies, beautifully decked out, dance with each other, and gladly waltz with the club customers. We scrutinize them, itemizing each body part. Every time we seem to discover one glaring defect. Some of these camouflaged Eves are betrayed by a neck too muscular, a hand too wide, an ankle too thick. Others attain near perfection: Two lovely girls, one blonde, the other auburn, dance the Valse Boston faultlessly. They are slim, nearly without hips; their slender frames are extenuated by their long dresses, which reveal exquisite pairs of shapely legs. Unfortunately, they are men!

The most bewildering of these perverts are not the most perfectly feminine. There are, in the crowd, two or three big *dondons* (fat women) with short, thick-fingered hands, drooping breasts, huge behinds, Adam's apples, and five o'clock shadows. One oversized *dondon* says about another, "The poor girl, how seedy she appears tonight!"

The life of these "transvestites" is interesting to observe: Most live in couples with a thousand jealousies and intrigues. Some are small-time prostitutes, others husbands, and a few are fathers with families. And the prostitutes are treated like members of any other respected profession.

Like ragged circus clowns who inexplicably bring tears to children, male transvestites furtively evinced an underground fraternity of ineffectual, castrated fathers.

Militant Homosexualists shared this one hateful belief with the right-wing and religious opposition. *Ladies* (and feminized males in general) were despicable; their soft, depilated bodies and mocking antics were an affront to German strength and German manhood. In the ethos of Brand's disciples, male transvestites projected a weak, jaded, and mocking reflection of same-sex male desire; a dangerous and irreparably haunting challenge to phallocentric gays and their Hellenistic theories of male supremacy and the soldierly rectitudes of man-boy love. Men in drag were regarded as disgusting *Untermänner*. Women were born into their hapless gender. *Aunties* and *Ladies*

enthusiastically adopted the dress, "soul," and even the Christian names of the lowly sex.

Still a hardcore community of transvestites flourished in Berlin despite all efforts to suppress and sharply restrict their presence and nighttime pursuits. In fact, it was drag entertainments in the forms of balls and *Dielen* that customarily marked Berlin Weimar's erotic vitalism, its taunting masquerade of tangled and flipped carnal lust. Deco line-drawings of men in taffeta dresses and women in top hats signified only one Jazz-Age metropolis. The actual demographics of sometime drag queens and kings in Berlin, however, remained a mystery. (There were probably more secret cross-dressers in London and New York during the Twenties.) What made the city Transvestite Central was the sexological work of Magnus Hirschfeld, who did for cross-dressing what Freud had already done for modern neurosis: define it.

"The Erotic Urge to Cross-Dress"

The impulse to dress and exhibit oneself in the clothing of the other gender was thought to be a transcultural phenomenon. In the preliterate world, wonder-working shamans traditionally wore garments

In the room are some bourgeois couples and curious families from the neighborhood. They look upon the spectacle with wonder and fascination, like going to the movies.

The other Eldorado [on Motzstrasse] is more elegant. Sophisticated types spend the evening there for the performances and to savor a bottle of German champagne. On a small stage, some danseuses in tutus twirl on point: Again transvestites. (Many are from Paris.)

The main attraction is the "Dance of Héliogabal," executed by a lissome and naked eighteen-year old beauty. Not a disciple of [André Gide's] "Corydon." One can easily recognize that he is a little-cousin of Nijinsky. His golden body and coltish grace are not unpleasant to watch.

At an adjoining table, before a small cup of "mokka," sits a redheaded woman with Persian eyes. "Is this a man?" I ponder. After almost a half-hour, I still can't decide, for the red-head has delicate hands and very pretty legs. When our mokka-drinking neighbor stands up to leave, I observe her from behind. Her forearms reveal the ruddy smooth complexion of a female chef but her posterior displays something different: the unmistakable solidity of a male buttocks. So? So, one doesn't know anymore!

Bewildered, we leave for the lesbian lounges, the "Domino," "House of My Sister-in-Law," and "Mali and Ingel." In these nightclubs, women dress like miniature gentlemen. At three in the morning, tired of deciphering the perpetual riddle of "who is what sex," we depart for the safety of our hotel, confused and frustrated.

forbidden to those of their sex. In Asia, court theatres alternately encouraged and savagely proscribed gender-reversed presentations. Severe Biblical prohibitions against cross-dressing attested to its ancient Western roots. And Roman chapbooks famously detailed orgiastic spectacles where demented emperors openly flaunted their peculiar lusts, disguised in the perfumed wraps of mythic fertility goddesses or bejeweled harlots.

From the early Renaissance onward, a great folklore developed in Europe about cross-dressed women who lived fantastic lives as men, including great military and religious figures. In general, transvestism was viewed as an expansive form or feature of sexual inversion. The need to parade in the accouterments of opposite sex graphically "disclosed" a homosexual inclination. Central European psychologists, at the end of the nineteenth century, published hundreds of case histories establishing the obvious link between cross-dressing and classic uranism, or homosexuality.

Dr. Hirschfeld had a different take on these puzzling enactments. He also studied hundreds of cross-dressers in Berlin (but with surprising empathy) and theorized that the irrepressible urge to costume oneself with articles of clothing identi-

fied with the opposite sex fell into a new and independent erotic category. In 1908, he coined the word to describe this "intermediate sexual" behavior as *transvestism* and further popularized the provocative theory with his influential text, *Transvestites: the Erotic Drive to Cross-Dress.*

According to Hirschfeld, only 35% of the male and female transvestites he observed could be classified as practicing homosexuals; an equal percentage were, more or less, congenital heterosexuals, with the remaining 30% being split between cross-dressers who exhibited bisexual tendencies and "auto-monosexuals," a narcissistic type for whom the very act of pasting up an artificial beard or sporting false breasts before a mirror accompanied an autorerotic rush. Even among the cross-dressing bisexuals, Hirschfeld found a strong psychological tilt toward heterosexuality: they were mainly married men, who reluctantly allowed themselves to be penetrated by *Cellar-Masters* because of a desperate need to wear feminine clothing during intercourse. By engaging in this particular activity, bisexual transvestites claimed that they had maintained a heterosexual fidelity to their unknowing spouses.

Hirschfeld culled from the literature of cross-dressers and explored the wide, and naturally hidden, world of transvestite life in Berlin. In doing so, he was able to devise discrete typologies and innovative classifications

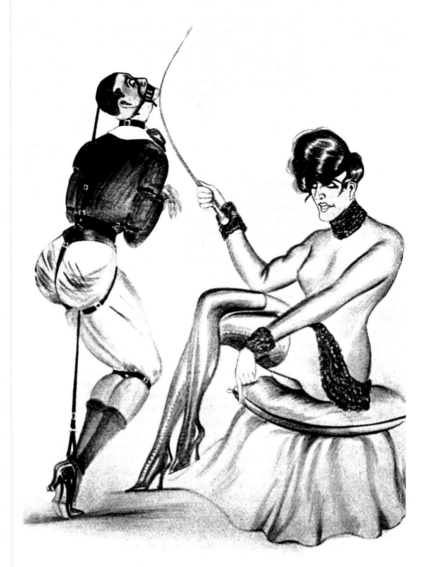

for gender reidentification and illusionism. These were based on the intensity of the erotic fixation and its relationship to sexual release (some male transvestites, for instance, desperately needed female attire to maintain erectile status; others suffered from spontaneous ejaculation when lipstick or other female makeup was forcibly applied to their faces); the duration and scope of activity ("Silk panties worn only after office-hours, sir?"); the full, partial, open, or veiled nature of the clothing or behavior ("What do you feel when the young woman seated next to you realizes that your

Opposite:
The New
Eldorado, 1928

Above:
Kamm, *Training*

123

vate counseling there, filling out cards that described their erotic compulsion in minute, near-pornographic detail. And it was long rumored (and reported in the reactionary press) that the otherwise strait-laced medical physician and cultural celebrity himself metamorphosed into a charming full-figured *Auntie* at Institute tea parties and secluded, smutty evening gatherings.

The Transvestite Demi-Monde

Despite Hirschfeld's scientific announcements, male and female transvestites were universally seen as a colorful subset of queer Berlin. Cross-dressed heterosexuals, except as one-time *Doll-Boys* or girlish *Line-Boys*, remained closeted and invisible to the general public. Straight and bisexual transvestites, reportedly the majority, had little interest in socializing or even communicating with one another. *Der dritte Geschlect* ("The Third Sex"), Friedrich Radszuweit's upbeat periodical for "ordinary" [straight?] cross-dressers, couldn't find a reading public and folded after two or three issues in 1929.

arm is not that of a man's?"); and significantly, how the altered gender appearance transformed the transvestite into a more authentic, sexually charged and psychologically fulfilled individual.

At his Institute of Sexology, which opened in 1919, Hirschfeld employed several transvestite maids and servants of both genders. Hundreds of Berlin cross-dressers, including Nazi Party members, received pri-

Heterosexual *Ladies,* according to Hirschfeld, often married women with pronounced masculine traits (often themselves partial cross-dressers). Shame and fear of social ridicule kept straight transvestites' distinct peccadillos indoors or coyly sublimated except during Carnival season. Undecided or borderline types were, of course, a lucrative cash cow for *Minette* callgirls, who graciously offered their special therapeutic services.

The normal life of queer male transvestites, the obvious drag queens and divas, who frequently lived as couples, was further complicated by Paragraph 168, a Prussian statute that forbade the appearance of cross-dressers on Berlin's thoroughfares. This gave rise to private transvestite *Dielen* and bars, where patrons entered as dowdy men and women and then re-emerged from the bustling restrooms as splendid specimens of the opposite sex. On occasion—and as a favor to crime reporters, usually their drinking buddies—Berlin vice commissioners staged phony raids on these establishments, maliciously forcing the transvestites out into the street, where they were subject to instant arrest and a battery of tabloid paparazzi.

Above:
Expressive drawing by Voo-Doo, a *Lady* dancer

Transvestite Nightlife

Private lounges and nightclubs formed the nucleus of Berlin transvestite social activity and interaction. The first club that catered to cross-dressers, the "Hannemann," opened in 1892 on Alexanderstrasse, and welcomed both men and women. It was also a Boy Bar, and its mixed queer clientele typified a communal openness of same-sex pursuits in the Wilhelmian era. Frequented by

off-duty German soldiers, low-level bureaucrats, *Line-Boys,* and hard-drinking *Bubis,* it was soon replaced by the infamous "Mikado Bar" and the "Bülow-Kasino" (on Bülowstrasse).

After the Collapse, drag queens appeared everywhere and added much to Berlin's local color. The American writer Robert McAlmon, who visited the city during the desolate winter of 1923, reported, "Several Germans declared themselves authentic hermaphrodites [*sic*—transvestites], and one elderly variant loved to arrive at the smart cabarets each time as a different type of woman: elegant, or as washerwoman, or a street vendor, or as a modest mother of a family. He was very comical and his presence always made for hilarity."

Yet there was a corresponding pathetic side to that transgender illusionism: boys forced into the role of Situational female whores. Again McAlmon on a melodramatic note: "At nights along the Unter den Linden it was never possible to know whether it was a woman or a man in women's clothing who accosted one. That didn't matter, but it was sad to know that innumerable young and normal Germans were doing anything, from dope selling to every form of prostitution, to have money for themselves and their families, their widowed mothers and younger brothers and sisters."

Transvestite acts, a standard feature of nineteenth-century German music-hall and variety, became more plentiful after 1919 and could be found in most gay cabarets and amusement halls. Performing before a mostly young, randy, and mostly liberated queer audience absolutely changed the *outré* nature of the enactments and their dramatic meanings. But growing political tension between the organized gay community and the theatrical drag queens and kings in the mid-Twenties forced a mass exodus of cross-dressers from homosexual *Dielen* to a different Berlin sensation, the public transvestite nightclub.

Although there were never more than a dozen such "licensed" outlets at any one time, transvestite entertainment palaces and cabarets quickly revamped the city's boastful "Once in Berlin" nightlife. And since straight tourists were usually cherished customers,

transvestite clubs appropriated the hard-currency draw of less humble and physically insecure posts of "divine decadence." Hotel brochures, tourist guidebooks, even intellectual monthlies promoted the major drag clubs, and in return received substantial advertising. The Nationalist, middle-of-the-road, and Catholic political parties, of course, raged. Again the greatest opponents of the clubs were Berlin's militant gay organizations and societies, who found them so distasteful and degenerate that not one male homosexual publication ever accepted a paid ad from them.

On the other hand, many hip Berliners and foreign tourists wrote admiringly about the transvestite vestibules. Typical description of the hotsy-totsy "Eldorado" from a Berliner: "You'd see always famous people there, like Max Pallenberg. Not much of a show, but

the most fascinating thing was ... you had lesbians looking like lesbians with short hair, lesbians looking like beautiful women, lesbians dressed exactly like men and looking like men. You had men dressed like women so you couldn't possibly recognize they were men, it was so realistic. Then you would see couples

Above:
Benari,
Eldorado Dancers

Left:
Melchior,
Meyer-Stube

127

the old man's otherworldly enchantment with the place. Leaning between the club's backroom columns were the Eldorado's stunning males in drag. To the provincial Artur, they resembled nothing so much as pale princesses out of children's storybooks. The raucous atmosphere of gender confusion, for one guileless German, had crossed over into the realm of poetic theatre.

American *Vogue* also attempted a sendup of Berlin's transvestite clubs. For their May 1932 issue, a

dancing and you wouldn't know any more what it was." (quoted from *Mankoff's Lusty Europe*).

Among Rumpelstilzchen's many journalistic gimmicks was his annual fall *Bummel*, where he accompanied his fuddy-duddy uncle from the sticks to some bizarre or naughty Berlin institution. In September 1931, the roguish, *Schnauze* columnist brought Uncle Artur to the Eldorado at midnight. Artur, of course, got everything wrong but Rumpelstilzchen understood

reporter scoured the city in search of Berlin's single most perfect female. Starting with the grand hotel lobbies, the voyeuristic safari took the writer through an assortment of chi-chi cafés and Pleasure Palaces. Using a beauty chronometer that rated everything from up-to-date shoe accessories to ideal nose length, *Vogue*'s travel specialist failed to detect a stylish *Berlinerin* worthy of the title. Then, at the suggestion of a local, he took a chance at the old Eldorado, where a non-biological femme finally complied with the American's exacting requirements.

Vogue did not know it but, by the time their sardonic piece was published, Berlin's drag *Dielen* had already been banned and shuttered. The growing Nazi and Nationalist menace nationwide began to affect the Berlin social climate.

In March 1932, the city's frightened liberal vice establishment declared male transvestite nightclubs an affront to public morality and, under Paragraph 168, used their authority to close them permanently. Seven months later, the Nazis made a poignant effort of transforming the Eldorado on Motzstrasse into one of

their district electoral headquarters. It was as if a desecrated Nordic temple had been thoroughly cleansed of polluted influences and re-sanctified for the virtuous torch-bearers of Adolf Hitler's New Germany. ■

Above:
Muguette

I have just come back from the Land of the Naked, where men, women, children, oldsters, fathers and mothers of families, virgins and adolescents come and go quite nude, where they bathe, laugh, eat, drink and cook their meals, in a state of total, stark, utter nakedness. Do not go and search for this earthly paradise at the Antipodes. It is situated at a distance of twenty hours from Paris. In the very heart of Europe, in Germany, to be exact.

Louis-Charles Royer, *Let's Go Naked*, 1932

"MORE SUN + MORE AIR + MORE NUDITY = MORE LIFE!"

Berlin Naturalist Slogan, 1926

LAUGHING NUDITY

Modern nudism, or *Nacktkultur*, developed into a mass German movement shortly after the Armistice and continued well into the Nazi era. Like many Central European social innovations, it fused modernist and reactionary beliefs in such a way that it defied easy definition and appealed to people on the political fringes who had little else in common. Hirsute revolutionaries, primitive Christians, Aryan mystics, middle-of-the-road Socialists, free-thinkers, Nationalist academics, health fanatics, eye-fluttering gurus, unrepentant feminists, pseudo-Buddhists, and flat-out hedonists all joined arms to promote the cult of the naked human body.

The peripatetic leaders and theoreticians of the *Nacktkultur* program adroitly stitched together a dedicated underground community of "Life Reformists" and visionary utopians from Germany's disaffected. Their web extended everywhere. It was particularly strong in Northern Germany, where several dozen nudist sites and colonies dotted the

GERMAN NUDIST AND LIFE REFORM MAGAZINES

Die Aufklärung ("The Enlightenment"), "a Monthly Journal for Sex and Life Reform." Edited by Magnus Hirschfeld and Maria Krishe from the Institute for Sexology. An upbeat zine designed in a pop/Bauhaus format, it mixed enthusiasm for *Nacktkultur* with sexological exposés and anthropological/historical material. Supportive of Adolf Koch's "Free Men, Union for Socialist Life Reform" and sympathetic to homosexual and lesbian aspects of nudism. [1929–1931]

Der Eheberater ("The Marriage Counselor"), a "Monthly for Hygienic People's Instruction." A women's magazine that promoted nudism, natural medicine, graphology, and sexy fashions. Interesting advice columns. [1928].

Das Freibad ("The Open-Air Bath"), a "Monthly Journal for the Promotion of Naked Bathing." A glossy magazine with a nonpolitical and clearly hedonist appeal. Affiliated with Birkenheide. Edited by Charly Straesser. [1927–1932]

Figaro, "Bi-Monthly Journal for Politics and Culture." Motto: "Fights in Word and Picture for Cultural Freedom." Illustrated popular magazine promoting *Nacktkultur* from both historical and international perspectives. Famous for its satirical *faits divers* and political cartoons. Affiliated with the FKK. [1924–1932]

Freikörperkultur und Lebensreform ("Free Body Culture and Life Reform"), "Magazine of the Reichs Union for Free Body Culture." Conservative intellectual journal open to middle-class and Catholic points of view. Affiliated with the New Sunland League. [1929–1930]

Die Freude ("The Joy"), a "Monthly Journal for Free Life Reform." Artistic journal, embracing both Socialist and Nationalist points of view. Expressionist in design and thought. [1924–1925]

Ideal-Ehe ("Ideal Marriage"), a "Monthly for Spiritual and Corporal Education in Marriage." Edited by Edgar Schulz. A glam women's magazine with a progressive slant. Lots of articles on modern living, nudism, body development, and problems in marriage. [1927–1929]

Körperbildung/Nacktkultur ("Body Development/Naked Culture"), the "Organ of Free Men." An Adolf Koch periodical devoted to intellectual currents in the *Nacktkultur* movement. Filled with manifestos and recipes for good

North and Baltic Sea coastlines. By 1931, even landlocked Berlin had some 40 competing *Nacktkultur* societies and clubs.

What united the multi-hydra leagues, associations, unions, and brotherhoods was a shared enemy: modern capitalism. The weakening of blood ties and individual purpose, excessive fluctuations in birth rates, factories spewing toxic wastes, prostitution, the inhuman rationalization of medicine and education, alcoholism, the unbridled accumulation of paper assets, and a general decline in physical health and happiness were the inevitable products of the Industrial Revolution and the rampant urbanization that followed.

The *Nacktkultur* philosophers wanted nothing less than a wholesale reformation of German life. In their nude encampments, they promised, sacred space and time—beyond the numbing boundaries of work and pew—could be reestablished. By merely removing their clothing, strangers could shed their social markings, toss aside all sexual taboos, and enter into an exalted state of Adamite consciousness. Peace, emotional tranquility, physical health, and corporal beauty would reign in the Naturalist communes.

health. Especially concerned with children and women's issues. [1925-1933]

Kraft und Schönheit ("Strength and Beauty"), "Journal for Body Culture." Edited by Heinrich Pudor. An early *Nacktkultur* monthly magazine that increasingly promoted nudism as a form of regeneration for the "Nordic" race. Mostly drawings and text. [1900-1919]

Lachendes Leben ("Smiling Life"), a "Magazine for a Healthy World-Philosophy." A nonpolitical, nudist pictorial with short upbeat pieces, celebrating the family *Nacktkultur* lifestyle and Rhythmic Gymnastics. [1925-1933]

Leben und Sonne ("Life and Sun"), a "Monthly of the Free Body Culture." An independent intellectual Socialist journal concerned with children's health, sports, and nudity. Not affiliated with the Union of Free Men. [1925-1926]

Der Leib ("The Body"), "Picture Book of Ideal Nudity," [Earlier, "Organ for the Understanding of Spiritual Living Through the Knowledge of the Body."] Artistic journal edited by Max Tepp. Concerned with social issues, like female health, prostitution, and the Jewish Problem. Promoter of Rhythmic Gymnastics and *Ausdruckstanz* (Expressive Dance). [1919-1927]

Lichtland ("Light-Land"), "the "Official Organ for the League for Free Life Improvement." A magazine with innocuous nudist photographs but increasingly National Socialist orientation in text and design in the Thirties. [1923-1933]

Licht-Luft-Leben ("Light-Air-Life"). Combined with *Der Mensch*, "Monthly Journal for Beauty, Health, Spirit, Body Development." *Nacktkultur* supplement of *Die Schönheit*. A cooperative journal for twenty-some German and Swiss organizations. [1920-1933]

Nacktsport ("Naked Sport"), "Illustrated Journal for the Theory and Praxis of Healthful Development Through Sports." Edited by the German Nationalist Artur Fedor Fuchs. [1919-1923]

Die neue Zeit ("The New Era"). International Body Culture journal with color photographs. Edited by Swiss nudist Edi Frankenhausen. [1929-1933]

Soma, a "Monthly with Beautiful Photographs from the Naked and Free Air Movement." Small glossy zine with virtually no text or political point of view. [1931-1932]

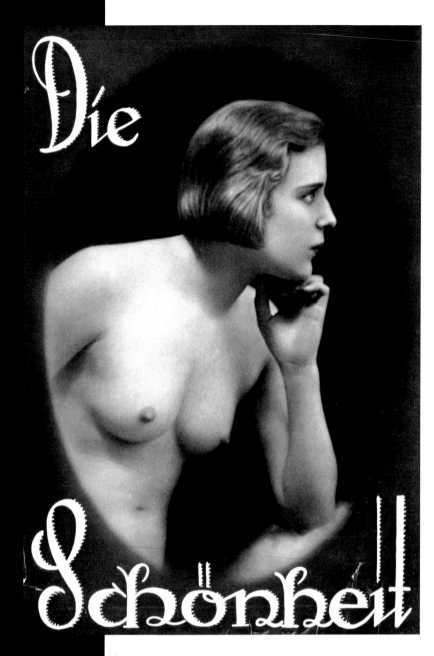

The message of organized nudism spoke compellingly to the nascent radicalism of the German-speaking world. Already there were separate attempts, like the *Wandervogel* movement, to rethink the conventional patterns and hierarchies of bourgeois life. Holistic methods of healing and amateur sporting leagues challenged the notion of high professionalism and the feudal divisions of labor. The *Nacktkulturists*, however, offered, in addition, spiritual uplift, community values, and all the wallop of a new religion.

Urban youth, according to Naturalist precepts, could attain a more profound sense of well-being without the blandishments of clergy or Gymnasium master. German boys and girls needed only nature (in the form of clean water, air, and sunlight), vigorous exercise, an improved diet, and the new awareness that the naked human body alone radiated perfection and supreme beauty.

Beginning in 1919, the illustrated periodicals and manifestos of *Nacktkultur* movement, of course, harped on the contrasts between their hale and robust life-styles and those of decadent Berlin. One pictorial theme appeared repeatedly: the Naturalist Girl and the Bad Girl. Typically, a photo-montage spread would juxtapose a series of carefree women in the nude tossing medicine balls with nighttime shots of smirking *Tauentziengirls* posed before the display windows of the Kadewe Department Store. The disparities, for the Life Reformers, could not be presented more starkly.

To most Berliners, accustomed to the vagaries of erotic dissonance, *Nacktkultur* and its celebration of the naked body manifested another interesting possibility in the ethos of sexual freedom. Nudist debates over chaste living, racial hygiene, "healthy desire," and moral purity, however, irked the free-spirited city dwellers. And, in the minds of the Girl-Culture consumers, these provincial platitudes wrapped the movement in an antiquated Puritan code.

Opening Left:
Daughter of Adolf Koch and friend, 1932

Opening Right:
Member of Artur Fuchs' Nationalist FKK

Previous Right:
Johannes Arz, *Weekend*

("The Beauty"), the most popular German monthly promoting all aspects of Body Culture. Edited by Karl Wanselow. Noted for its striking Art Deco design and aesthetic depictions of female nudity. Many articles on artists and scientific discoveries. Only *Nacktkultur* periodical with an interest in science fiction and sexual aids. Great classified section. [1902–1936]

("Sun Land"), "a Journal for Air Body Culture." [1931]

("Sunny Land"), "the Great, Illustrated Journal of the Free Body Culture Movement." A general nudist pictorial devoted to outdoor life. [1929–1933]

, a "Monthly for Nature-Consciousness and Social Learning." Socialist periodical with a heavy emphasis on nudism, German mysticism, and Buddhist teachings. [1925–1926]

After all, Naked Dance and "Beauty Evenings," which the *Nacktkulturists* vehemently condemned, also exhibited the nude body. But their prurient appeal violated the essence of modern German nudism. The healthy naked physique was not meant to be an object of male/female gaze or lewd entertainment, according to German Life Reform doctrine. Men and women who patronized Berlin's *Nachtlokals* and *Dielen* were obvious perverts, sick relics of a commodity-driven society. In the stirring words of the *Nacktkultur* manifestos,

shame and guilt—which unnaturally stimulated the sexual impulse—needed to be uncoupled from the display of the exposed human form.

Unfortunately, thrill-seeking Berliners too often reveled in their shame and guilt. With the air, it animated their nightly *Bummels*. And, during the Weimar period, at least two versions of organized nudism arose in the city: one for prudes (allied with the national federations) and one solely for Berlin's primitive sophisticates.

German Life Reform and *Nacktkultur*

The jumbled and contradictory nature of the Weimar German Life Reform and *Nacktkultur* movement is usually explained by its divergent nineteenth-century roots. Between 1870 and 1900, over 200 alternative therapies and patented health regimens—some fantastic and others with a scientific underpinning—sprang up in Central European clinics and spas. Homeopathy, mud and sea-air baths, hydrotherapy, "curative gymnastics," medical massage, physical culture programs, colonic cleansing and supervised fasts, sun worship, whole-grain, sour-milk or single-fruit diets, naked swimming, hypnotic and electrical wave treatments, all competed with the conventional medical wisdom for the soul and physical restoration of the German people.

In 1903, Heinrich Pudor, a devotee of air-bathing, combed the alternative, commercial muck and extracted from it the most outdoorsy and naturalist elements. He gave these nude therapies and philosophies an intriguing modernist name, *Nacktkultur* (Naked Culture),

Opposite:
At Birkenheide, 1926

Above:
Cover of *Die Schönheit* nudist calendar

of natural health and extolled his Manichean division of Germany into wholesome, young nudists—or potential nudists—and their envious opponents.

Naked-bathing was the most ubiquitous activity of the early *Nacktkultur* groups. The nude human body in free-flowing water provided arresting photographs for the aesthetic journals and echoed the German Romantic notion of man in joyous harmony with nature. Pudor even attacked the over-the-chest bathing suit as a Philistine invention. He harangued swimming trunks as the contemporary "mark of Cain," created and worn by people ashamed of their genitals. No wonder the most popular color was red, Pudor wrote; the anti-Naturalists who covered their pasty bodies with them were in a perpetual state of blush.

Above:
Boys from
New Sunland

which effectively separated them from their folk and quack-cure sisters. Two artistic monthlies, *Die Schönheit* and later *Kraft und Schönheit*, advanced Pudor's vision

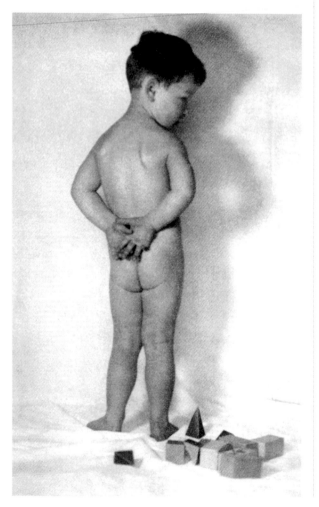

Several private *Nacktkultur* lodges in Berlin opened in 1907 as a result of *Die Schönheit*'s persuasive propaganda. The same year, Richard Ungewitter published *Nudity and Culture*, the first in a long string of intellectual pamphlets (with a total sales of 100,000) that lauded Pudor's dream. Ungewitter also affixed mystic Aryan and temperance features to the simple *Nacktkultur* philosophy: nudism, abstinence from alcohol and tobacco, and vegetarian diets were the means by which the German race would regenerate itself and ultimately prevail over its neighbors and the diabolical Jews, who were intent on injecting putrefying agents into the nation's blood and soil.

While Wilhelmian Germany's vice police checked the growth of the *Nacktkultur* societies and their ability to proselytize, Ungewitter turned the movement upside down with his cultist screeds. *Nacktkultur* enthusiasts were forced to consider the deep political meaning of their Edenic pursuits. The German Life Reform league splintered into hostile ideological camps in those years. Even the apoliticos had to explain their national purpose.

At first, the linkage of nudity to the dogmatic issues of German public policy and social renewal seemed over-reaching and blunted its unvarnished allure. The *Nacktkultur*, for the most part, was a reaction against the stultifying bourgeois existence, an indolent lifestyle that corporally terminated at the shoulder-blades. Bathing naked in a stream with one's family didn't normally attract the mokka-and-newspaper crowd from Berlin's smoky gentlemen clubs. But, starting in the Weimar period,

1. heft deutsche rm. 1. , schweiz. fr. 1.40, öster. schilling 1.80, holl. fl. .65. ckr. 9. **2. jahr**

everything changed. Nudism joined the political struggle and Germany's extremist parties embraced the *Nacktkulturists*.

During the Twenties, nudist societies formed in Scandinavia, the Baltic countries, Austria, Czechoslovakia, and France, but their overall membership was quite small. Only in Germany did Life Reform

AN AFTERNOON AT ADOLF KOCH'S "SOCIETY OF FREE MEN"

I saw one of the worst groups: skeleton-like adolescents and varicose old men; women with pendulous breasts and others whose posteriors might well vie with those of a Hottentot Venus. There were even consumptives who came back from their "sun showers" with great red moons on throat and backs.

Koch makes them dance—and they dance.

Awkwardly at first—and pitiful, it is, to see such efforts towards harmony made by these unshapely creatures.

They dance ...

And gradually, it seems to me, the charm begins to work. The pervading rhythm, Koch's persuasive words, the warm emanations given forth by all these bodies, intoxicate them. The pace quickens. They forget their ills, which yet permit them this physical lightness.

Some have lost their look of sad resignation; that expression of envious revolt, which characterized others, falls away. One of the women, with gnarled legs but with beautiful breasts, tenses her torso as though in dedication to some invisible male.

These too, then, amid the intoxication which music and feverish dance arouse in all their senses, these too may dream for one instant that they are—who knows?—beautiful and strong, or at least like their fellows.

"When they are together," Koch tells me, "they suffer less from their infirmities. They are mostly poor devils who toil hard for their daily bread. Some are 'pariahs.' They come here to forget their miseries, all their miseries. They feel equal, being naked. I believe they leave this place, not only the better for their bodies, but for their souls as well."

from Louis-Charles Royer, *Au Pays des Hommes nus*
(Paris: Editions de France, 1929)

organizations and their many periodicals enter into the public sphere. It was claimed that at the end of Weimar over one million German families belonged to *Nacktkultur* societies.

Nude Berlin

While Hamburg weighed in as the demographic champion of the *Nacktkultur* movement, Berlin claimed its intellectual heart. Quartered all through the Friedrichstadt were the national offices of the left- and right-wing nudist associations and their publishing arms. In Berlin's parks, enclosed swimming pools, and rehearsal halls, societies of the naked conducted weekly exercise classes in full public view. And, outside the city, surrounding Lake Motzen emerged 40 to 50 individual nudist "territories." Jan Gay, an American journalist, wrote in 1932, "A stranger in Berlin desiring to visit a nudist group has an embarrassment only of choice."

The Berlin groups heralded fanciful names that rarely disclosed their political leanings or size. (Only the Socialists included their party's affiliation in their *Nacktkultur* mastheads.) A few titles of the Nationalist and proto-Nazi outfits: "Berlin League of Free Body Culture" (FKK), "Concerned Community of Free Sunland and Naked Sports," "Federation of the Faithful," "League for Free Life Improvement," and the "Union of Free

Above:
Free Sunland

Below:
Territory
Adolf Koch

Sunland." Independent Marxist and Communist organizations: "Federation for Body Culture and Nature Indoctrination," "Federation for Body Culture and Nature Refuge," "Federation for Free Body Indoctrination," "Federation of Itinerant Youth," "German Air Bathing Society," "Sparta Sports Union," "State Federation for Free Body Culture" (AFK), and the "Union of Social Life Reform." Centralist, Catholic, Republican, and apolitical groups: "Federation for Natural Healing," "Federation of Free Light," "Friends of Nature," "Light-Federation Fairy Meadow," "New Sunland League," "Reichs Federation of German Youth Nudist Colonies," "Reichs Union for Free Body Culture," "Union for Body Culture," and the "Youth Reform Birkenheide." Socialist groups included: "Circle of Free Men," "Free Men, Union for Socialist Life Reform and Free Body Culture in the Federation of People's Health," "Socialist Cultural Society," and the "Workers Society of Outdoor Campers."

Many of the heroic-sounding—in fact the most heroic-sounding—"Federations" were one-man or one-

FIGARO

Aus dem Inhalt

(Heft 13, IX. Jahrgang)

15
Akt- u. Freilicht-Aufnahmen

—

Im Textteil:

Die verunglückten Jugend-
ämter — Jugend, die an Liebe
stirbt — Auch die Kehrseite
betrachten — Welch ein Segen!
Fern im Süd.... — Familie
bittet um Abtreibung — Ge-
fährdete Jugend — Darf ein
Erwerbsloser heiraten? — Kul-
turbolschewist Hugenberg —
Schwarze Lügenhetze — Erben

**Die Ehen
der Arbeitslosen**

**Das erotische Problem
im Film**

Fred Stelner:
**Kleine Tragödie
der Liebe ...**

Gerhard Lindner:
**Volk ohne Raum
vor 100 Jahren**

Paul Reboux:
DIE PERLE

**Weiche Männer und
harte Frauen**

**Wo bleibt die Liga für
gute Sitten?**

Natron und Geschlechtskraft
Vom Hängen allein kann man
nicht leben — Der Gegen-
satz — Der Kurpfuscher
Amerikanisches

**IX. Jahrgang
Heft 13**

Preis: 60 Rpf.
Oesterreich 1 Schill.

Adolf Koch and the "Society of Free Men"

Adolf Koch, like many of the founders of *Nacktkultur* associations, began his career in scandal. A principal in a state-run elementary school outside Berlin, he insisted that his young wards arrive in the classroom with clean hands, then clean feet, and finally thoroughly washed bodies. After introducing public showers, Koch noticed the giddy excitement it caused when students ran around naked to warm up. He introduced nude mat-exercises as a substitute and, to combat vitamin deficiencies in the proletarian children, brought the drill sessions outdoors under the health-giving sun.

When a government observer made a scathing report, with pedophilic overtones, on his students' rhythmic gymnastics—she called them "nude dancing"—Koch decided to resign rather abolish the program. Like other pedagogues in the *Nacktkultur* project, he was troubled about the physical and spiritual well-being of German youth and sought a means to elevate it.

In 1920, Koch inaugurated a *Nacktkultur* school in Berlin, which combined elements of Swedish Physical Culture, a pale form of *Ausdrucksgymnastik* (Expression

shot affairs with vivid logos and impressive promotional packaging. In Berlin, three men dominated the authentic *Nacktkultur* scene and were well known to the foreign press. Each represented a corner point on the Socialist, Nationalist, and anti-political triangle. These were Adolf Koch, Artur Fuchs, and Charly Straesser.

Gymnastics), nudity, and hands-on socialism. Everyone was addressed in the familiar German form of "Du" and under artificial, indoor lighting they exercised, listened to political and hygiene lectures, and swam naked. Later schools in five other cities and an outdoor campground on Lake Motzen, "Territory Adolf Koch," were added.

Koch's Body Culture schools recruited from Germany's powerful Socialist Party and the politically uncertain working class. All were welcome, without regard to income, profession, ethnic background, physical shape, or age. "Free Men" members were tithed five percent of their income as dues; the unemployed attended for free. The entire enterprise, which soon included nudist magazines and books, was a tremendous success. The Socialist "Alliance of People's Health" boasted 300,000 paid members in 1932.

The village schoolmaster, however, never left Koch. His classes began punctually and were highly structured. Although he personally trained his growing staff and often gave individual attention to special problems, his professional attitude was usually officious and chilly. The lecturers he chose pontificated on serious social and medical stuff. Nude adolescent boys were admonished for uncontrolled erections and compelled to attend a psychosexual clinic, where their churlish behavior was "studied and addressed." For the

politically correct Koch, the naked torso was not to be an instrument of sexual desire.

Despite its institutional, chaste environment, Koch's Body Culture Schools and their public demonstrations were sometimes viewed by outsiders as highly erotic. The mayor of Chicago, Anton Cermak, visiting Berlin in August 1932, remarked to Sefton Delmer during one demonstration, "You know somep'n? In Chicago, you couldn't get a show as good as this for a thousand bucks!" Nationalist and Nazi politicians agreed with the crime-busting American's

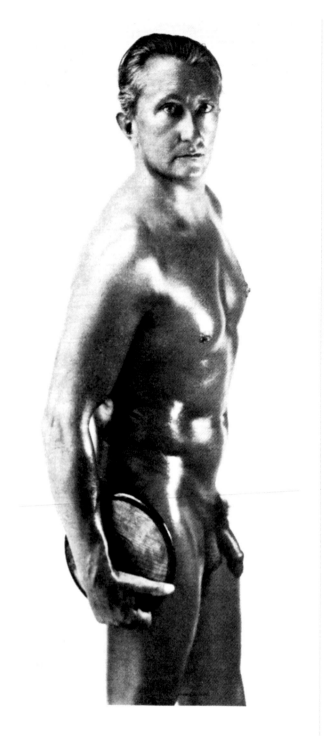

In three months' time, the Alliance's legal maneuvers against censorship and accusations of lewd behavior would hardly matter.

"League of Free Body Culture" and Surén's "Suncult"

Koch had many adversaries in the *Nacktkultur* world of Berlin. His tendentious Socialist teachings, skill for generating publicity, acceptance of all body types, and astonishing prosperity disturbed his opponents, who promoted nudism as an aesthetic as well as a health regimen. Mostly it was the reactionary *Nacktkultur* organizations that defined their programs in counter-distinction from the "Free Men."

In 1920, the Nationalist physician Artur Fedor Fuchs attempted to draw members for his "League for Free Body Culture" (FKK) from the same family and *Lumpenprol* pool that Koch had already reached. Staking out the first *Nacktkultur* Territory on the Lake Motzen army and offering a full calendar of sporting activities in the nude, Fuchs did find a lower- and middle-class audience. But it was limited.

Over the next few years, the FKK attracted a considerably more upscale and fashion-conscious crowd, Berlin's Girl-Culture denizens. At Fuchs' "Free Sunland" encampment, professional athletes, balding aristocrats, and glam film starlets—wearing just gold bracelets or

humble assessment. Two months later, they adjoined the Berlin City Council to close down Koch's establishments, citing they inspired nude orgies among the young and hundreds of spectators "to slake their carnal thirsts." Koch, like the *Ladies* club owners, fought the municipal injunctions, but the skies were darkening over freewheeling Berlin in the late fall of 1932.

sexy flat footwear—mixed on the volleyball and tennis courts. While the portly and bespectacled Fuchs himself had the reputation as a morose ideologue, the FKKers were basically apolitical and sexually hip. Unlike Territory Adolf Koch, Free Sunland provided ample opportunities for gawking at the eye candy during daylight hours and swinging in the nudist "fuck huts" at night. The food, although vegetarian and still Germanic, was several notches above the mucky Socialist fare.

For his can't-get-away-from-the-city members, Fuchs rented the multi-storied Luna Bad in Berlin East. There every Sunday and Wednesday, naked FKKers exercised, swam, received electrical tanning and massage treatments, and ate. The sight of moneyed aristocrats dining in the semi-nude (most retained one small indication of class, like a monocle or silver hair brooch) amused foreign journalists, looking for those Only-in-Berlin social mores. Former military officers, sans uniform, bowed to kiss ladies' hands and then dashingly clicked their bare heels together. Society types main-

tained their elegant manners although their protruding flesh sometimes got in the way.

A cynic writing for the American newsweekly *The Outlook* spotted a fat society matron at the Luna Bad one morning who became so engrossed in her companion's repartee that she failed to notice the soft-boiled egg matter falling from the spoon she held in front of her mouth. The errant yolk drops rolled down her breast, hung from her nipple for an instant, and then splattered over the folds of her stomach.

As the FKK expanded, its softcore Aryan message became more stringent and pronounced. *Nacktkultur,*

Licht ✦ Luft ✦ Leben

vereinigt mit „Der Mensch", Monatsschrift für Schönheit, Gesundheit, Geist, Körperbildung

Above:
New Sunland,
1927

**Opposite and
Following:**
Surén
followers

lecturers illustrated in pulldown charts, was a natural reversion to pre-Christian folkways. Once the solar rays of the Nordic sky alone strengthened and healed the warrior nation. German tribes spent most of their summer daylight hours naked and carefree until evil missionaries from the south forcibly covered their bodies in shame. The awakening of Aryan might required a restoration of ancient forest practices.

Another German Nationalist, Hans Surén, pulled the reactionary *Nacktkulturists* even farther to the right. In his Berlin studio and influential publications, Surén proposed a cult of the sun and the naked male body. A celebrated officer from the German colony of the Cameroon, Surén instilled his followers with strict military discipline and designed a vigorous system of gymnastic drills. For Surén, *Nacktkultur* living was not a therapy for the weak and undernourished but a means of soldierly conditioning and sun worship. The salvation of the German people did not depend upon weekend armies of nature-lovers and naked sunbathers; it demanded a race of toned and greased-up supermen. Surén's first book *Man and the Sun* (1924) sold over 235,000 copies and was reissued in 68 editions by 1941. Despite its unmistakable homoerotic imagery—floppy-dicked muscle-men wrestling bright-eyed boys on the grassy plain—*Man and the Sun* was a favorite Aryan read for the Hitler faithful and Nazi culture-mavens.

"New Sunland League" and Birkenheide

Between Naked Marxism and Naked Fascism stood the bulk of the Berlin *Nacktkultur* supporters. They came from solid middle-class backgrounds and equated nudity with recreation and pleasure. The first Territory established for Berlin's nude hedonists was Fritz Gerlach's "New Sunland." Unlike the FKK Free Sunland, from which it seceded, the New Sunland had few rules or political slogans tacked to birch trees. Hanging over its admission table in front was a poster declaiming: "HAPPINESS—the Imposed Order of the Day." Instead of shaming boys out of their erections or stealing away in "fuck huts," New Sunlanders were encouraged to display their affections quite openly. All in all, the atmosphere in the New Sunland was unpretentious and pleasant, like the nudists themselves.

Less respectable was Hans Heinz Rassow's "Naked Club," which limited its membership to only the most beautiful and socially-connected youths. Meeting in Rassow's spacious Berlin West quarters, the Naked Club clique traveled en masse to *Wandervogel* sites, where they swam, hiked, sang folk songs, and generally partied nude in the woods.

Charly Straesser, a sometime participant in New Sunland League and the Rassow group, decided to create his own nude Territory on Lake Motzen in 1924. He called it "Birkenheide." Here *Nacktkulturists* could do anything they pleased. There were no official-looking identity cards, annual fees, psychological questionnaires, lessons in hygiene, group diets, campfire anthems, or political-ethnic profiles. Birkenheide's nudists weren't even required to have fun.

Photographers and gawkers who refused to disrobe were not admitted to Birkenheide. Anyone else was welcome. Patrons merely had to pay at the gate and agree to perform a short work assignment during their stay. Consequently, Birkenheide had the most varied and unconventional nudists. Straight perverts and gay men conducted their consensual activities unimpeded. Gigolos from the Resi and Femina nightclubs found Birkenheide most congenial to their daytime occupation. And Berliners out for a nonurban, fresh-air *Bummel* swore by the place. Charly Straesser's invention was a bit of libertarian paradise. It prospered until Berlin's *Nacktkultur* societies and Territories were reorganized as National Socialist institutions. ■

Licht-Land

Offizielles Organ der Liga für freie Lebensgestaltung
Illustrierte Blätter für Körperkultur und Lebenserneuerung·

Nr. 4 ★ V. Jahrg.   15. Februar 1928

der Lie... ...iesst, sprosst ...em Leben Liebe

I was led into the office of the "Wise Man of Berlin" (as he liked to be called) and what I saw filled me with horror. Sitting on a velvet armchair, his legs crossed beneath him like a Turk, was a man with bloated lips and crafty, lust-filled eyes. He offered me his fleshy hand and introduced himself as "Dr. Hirschfeld."

Hans Blüher, *Works and Days,* **1952**

Christopher giggled nervously when Karl Giese and Francis took him through the Institute's museum. Here were whips and chains and torture instruments designed for the practitioners of pleasure-pain; high-heeled, intricately decorated boots for the fetishists; lacy female undies which had been worn for ferociously masculine Prussian officers beneath their uniforms.

Christopher Isherwood, *Christopher and His Kind,* **1976**

THE NEW CALCULUS OF DESIRE

During the Great Inflation, as Berlin metamorphosed into Europe's garish midway of smut, a different, more respectable enterprise surfaced in the erotic city: "Sexual Science." A hodgepodge field that had its origins in Wilhelmian times, Sexology was nothing less than a mammoth attempt to excavate, classify, and then cobble together all things sexual into a single body of knowledge. Nearly every area of the humanities and medical science fed the novel endeavor: cultural anthropology and folklore; anatomy, biochemistry, and eugenics; endocrinology and psychotherapy; religious and art studies; social psychology and public health, criminology and prison reform. Even hypnosis, graphology, folk medicine, and nineteenth-century phrenology were analyzed for their sexual relevance.

SAMPLE QUESTIONS **FROM DR. MAGNUS HIRSCHFELD'S**

"PSYCHO-BIOLOGICAL QUESTIONNAIRE"

No. 17: In your immediate family, are there any females who look like men; or males with obvious female characteristics? Do any of your siblings exhibit any aspects of the opposite sex?

No. 44: Can you whistle?

No. 61: Are you left-handed?

No. 90: How do you feel about the Great War? What part did you play in it?

In Vienna's scientific circles, particularly among the bickering founders of psychoanalysis, there was great skepticism (later mixed with envy) over the ever-expanding scope and public acceptance of Sexual Science. The Berlin upstart, according to the Freudians, received far too much lay support and renown during its recklessly short period of incubation. The infant science had merely hacked off tiny offshoots from established disciplines (as it highlighted all their fringe minutiae) and grafted them onto some hulking, synthetic beast.

More irritating was the professional attitude of Sexology's leading practitioner, Dr. Magnus Hirschfeld. The Berlin educator acknowledged the opinions of his many detractors, considered their scientific validity, and frequently embraced them. "Papa" Hirschfeld was the liberal spirit of the infinitely tolerant metropolis. Debating him was an exercise in maddening futility, like passing bad notes on to an old-time counterfeiter or boxing an ancient but improbably nimble kangaroo.

"The Einstein of Sex"

Trained as a physician, Hirschfeld acquired other skills during his long career as the international spokes-man for Sexology. He was an energetic defender for sexual minorities and women, prolific science writer, legal authority, behind-the-scenes politician, and mas-ter showman. Hirschfeld was widely credited in his lifetime and after as the primary inventor of marriage counseling, Gay Liberation, artificial insemination, surgical gender "reassignment," and modern sex therapy.

In 1897, Hirschfeld founded the Scientific-Humanitarian Committee, the first organization anywhere devoted to the protection of homosexual rights. As a young doctor, he studied the riptide affects of alcoholism and unwanted pregnancy on Berlin's families and their neighborhoods. Prussia's comprehensive program for health and social welfare, considered to be the most enlightened in Europe, was designed by Hirschfeld in 1916. He also served as the first President of the World League for Sexual Reform.

Hirschfeld's judicious writings included more than 200 titles. Their range was broad and the research

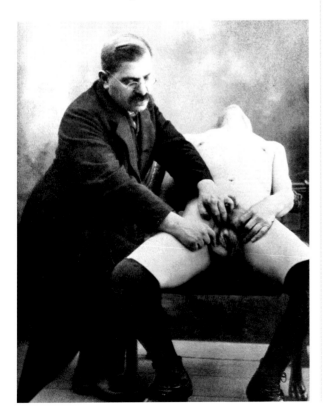

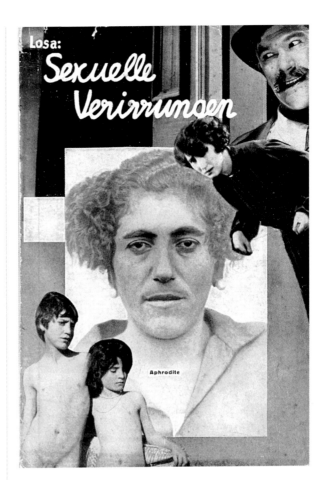

Aphrodite

insightful. Besides sexual variation, Hirschfeld methodically investigated pornography, traditional aphrodisiacs and sexual aids, the relationship between crime and illicit sexuality, social mores and fetishism, the etiology of pleasure, and the erotic basis of warfare. His goofy persona and conscientiousness transformed Sexology from an anthropological curiosity into a popular German science. The Berlin monthlies, starting in the mid-Twenties, referred to Hirschfeld solicitously as "the Einstein of Sex."

"Sexual Intermediates"

Hirschfeld embraced a doctrine known as "sexual relativity." He wrote that it was "unscientific" to speak of only two sexes. Between "full man" and "full

No. 92: Do clothes occupy an important part of your thinking? Do you prefer a simple or multi-layered look, tight or free-flowing garments, high-collared or open shirts? Do you wear any accessories or jewelry? Do you have a favorite color? Which?

No. 93: Do you normally carry in your pockets or purse: a knife, make-up kit, lighter, or photographs? What objects do you like to always have with you?

No. 97: Have you ever been aroused by a member of your own sex?

No. 99: Which sexual partners do you normally prefer: people older than yourself, younger, or—more or less—the same age? What was the most extreme difference in age of someone to whom you were attracted? Do differences of age and generation have no importance for you?

No. 100: Which do you find more exciting: the naked body, the clothed body, or the partly-clad body? Does the smell of perspiration from certain people ever excite you? Repel you?

No. 102: Have you ever fallen in love with someone solely because of an idiosyncratic trait, like the way that person wore something, their body shape, hair color, or spiritual demeanor?

No. 104: During sex, have you ever fantasized you are with another partner?

No. 123: Have you ever wished that your beloved treated you in such a way as to cause physical pain? Allowed or commanded him/her to hit you?

No. 131: Have you ever been tempted to have intercourse with three partners? In which combination of men and women?

No. 132: Have you ever been sexually aroused by an animal?

No. 133: Does it bother you when someone refuses to talk about their sexual peculiarities?

woman" was an infinite string of sexual/gender possibilities. Male and female hormones, which Hirschfeld believed determined basic sexual type, were never carried in the blood as pure agents within any individual.

Each body manufactures andrin and gynecin (male and female) compounds in various proportions. When the glands that regulate these secretions produce too few andrins or gynecins—or are metabolized incompletely—a sexual "indeterminacy" develops, according to Hirschfeldian analysis. By puberty the hormonally-imbalanced individual exhibits psychological or physical signs of the opposite gender.

Around 1919, Hirschfeld estimated that two percent of humanity could be characterized as constitutional Sexual Intermediates. But his field studies in Berlin and use of more refined typologies during the Twenties and Thirties caused him to upgrade that initial calculation repeatedly. Toward the end of his career, he believed that about 15 to 20% of any observed population manifested aspects of Sexual Intermediacy.

At first, Hirschfeld identified four main Intermediate groups: Hermaphrodites, Androgynes, Transvestites, and Homosexuals. And within each of these classifications were many subgroups and lesser categories. For instance, he divided Hermaphrodites into: 1) men with female organs, 2) women with male organs, 3) people with both sets of sexual organs, appearing in some

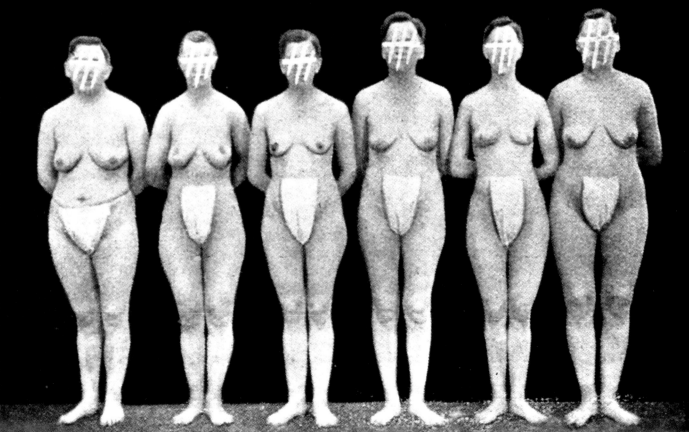

BAUER'S SHOE-AND-WHEEL MASTURBATION MACHINE
(AUGSBERG, 1920)

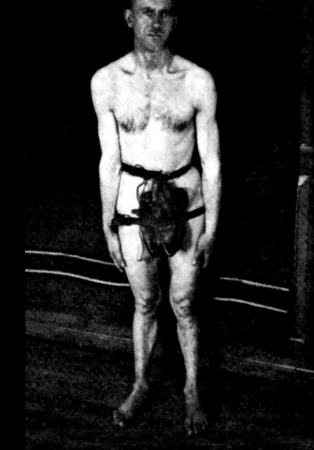

Ben Bauer (41) confessed that he built this Masturbation Machine. He willingly demonstrated its unusual mechanism and allowed himself to be photographed while doing so.

At an earlier age, Bauer was observed rubbing his penis against a cow's stomach until it became fully erect. He then inserted his member into the vagina of a nearby calf. On another occasion, Bauer's 72-year-old mother was found naked and unconscious with her legs spread open. Authorities suspected the son had intercourse with her. These allegations of bestiality and incest were, of course, vehemently denied by the young Bauer.

Description of the Picture:

Bauer built the Masturbation Machine with the following items:

1. Two Sewing Spools
2. A Bicycle Rim
3. Three Pairs of Used Women's Shoes
4. One Chain Gear
5. Two Leather Ties

Bauer strapped the first leather piece around the small of his back—with the slack taken up by a spool over the spine. The other spool was placed vertically near his anus. The second leather piece held the soles of the three shoes firmly against his stomach. This allowed the head of his penis to penetrate the middle shoe. By rolling the bicycle rim forward and back, Bauer created the proper thrust and friction for a full ejaculatory release.

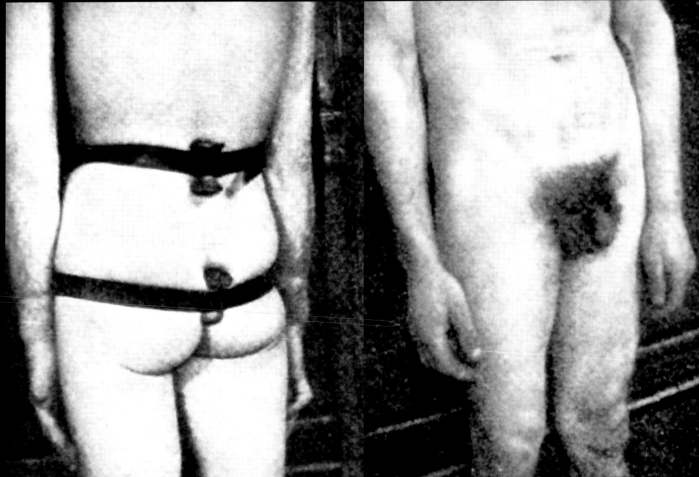

rudimentary or arrested state, and 4) people possessing functional duel male-and-female genitalia.

What united all types of Hermaphrodites, Hirschfeld maintained, was their confused sexual self-definition, a psychological state that was conditioned by a sustained ability to shield their abnormality from the world around them. He found cases of female-with-male sexual characteristics (Number Twos) particularly difficult to investigate because such individuals habitually altered their sexual identities two or three times during their troubled adolescence and adulthood.

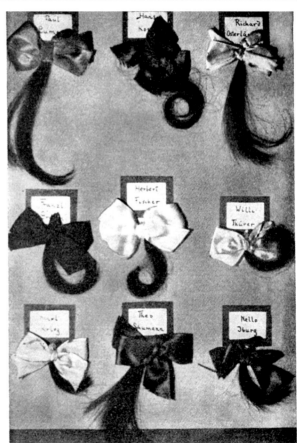

One of Hirschfeld's many astonishing case studies on Hermaphroditism: "Bertha D.," a seamstress, was taunted as a child for her masculine voice. Later when she discovered that her face was sprouting facial hair, "D." soon tired of shaving twice a day and began wearing male clothing and assumed a male identity. By 18, "Bert" successfully engaged in sex with teenage girls, but she suffered from fierce, premature ejaculations. Around age 20, "D.'s" sexual orientation included boys as well. Although "D." was unable to maintain an erection with the young males, her engorged clitoris-penis discharged spermatic fluids during intercourse with them. "D." told Papa that her desire for men peaked right after menstruation but she normally derived more intense sexual pleasure from female partners. Was "D." a true bisexual, a lesbian with male homosexual tendencies, or a pansexual with straight urges? Hirschfeld merely assured her a coveted point on his Intersexual spectrum. "D." was what she was (*Hermaphroditismus femininus* #1,982).

Hirschfeld's other Intermediate types cropped up more frequently in the general population. Androgyny involved the growth or adaptation of secondary sexual characteristics from the opposite gender. Male Androgynes, typically, lacked facial hair, had feminine breasts, sensitive nipples, soft fatty skin, and rounded pelvises. Female Androgynes, correspondingly, had

flat breasts, little sensitivity around the nipple, and possessed a masculine build, vocal range, and distribution of hair. Unlike Hermaphrodites, both male and female Androgynes were likely to enhance, rather than hide, their constitutional state and seek the sexual company of their heterosexual or homosexual complements.

Hirschfeld punctured the Renaissance myth that Androgynes were divinely bisexual creatures—the vast majority he met were utterly "straight." One of Papa's favorite patients was a bearded lady who appeared in local freak shows. In spite of her super-masculine appearance, she was a tender and self-sacrificing mother. (When she was about to give birth to her fourth baby, the midwife naturally mistook her for the father.)

Transvestites were psychological Androgynes, people who voluntarily acquired the look of the opposite sex through dress, exaggerated mannerisms, and corporal deformation. While an apparent psychic phenomenon, Hirschfeld believed Transvestitism required an entirely separate psychosexual nomenclature, since its practitioners were neither exclusively heterosexual or queer. Among his clients, for example, was the Chief of Police of a Central European town, who was married and fathered several children. While normal in every other aspect, the Chief was never content in masculine attire. He liked to visit Papa during his vacations and spend the rest of the day dressed as a woman on the welcoming streets of Berlin.

For other Transvestites, only particular costumes satisfied their deepest urges. One *Lady* confessed to Hirschfeld that his mother's cream-colored damask dress, which he furtively wore on the day of his church confirmation, stimulated his first erection and was a necessary sex aid ever since. Another patient wrote that the mere donning of a frilly lace skirt caused him to orgasm uncontrollably. No other clothing or sexual companionship did the trick.

Hirschfeld's designation of Homosexual men and women, the so-called Third Sex, as Sexual Intermediaries, created the most controversy. He believed they,

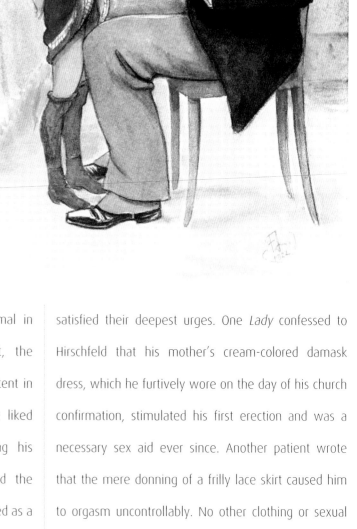

HANS LUNGWITZ

EINER
MUTTER
LIEBE

like the other Intersexuals, were constitutionally predisposed in their sexual desires as "incomplete" mature males and females. The theory enhanced queers' legal status as helpless victims of faulty chromosomes—and the mass struggle against Paragraph 175—but its scientific and social value was challenged on every front. Militant Homosexualists ridiculed the secretive Papa as "Auntie Magnesia," a cross-dressing sissy and cosmopolitan Jew. Of course, it was hardly noticeable to Hirschfeld's antagonists, that the ever-protean and

devoted sexologist incorporated their scientific objections into his evolving grid of transsexuality.

Derangements of the Sexual Instinct

Hirschfeld also conducted extensive research in more traditional sexual behavior, especially in the field of sexual pathology, which he cataloged as the "Derangements of the Sexual Instinct." His sweep here ran from the study of self-castration and impotence to "hypereroticism" and "coital hallucination."

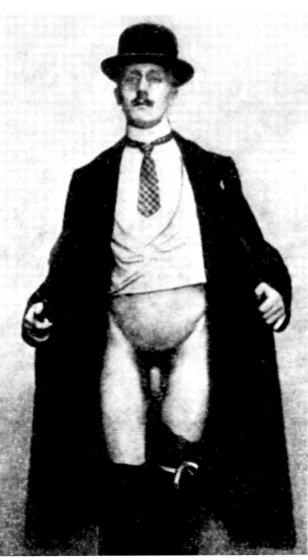

Left:
Exhibitionist displaying his "working uniform"

161

Dein „Riesenrad" wie [du] Dir es im Prater gewünscht
hast! Hoffentlich gefällt es Dir! Dein Bohumil
Wien 15/XI
1930

Above:
Flagellation
drawing by a
17-year-old
sadist, 1930

childhood eroticize their morbid attachment to the charged article?

To explore the problem, Hirschfeld prepared an exhaustive 140-part "Psycho-Biological Questionnaire." The 18,000 Berliners who responded to the survey were asked to reveal their innermost erotic secrets and family background, as one would expect. But also in the sexual profile were inquiries on seemingly isolated topics like shoplifting, color preference, stuttering, feelings on capital punishment and war, left-handedness, and diet. For Hirschfeld and his trained associates, their candid replies were the initial step in correlating heredity, child-rearing, and education with everyday expressive behavior and unconscious sexual desire.

The Psycho-Biological Questionnaires served several purposes, besides their obvious research benefits. Hirschfeld used them clinically to diagnose deeply imbedded sexual disturbances and for premarital counseling. The Einstein of Sex proclaimed that he could help prevent unhappy marriages through his interpretation of the sex surveys. Long-term attraction involved the joining of complementary erotic temperaments.

Why individuals would choose to obliterate or compulsively bind their sexual desires to inanimate objects or childhood/sadomasochistic/power-exchange scenarios fascinated Hirschfeld. For Central European psychologists, the answer touched upon the fundamental twentieth-century issue in human behavior: how much anti-social activity is caused by "natural" elements (genetics and chemical imbalances), and how much by sheer nurture. In other words, were glove fetishists people with obsessive inherited or hormonal traits, like Transvestites, or did some event in their

STRAFRAUM III

Once the "false fire of passion" diminishes, Hirschfeld stated, coital disappointment naturally occurs. By gazing into the "sexual souls" of the couples, scientific predictions about their overall psychological and physical relationship could be made. While not infallible, Sexual Science at least attempted to point out the barriers to and possible aids for wedded bliss.

In a famous quote, "Happy marriages are not made in heaven, but in the laboratory," Hirschfeld inaugurated hard science's entry into the matchmaking business. According to the publicity-savvy Papa, even love-at-first-sight did not have a real physical basis. At the end of the day, it was all genes and chemicals, racing through the bloodstream, that kept relationships intact and produced babies.

Above:
My Invention, fantasy drawing of a sadistic intellectual

Below:
Pedal-driven female masturbation machine manufactured in Dresden, 1926

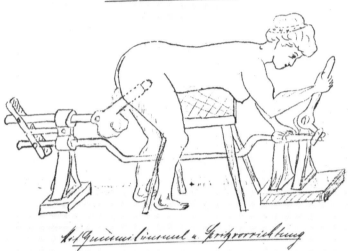

The Institute of Sexology

In July 1919, Hirschfeld opened his Institute of Sexology in Berlin. It quickly became one of the city's most curious attractions. The Institute's buildings, including a former mansion, were divided into areas for lectures, consulting offices, study rooms, laboratories, medical clinics, and a museum space devoted to sexual pathology and erotic folkways. George Gershwin, Ben Hecht, Douglas Fairbanks, André Gide, Sergei Eisenstein, Anita Loos, and Christopher Isherwood (who worked at the Institute) were among the many enthused visitors to Hirschfeld's Institute, leaving fascinating accounts about its strange inhabitants and artifacts.

Hirschfeld's Institute functioned as a hospital and a free university under one roof. Medical advice was offered without charge, and scientific lectures by leading sexologists were open to the general public. The Institute's library, which contained the largest sex and pornographic book collection in Europe, remained acces-sible to all readers. The Institute also housed Germany's first Marriage Bureau and clinics for the treatment of venereal disease and other sexual maladies. Politically, the Institute provided a forum for progressive lawyers and government officials who sought to eradicate the laws against homosexuality and defend Germany's legal abortion rights from the growing onslaught of fascist and religious parties. Most of the legal work involved suits protecting gay men against threats of petty black-mail. These services were also rendered pro bono.

Above the gate of his Institute was the inscription: "*Amori et dolori sacrum*" ("Sacred to Love and to Sorrow"). It was one of many rather banal mottos and plaques that Hirschfeld posted around and inside his foyers and offices. Other Hirschfeldian banners: "Justice Through Science," "To Understand All is to Forgive All," "Nature Does Not Make Leaps," "What the World Calls the Soul, We Call the Endocrine System!"

The Institute itself was a font of sexological activity. Pediatric care, abortions, "sexual rejuvenation" and sexual "correction" operations were conducted on the lower level of the main building. Psychological consultations and tours took place on the upper levels. In the adjoining Ernst Haeckel Hall, films, demonstrations, and public health panels were held for the 1100 physicians who visited the Institute annually. Hirschfeld himself produced and advised on several groundbreaking

Left:
Fantasy drawing of a 12-year-old masochist

medical documentaries and silent features, including Richard Oswald's *Different From Others*, a *film à clef* about the torturous life a closeted male violinist. (The title of the 1919 melodrama was later immortalized when it resurfaced as a refrain for the Toppkeller sing-along, the "Lilac Song.")

Mostly what visitors remembered from Hirschfeld's Institute were the museum exhibits displayed in the "Gallery of Derangements of the Sexual Instinct." Hanging from ceiling hooks were wooden boards that illustrated Hirschfeld's case studies. The multitudinous sexual personae of his Sexual Intermediaries were disclosed in arresting photographic series. Glass cases of fetishistic objects and sex aids from preliterate, Asian, and European cultures filled two other rooms. In the open counters and boxes were collections of

Mandigo dildos that squirted a milky solution, Moché water bottles with penis-shaped spouts, Sanskrit sex manuals, miniature shoes worn by bound-foot Chinese courtesans, medieval chastity belts, torture instruments from a German brothel, sadistic drawings and assemblages created by *Lustmord* convicts, an entire picture window of ankle boots donated by a local fetishist, antique steam-driven vibrators, fake rubber breasts and vaginas taken from transvestite prostitutes, lacy panties found on the corpses of von Hindenburg's heroic officers, and other such incontrovertible evidence of Hirschfeld's new calculus of desire. There were also free-standing sex machines and masturbation devices of every shape and variety.

Eisenstein especially enjoyed the Institute's collection of sailor-dolls—homemade paper toys that German

O FLEIZGHEZLUZT WIE HAZT DU MICH VERBRANNT
NU BIN ICH GAR INZ ZUCHTHAUZ VERBANNT

homosexuals fashioned during the Great War. The figures were drawn naked, except for their caps and boots, and designed to show off the marines' aroused genitals and smiling faces. Tiny red paint drops were splattered over the blithe forms to give the incongruous appearance of deadly wounds. After bringing them out of their case, a delighted Papa asked Eisenstein and his friends if they carried any penknives in their

pockets. When the entourage failed to turn up any, Hirschfeld explained the reason for his inquiry: homosexuals rarely packed them.

Hirschfeld employed Sexual Intermediaries for his museum docents and assistants. "Herr Alfred" was a slim, fortyish Bavarian peasant woman, the mother of one child with a normal het sex interest. Her only abnormality was wanting to live in the clothing of a man. The Institute hired her along with two dozen other inside-the-spectrum types. André Gide almost bolted from the Institute when Papa had a "Sexual Intermediate: Grade Three" employee unbutton his shirt and reveal two perfectly-shaped female breasts.

How Hirschfeld's Institute of Sex Science paid for its huge staff and many house expenses remained a carefully guarded secret. Only a fraction of the Berlin patients compensated the Institute for their immense needs. The city chipped in here and there, but never enough to keep the place running at full throttle. Rumors abounded that German gay magnates channeled funds in sealed envelopes or that a famous Ruhr industrialist, known to be a closeted infantilist, forked over a fortune to Hirschfeld for the construction of a private nursery, laden with sex apparatuses in the shape of old toys.

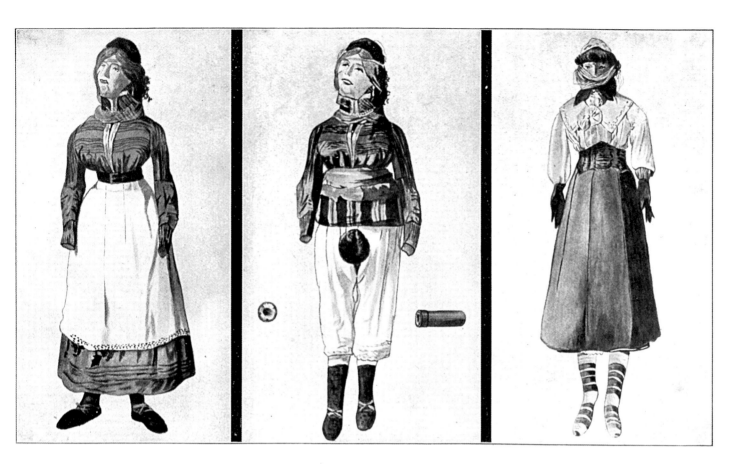

More likely, Hirschfeld used his own inheritance to support the Institute. He also formulated and patented several heavy-duty aphrodisiacs and Viagra-like anti-impotence tablets. The best known of these was called Testifortan, a concoction of yohimbé bark from French West Africa and clamshell from the North Atlantic. Hirschfeld advertised that Testifortan stimulated the centers of hormonal production, chemically charged the synapses of the nervous system (especially those along the spine), and regulated the restricted blood flow into the male genitals through dilation and engorgement of the *corpora cavernosa*.

Testifortan and Hirschfeld's "Titus Pills" were marketed in *Galante* magazines, at German pharmacies, and

Above:
Life-size
sex dolls

Below:
Homemade
"Penis
Shoes"

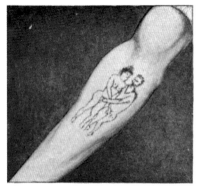
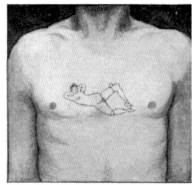
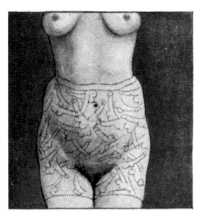
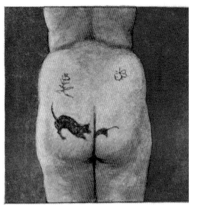
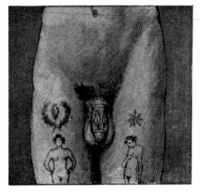
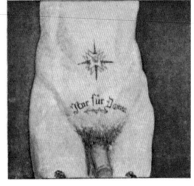

Above:
Erotic tattoos of sailors and criminals

in the Museum gift shop, where visitors could purchase other enhancers, *Sittengeschichten*, and an array of scientifically-tested sex remedies. The Nazi and Allied-installed German governments thought highly enough of Hirschfeld's patented compounds to claim his formulas for themselves and sell the licensing rights to Swiss pharmaceutical firms. They were a source of state revenue for German health ministries until 1962.

Hirschfeld's Enemies

Hirschfeld's outsized personality and quasi-scientific proclamations drew an endless stream of critics. Some ranted against Sexology as a legitimate science. Others, like the homophobic Dr. Albert Moll, questioned Papa's objectivity and found ingenious methods to blunt Hirschfeld's international standing. He usually accomplished this by denying the doctor's medical credentials at world congresses. Freud, whom Hirschfeld adored, avoided the entire topic of endocrine-based sexology despite the hearsay belief that he received a sexual rejuvenation operation at Hirschfeld's Institute in 1922.

The renegade Freudian, Wilhelm Reich, transferred his clinical base from Vienna to Berlin in 1930. A fervent Communist, anxious to establish an Institute for Sexual Politics (Sex-Pol), Reich mocked Hirschfeld's egalitarian attitudes toward sexual morality. Good orgasmic sex, according to Reichian doctrine, was always uninhibitedly straight and the result of vigorous genital thrust. Intermediary erotic desire, like the capitalist system itself, was not immutable nor a natural aspect of human character. Homosexuality and other such perversions demanded a healthy revolutionary response, curative techniques that the Marxist Viennese claimed to pioneer. Hirschfeld's sexual nihilism, however well-intended, Reich harangued, was furthering fascism.

Of course, the Nazis did not see it that way; they tried to murder Hirschfeld as early as 1923. And when Adolf Hitler came to power ten years later, the Institute of Sexology was one of his first targets. Much of the leadership of the Ernst Röhm's Storm Troopers (the Nazi SA) covertly subscribed to Brand's Militant Homosexualism and feared that among Hirschfeld's Questionnaires were sexual profiles that might ultimately embarrass them. The liquidation of the Institute and its archives was doubly important for Röhm.

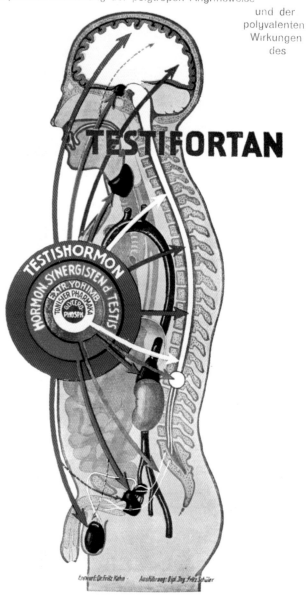
Hirschfeld lived for two more years outside Germany. He scurried around Europe in hopes of rekindling his career and Institute but knew his base of power could only reside in Weimar Berlin, a spiritual metropolis that had been excised from the map by National Socialism. In 1935, on his 65th birthday, Magnus Hirschfeld, the fighter for sexual science and understanding, died a lonely death during his exile in the South of France. ■

Above and Left: Magazine advertisements for Hirschfeld's Titus Pills and Testifortan

There was always a feeling of violence about Berlin, which was not true of other capital cities. You felt that the rule of law was skin deep and people were capable of a greater degree of physical violence than one was accustomed to live with elsewhere.

Alec Swan, quoted in *Weimar Chronicles*, 1978

Homosexuality, sadism and masochism, and generally perverse practices
are gaining a powerful hold on the Germans.

Hendrik De Leeuw, *Sinful Cities of the Western World*, 1934

ALGOLAGNIA

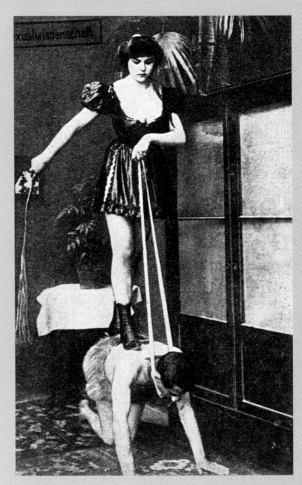

The pornography that circulated in Weimar Berlin was marked by its unusual emphasis on body worship, extreme fetishism, scatology, dark roleplay, and ritualized gender struggle. There was the soft stuff too but the most sought-after girlie mags and sex novels were usually imports or translated editions from Paris or Rome. Local imitations of the same, like *Reigen*, *Der Junggeselle*, *Lustige Blätter*, and *Berliner Leben*, always started off with perky Gallic charm but succumbed, even in their erotic cartoons and short stories, to menacing visions and S&M fantasies. Berlin Girl-Culture was inextricably mixed with eroticized violence.

Algolagnia (the "Craving of Pain") was a Latin term coined in 1894 by Albert von Schrenck-Notzing, a Berlin physician better remembered for his investigation of the paranormal. Although Algolagnia encompassed what we normally think of as Sadism and Masochism, Schrenck-Notzing also intended it to define a much larger terrain of sexual perversion, especially psychological

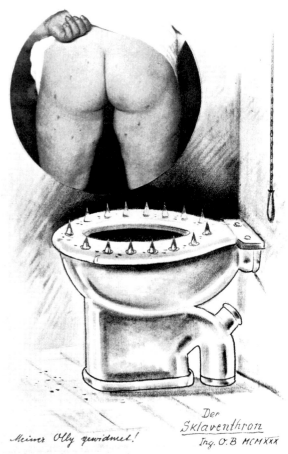

Der Sklaventhron
Ing. O.B MCMXXX

Meiner Olly gewidmet!

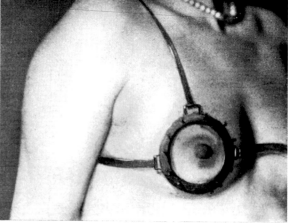

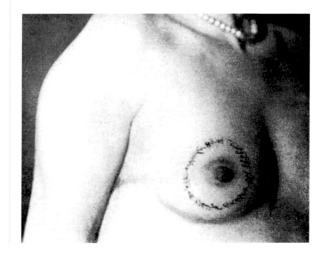

Previous Left:
Amateur photograph, 1932

Previous Right:
Zoomimic Masochism scene

Above:
Drinking Nectar

Above Right:
The Slave Throne, 1930.

Center and Below Right:
The barbed bra

domination, erotic servitude, forced gratification, bondage and discipline, infantilism, humiliating role-reversal scenes, and "morbid" fetishism. Schrenck-Notzing, Wilhelm Stekel, and Albert Eulenburg each attempted to explain the mysterious aberration that tied sexual pleasure to suffering or to compulsive symbolic play. Like their contemporaries, Richard Krafft-Ebing and Freud, they knew the phenomenon was growing rapidly throughout the German-speaking world.

Hirschfeld noted that physical aggression during puberty and sexual courtship were intercultural universals. Boys naturally fought other males in order to "take" or "possess" their mates; and girls were expected to surrender, accede, "give in" to the most virile male who lusted after them. Aggression and submission in the service of sexual conquest were instinctively short-lived and restrained acts, final steps in the procreative dance. But Algolagnia upset the rules of natural selection. It forced an ongoing recapitulation of excessive violence and pain to achieve sexual excitement and release. People who exhibited these sadomasochist tendencies had consciously contaminated the normal sex drive with the psychic toxins of childhood trauma and the oppressive mementos of adolescent awakening.

Freudians had an elegant elucidation of the Algolagnia complex and its fetishistic components. It was

all a symptom of castration anxiety, penile substitution, arrested neurotic development, and repressed homosexuality. Of course. Yet psychoanalysis didn't adequate-

Above:
Richard Hegemann, *The Healing Sister*

Far Left:
Amateur drawings from an Algolagnist

Left:
Male Bra

173

Above:
A.Z.,
*In the Torture
Chamber*

Right:
Von Zabczinsky,
Modern Furies

Opposite:
A stained
glass fantasy,
The Mistress

ly explain why Algolagnia, particularly in its twentieth-century manifestation, Metatropism, had gained such a hold in Central Europe and how it affected women.

Metatropism

Metatropism referred to the psychological pairing of female sadists (Dominas) and masculine masochists (Metatropists). While the socially reversed roles of powerful women and passive males who acquiesced to them could be traced to sex cults in prehistoric Asia Minor and India, its incidence, according to Hirschfeld, was relatively uncommon until the end of the nineteenth century. Suddenly, fantasies of female vampires

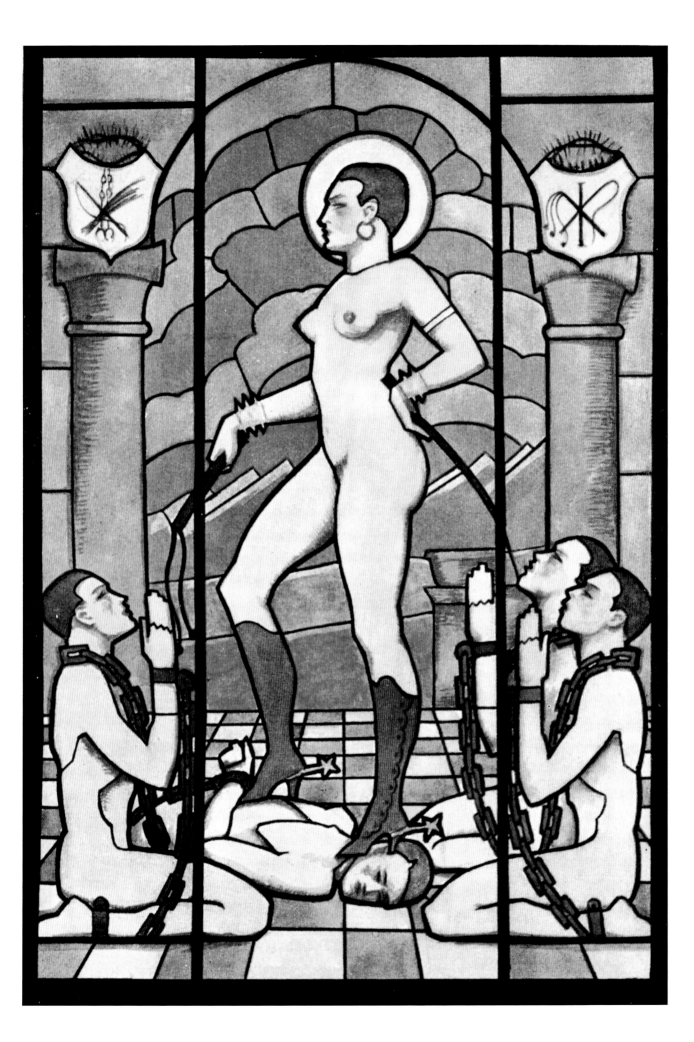

and male supplicants in their thrall jumped from the notepads and canvases of Austrian and German artists into the vast popular imagination. Metatropic sexual displacement, while observable elsewhere in Europe on a diminished scale, seeped into the mainstream of Berlin's erotic visual life and thinking.

Hirschfeld, who counseled hundreds of male and female Algolagnists, characterized the typology of Metatropism according to four fantasy scenarios of self-debasement: 1) *Servilism* (reduction of status), submitting to a *Domina* as her slave, servant, or page; 2) *Puerile Masochism* (reduction of age), wishing to be

Opposite:
Book Illustration for *The Bloody Countess*

Above:
Helga Bode, *Delicate Manipulation*

Left:
E.D., *After the Injection*

punished as an infant or schoolboy by an angry mother, strict governess, or "aunt"; 3) *Zoomimic Masochism* (transformation into an animal), being treated like a beast of burden by a mistress, who addressed the subject as an animal and then "rode" him, placing a saddle on his back, a bit in his mouth, and finally spurring and cropping him; and 4) *Impersonal Masochism* (transformation into an inanimate object), used by a stern mistress as an ashtray, footstool, coffee table, or animal-skin rug.

Opposite:
Schlichter,
My Domina

Above:
Arnim Horowitz,
The Trained Poodles

Left:
Amateur drawing,
1930

Above:
*The Strange
Professor*

Right:
*"You Must Also
Be Beaten"*

The Raised Buttocks

In the *Galante* monthlies, *Sittengeschichten*, sex encyclopedias, and private pornographic serials, one visual theme dominated and seemed to appeal to all sectors of Berlin's Algolagnic community. This was artistic enactment of a sadistic teacher administering a bare-buttocks punishment to a hapless student. The standard instruments of discipline could be as simple as a cane or whipping crop but more inventive fantasies

involved flagellation machines and paddles with cut-out numerals in the center, which left an outline of the number of whacks on the child's reddened derrière.

The forced application of an enema to the recalcitrant pupil was still another ubiquitous image. The characters and settings for these schoolroom whippings and anal torments were drawn or photographed in infinite permutations and weird variations: a shocked principal watches from the hallway as a comely Gymnasium instructor canes a cross-dressed boy while his classmates secure the boy's naked rump to a desk-top; a loving schoolmistress inserts an enema into the rectum of a hysterical 15-year-old girl as a grotesquely ugly nurse kisses the teenager's contorted face; an excited schoolboy, no more than eight, is taught to wield a cat-o'-nine-tails on the elevated posterior of his naughty little friend; and so forth.

Why fecal and buttocks fetishism prevailed in

Opposite:
Hegemann,
*Weekly
Punishment*

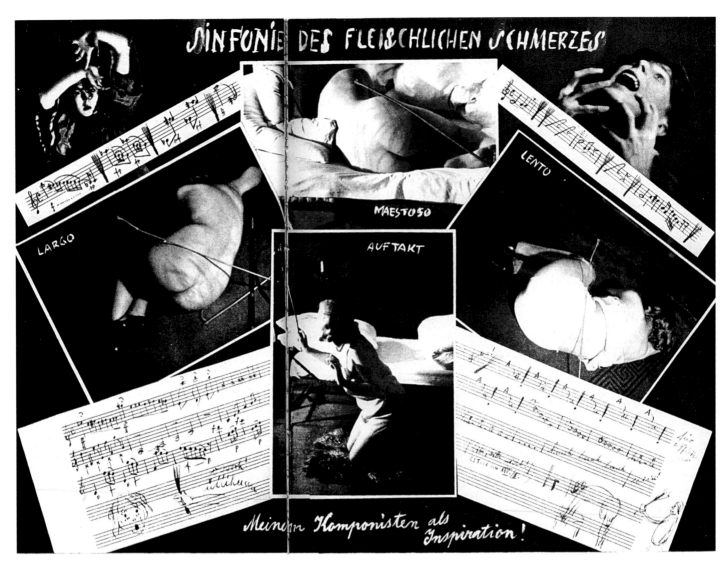

SINFONIE DES FLEISCHLICHEN SCHMERZES

LARGO

MAESTOSO

AUFTAKT

LENTO

Meinem Komponisten als Inspiration!

Above:
*The Symphony
of Corporal
Pain*

Right:
*A Womanly
Hand*

Weimar Germany is a question that was weakly addressed in the literature of the time. Some apologists wrote that spanking stimulated the blood flow to the constricted muscles of the gluteus maximus and outward to the sensation-deadened genitals. Ernst Schertel, a prolific pornographer from Munich and historian of the erotic, expounded on ritual flagellation as an ancient ecstatic technique and possibly the origin of religious experience. Others claimed the centrality of the anus as the source of infantile eroticism.

But not answered in these perverse treatises was the geographical issue. Scatological scenes and exposed

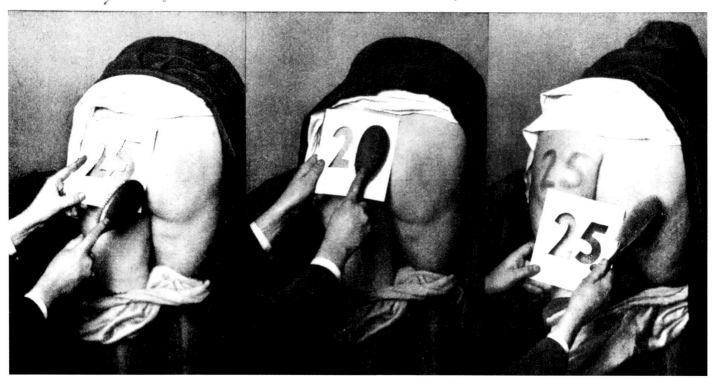

Ja, mein Lieber, weiß ich es wenn meine Kleine nicht brav ist. Ich kann dir diesen Razept bestens empfehlen

lower torsos abounded in Central Europe's straight, gay, lesbian, transvestite, and *Nacktkultur* publications. They appeared in non-German erotica but with maybe a fifth or a tenth the regularity. Presumably the heavy use of colonic irrigation to fight childhood diseases, specific pedagogical forms of punishment, and unexplored cultural symbolism shaped the strange fixation.

"Morbid" Fetishism

Other sexual fetishes in Weimar Berlin were shared obsessions of the Jazz Age. Heinz Schmeidler in *The Moral History of the Present* (Berlin, 1932) listed what he thought were the most prevalent objects of sexual compulsion in the city: Nose Fetishism, Mouth Fetishism, Ear Fetishism, Hand Fetishism, Leg Fetishism, Shoe and

Above:
Photos and a letter from a structural engineer to a fellow spanking enthusiast

Left:
Amateur photo from a buttocks fetishist

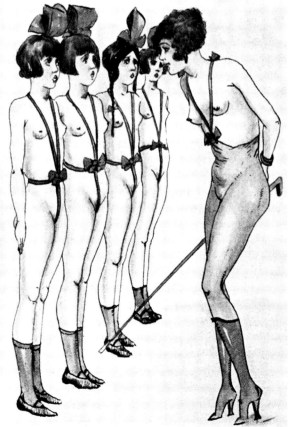

Stocking Fetishism, Breast Fetishism, Buttocks Fetishism, Hair Fetishism, Purse Fetishism, Music Fetishism, Clothes Fetishism, Underwear Fetishism, Bed Fetishism, Fabric Fetishism, and Flower Fetishism. To these, Losa in *Sexual Derangements* added Cold Fetishism and Voice Fetishism. (Cold fetishists found their jollies at ice rinks and in the back of speeding cabooses.)

Rumpelstilzchen felt the subject of sexual fetishes was of paramount interest to his provincial readers. Fashion among Berlin's *Beinls* was always related to fetishistic novelty. They needed to offer or emphasize some item or body part not readily available at home.

Opposite:
Fantasy drawings of a hair-pulling fetishist

Above:
Sadistic Teacher

Above Left:
The Bell-Boy's Last Duty

Left:
Bode, *Dance Hour*

earlobes, hairbobs, glossy eyeshadow, revealing blouses, men's leather ties, perfume, and, in 1929, to iridescent lipstick shades, to which he devoted four weekly columns.

When the Nazis came to power in 1933, Rumpelstilzchen again focused on street fashion. Hitler, who preferred the wholesome scrubbed peasant look, detested facial makeup on women. The *Kontroll-Girls* of Berlin responded accordingly. They appeared in the Friedrichstadt wearing long leather coats, opaque stockings, mannish hats, and freshly washed faces. Rumpelstilzchen waxed enthusiastic over that season's whore fashion. During the same April month, he also assured his readership that Berlin was more welcoming and less crowded now that the Jews were vacating their apartments for extended holidays in Paris and Vienna.

Above:
Fighting for Love, 1928

Below:
Sweet Punishment

Opposite:
From a series of 350 photographs, *Learning the Rules*

Between 1919 and 1924, Rumpelstilzchen provided detailed descriptions of exotic hosiery styles and high-heeled shoes, largely French imports. His gaze moved upward after that to powdered necks, shoulder lines,

"Scientific" Pornography

Clinical studies of sexual perversion, such as von Krafft-Ebing's *Psychopathia Sexualis* (Leipzig, 1901) and Stekel's *Sexual Aberrations* (Vienna, 1922), were printed by scientific publishing houses and produced principally for therapists and legal scholars in Central Europe. The numerous copies in multiple editions of these collections, however, revealed an unintended secondary

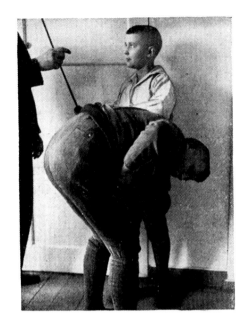
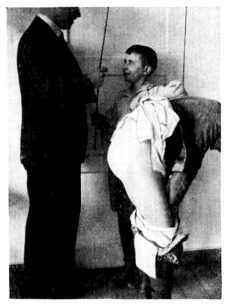
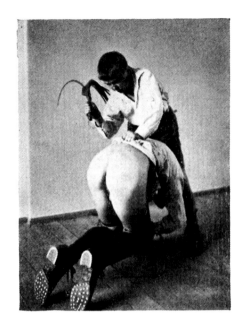

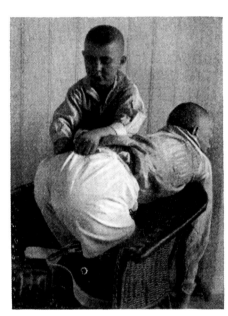

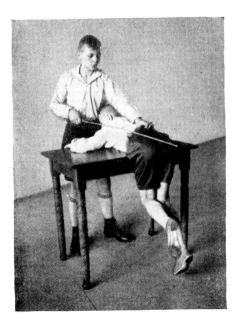
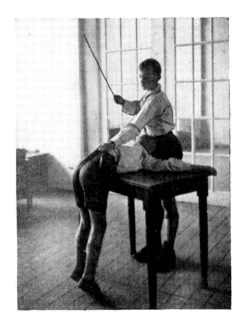

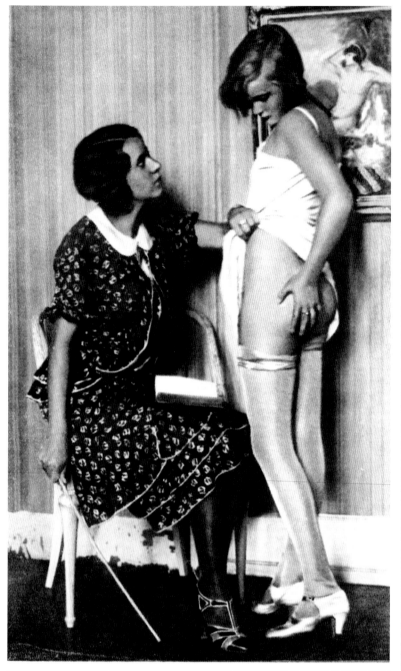

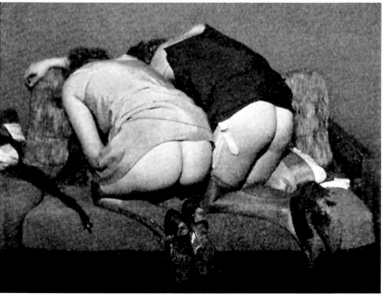

readership: other perverts. The salacious case histories of sadists, fetishists, Algolagnists, flagellants, and the like, formed a novel province in Weimar pornography.

Under the guise of psychological research, graphic photographs and illustrations were added to still other strange biographical confessions and fantasies. Berliners seeking stronger erotic sensations and instruction for weird sex scenarios merely had to peruse *Galante* journals for the current "scientific" offerings. Virtually every deviant practice had a layman's society and private publishing arm.

One "physician," Ernst Schertel, headed a hypno-erotic "Dream Theater" and several book clubs devoted to whipping and buttocks fetishism. Schertel's serialized periodicals explored the dark fantasy games and dramatics of animal lovers, worshippers of obese Dominas, sadistic teachers, bare-hand flagellants, incestuous necklace fetishists, urine drinkers, bondage freaks, high-heel stompers, and shit-sniffers. German authorities attempted to shut down his Parthenon-Verlag in 1931 and Wilhelm Reich publically opposed the perverse Dream Theater. But Schertel, working under foreign pseudonyms like Dr. F. Grandpierre, outwitted them all. His lavish works and those of his associates continued to be distributed into the early Nazi period. ∎

This Page and Opposite:
Maurice Carriere,
*Appreciating
the Need for
Discipline*

Following:
Manassé,
Das Magazin,
August 1932

The Headless Man

Last night I had a frightening dream. Standing by my bed was a headless man wearing a tuxedo. I jumped up and wanted to run but my feet were frozen to the floor.

The half man opened a suitcase, which was filled with detached heads.

"Here are the faces of the men who once loved you but you decapitated them with your cold heart," said the ghoulish voice. "Now match the correct face to my body." He emptied the suitcase and the heads rolled over my breasts. I awoke with a scream and hastened to my studio to illustrate my horrid history.

"Miss Bluebeard and Her Victims"

Seven heads she selected... But each one disconnected.

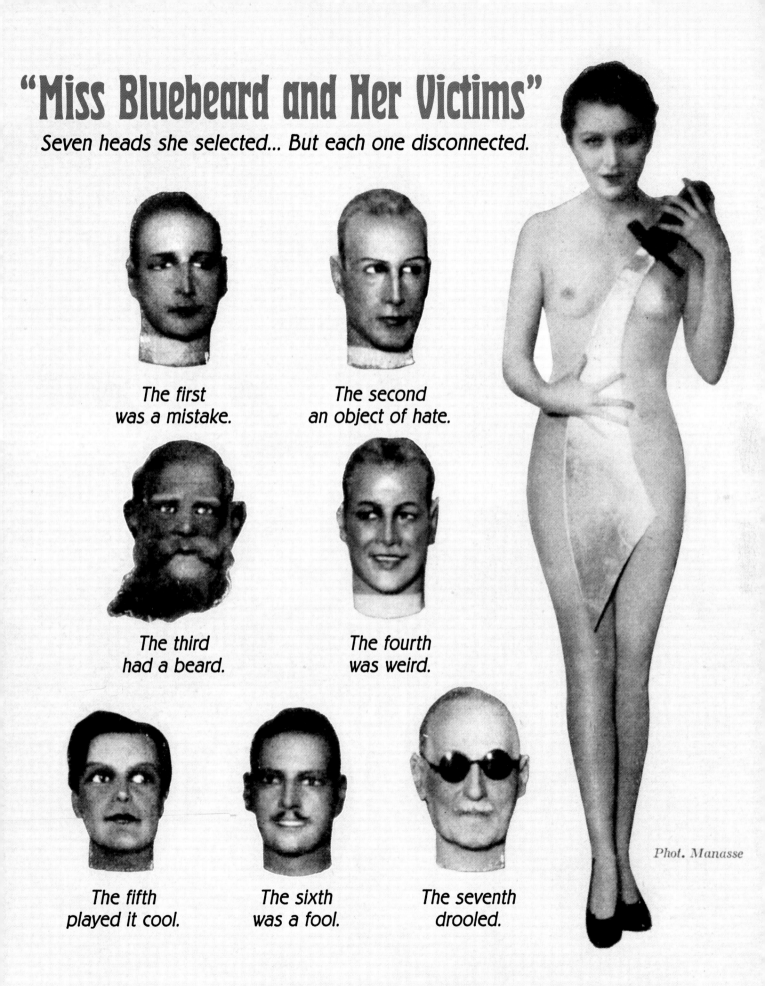

The first
was a mistake.

The second
an object of hate.

The third
had a beard.

The fourth
was weird.

The fifth
played it cool.

The sixth
was a fool.

The seventh
drooled.

Phot. Manasse

Every man she rejected.   Each technique was unperfected.

Of all the rites and ceremonies as practiced today by the secret love cults of the world, the most dreadful and least known is the Black Mass. [...] The Devil-Worshippers' infernal "underground" is comprised of people of otherwise superior intelligence. Its international center is in Germany, in the city of Berlin.

Marian Dockerili, *My Life in a Love Cult*, 1928

Contemporary religion can never ignore the embers of desire and sexual longing. Burning belief is always based on burning sex.

Ernst Bergmann, *The German National Church*, 1933

SEX MAGIC AND THE OCCULT

For many Berliners, sexual gratification was not primarily the end-game of courtship, a simple pleasurable pursuit, a nocturnal amusement, mammalian bond, or a natural expression of self. It was a sacred rite or miraculous proof of some paranormal lattice where supernatural fate and deviant desires had become intertwined. In Weimar Germany, sex—in all its untraditional, transgressive, and anti-familial manifestations—had become a religion as well as a pastime.

The antinomian groundswell that propelled nearly one quarter of Berlin's liberated denizens into the elegant vistas of erotic degeneracy dragged others into the dank chambers and communal embankments of sex-mad gurus and cultish mystery-sects. These homegrown creeds frequently mixed occult teaching with induced lust or carnal mayhem. Male/female intercourse was not just the very source of life—and therefore a shadow of God's creative function—it was also a supreme delight, and, when controlled, a heightened

Der Hellseher

Verlag
O.u.M.Hausser
Ludwigsburg
Ges gesch,

HUMORISTISCHES WAHRSAGE-&FRAGE-
UND ANTWORTSPIEL FÜR ERWACHSENE

209

Previous Left:
Erik Jan Hanussen
at his Palace of
the Occult, 1933

Previous Right:
Cult Dancer in
Berlin, 1926

Above:
The Clairvoyant,
an adult dice
game, where
players learn
their true sexual
characters and
erotic fortunes,
1926

form of prayer. Copulation and ejaculatory release for German devotees of Sex Magic had attained extraordinary and novel meanings; they were bodily manifestations of lost esoteric wisdom, techniques of Gnostic faith, flipped transmogrifications of flesh, even divine rungs for ultimate human salvation.

In his bestselling anthology about the contemporary occult in the German-speaking world, *The Miraculous, or The Bewitched* (Berlin: Rowohlt Verlag, 1932), Rudolf Olden compared magical belief systems to compulsions of physical attraction ("sex appeal") and unwavering love. Each of them had an irrational basis and was a publicly sanctioned sublimation of innate creative or sexual energies.

Outsider German political movements and religious cults tapped into the transcendent urge for ecstatic immediacy on a collective level. Hitler, for Olden, was no less a tantric god than Louis Haeusser, Otoman Hanish, Maria Raschig, Joseph Weissenberg, or dozens of other occult Führers with mass followings. Sexuality was the fuse and hidden spring of Weimar Germany's newest dogmas.

Revolutionary discoveries in behavioral science and technology in the last quarter of the nineteenth century, ironically, stimulated belief in "unseen forces" and their superhuman mastery. The empirical findings in brain chemistry, atomic physics, constitutional psychology, and, especially, wireless communication seemed to suggest—in the popular German imagination—that they were indeed invisible, virtually mystic, fields surrounding each individual body that, in turn, was dictated by solar or astral waves. International luminaries like Thomas Edison, Sigmund Freud, Carl Jung, Guglielmo Marconi, Marie Curie, Nikola Tesla, and Albert Einstein were heroes to both the scientific and psychic communities. Their baffling theories, Berlin parapsychologists claimed, were foretold by the nineteenth-century American Spiritualists and the Anglo-Indian Theosophists.

"Occult-Sciencism" was the strange Weimar prodigy that resulted from the blend of these two contrary world views. Increasingly, it acted as an effective substitute for traditional social discourse and long-established religious zealotry. By 1932, Berlin alone supported the flashy productions, séances, and publications of 20,000 itinerant telepathists, wonder-working healers, palm readers, storefront clairvoyants, Hollow-Earth adherents, alchemists, stage mesmerists, doomsday prophets, Gypsy-clad fortunetellers, and trance-performers.

Moreover, camouflaged feats of sexual dominance more suitable for ribald cabaret acts now ventured into the laboratory, church pew, and political street. After all, both hypnosis and mass suggestion traded on the principle of psychic seduction. Eroticized language and gestures, Olden wrote, had an unbridled capacity to influence crowd psychology and behavior. If channeled ritually or scientifically by experts, they resembled the incantations of pagan Sex Magic.

The Failed Crusade

Prussian obedience to Christian anti-materialist theology was slow and unsteady. Even after German princes and religious authorities embraced the Gospel's teachings in the 800s—usually in the form of public baptism—few Central European tribespeople remained staunchly faithful to the Roman papacy. As soon as the unsmiling Anglo-Saxon missionaries and preachers left their villages and towns, most Germans reverted to their original pre-Christian practices and traditions. Others integrated the Holy Mass into their heathen fertility rituals, invoking blessings from both Jesus Christ and the pantheon of Nordic forest gods. These ceremonies had to be performed secretly, and often perversely

Dr. Hans-Theodor Sanders
Hypnose u. Suggestion

Kosmos, Gesellschaft der Naturfreunde
Franckh'sche Verlagshandlung·Stuttgart

Above:
Fidus illustration
for G. Hermann,
*Saeming: Aryan
Sex Religion,*
1896

Below:
Fidus emblem
for *Trilogy,
Sex Religion,
Sex Mystery,
Sex Magic,*
1897

Opposite:
Fidus illustration
for Carl Hilm,
Satan, 1908

upended diocesan prohibitions against animal sacrifice and priestly intercourse.

For over 400 years, German bishops attempted to violently crush the perpetuators of paganism as well as the growing appeal of local heretic Christian sects. The

blasphemous leaders were frequently imprisoned, horridly tortured, and burned at the stake. But that did little to suppress the licentious folkways of the German peasantry. Free thought and sacred sexuality were too deeply rooted in their cultural ethos.

In the thirteenth century, Luciferians, who conflated the Nordic god Wotan with Satan (rather than Christ) in their midnight rites, openly challenged the German Catholic hierarchy and began to murder Franciscan monks and set churches ablaze. Militant anti-Christian Stedingers from the shores of Freesia joined the Prussian Satanists. Covens of German sorcerers and sibyls spurred the rebellion onward and prophesied the end of asceticism, Vatican martial constraints and councilor meddling. The old-ancient natural world, rife with lusty human-like deities, spirit communication, sexual desire, and physical attraction, was about to be restored.

In 1234, Pope Gregory IX issued proclamations against the growing German heresy. A European crusade to stamp out Satanism, witchcraft, Devil worship, nudist Adam-and-Eve cults, and Sex Magic resulted. Papal armies and inquisitional courts dispatched whole towns and communities into dungeons, torture chambers, and execution pits. In Spain and Portugal, Jewish and Muslim leaders were forced to confess their links to wizards and seers before their bodies were stretched on specially designed racks, broken on inquisition

Above:
Rhea Wells,
*Black Mass In a
German Town,*
1931

Right:
Witches'
Sabbath as
portrayed on
Berlin cabaret
stage, 1927

were dutifully recorded in church documents. Followers of the Anti-Christ reenacted Catholic and Lutheran services in twisted and perverted parodies. They drank urine mixed with hallucinogenic plants and swallowed wafers made from human feces, menstrual blood, and sperm. That was their Eucharist. Obscene prayers, orgiastic dance, and the worship of all things scatological—like the kissing of Lucifer's anus—replaced the Holy Communion. Even priests and prelates were implicated in the grand conspiracy.

Concealed in senators' cabinets, scholars' libraries, and rectory walls were handbooks on the Black Arts and occult Latin treatises that instructed the reader how to obtain demonic power. Apparently, no Germans—bishops, countesses, physicians, brewmeisters, or midwives—were completely immune to Satan's dark and sensual sway. Public exposures and civic persecution, an increasingly enlightened clergy, and the Scientific Revolution in the nineteenth century only tamped down the anti-Christian profanations.

wheels, and then incinerated in public squares. By 1492, all non-believers in Iberia were said to be killed, converted, or sent into exile.

But Satanism and its visceral appeal was not excised so easily from the German lands. Between 1500 and 1783, over 15,000 women and men were executed for engaging in necromancy or sealing compacts with the Devil and his minions. Graphic descriptions of Witches' Sabbaths and a new sacrament called the Black Mass

The *Hauptstadt* of Satan

Vestiges of pre-Renaissance superstition and Devil-worship were observed in the Central European countryside until World War I. Bavarian grandmothers continued to place horse and deer penises under their grandsons' beds to ensure their sexual happiness and fertility. Bohemian peasants, hoping to marry within seven years, avoided corner seats in taverns and, if their Biersteins toppled during the evening, splashed the spreading foam behind their ears for good luck. On Walpurgis Night, haggard women and men

still pranced around huge bonfires, where straw effigies were consumed and delivered to Luciferian proxies.

In Berlin, Satanist rituals dispensed with exhortations for robust health and pregnancy. Debauchery and orgiastic entertainment were the religious goals of the city-dwellers. The first known Black Mass in modern times unfolded at midnight in December 1919 at the Café Kerkau on Behrenstrasse. Five hundred celebrants stripped off their clothing in the club and circled around an altar covered with a black-and-red Pentagram. One hundred Polenta, with revolvers drawn, interrupted the solemn rite and the stark naked devotees were herded into police lorries. Among the law-breaking enthusiasts was the Crown Prince Friedrich Wilhelm, supposedly in exile with the Kaiser's family in Holland.

DIE GEISEL

Above:
Fidus,
Satana,
1896

Left:
Ernst Gerhard,
Captive,
1925

199

Marian Dockerill, a Swiss-born American journalist, described the activities of European and American occult sex societies in a sensational eight-part series, "Confessions of a 'High Priestess' in Notorious 'Love Cults.'" Her illustrated report was syndicated in the Hearst press in March and April of 1926 and later published in a re-edited pulp version, *My Life in a Love Cult: A Warning to All Young Girls* (Chicago: Better Publications, 1928).

The sister of Lea Hirsig (Aleister Crowley's "Scarlet Woman") and a strikingly beautiful woman herself, Dockerill was able to infiltrate and participate in several private Berlin ceremonies in the spring of 1923. Her eyewitness portrayals were unusually graphic and detailed. No contemporary German reportage could rival Dockerill's astute and in-depth accounts.

Marian remembers entering an elegant Berlin apartment, remade into a hellish sanctuary, lined with black and crimson silk curtains. Blue and red lights created an otherworldly chapel-like atmo-sphere. Men in black hooded robes, and women in white, sat silently on church pews, where they faced a black-curtained altar. Flutes and violins could be heard playing in an adjoining studio room. The "Priest"—reportedly a real defrocked Catholic priest—entered slowly from a side entrance. Inscribed on his black cowl was a red Satanic pentagram. Behind him was a bare-footed "High Priestess," wearing a revealing, diapha-nous scarlet gown. She swung a censer of burning incense as the "Priest" intoned Latin phrases. It sounded like a traditional Catholic Mass; only the words "Satan" and "evil" were substituted for "God" and "good." From the ceiling hung an upside-down crucifix.

The "Priest" pulled the altar curtain open. On a tiny black-velvet platform lay a naked 18-year-old girl, the daughter of two cult society members. Her neck and limbs were contorted in severe right angles to her stun-ning face and torso. The "Living Altar's" blonde hair touched the floor. Balanced on her smooth breasts stood a golden chalice. The girl appeared to be in a trance, lifeless, like a wax statue. The blue and red lights struck her translucent body in such a way that she seemed to be a Biblical figure in a stained-glass window.

While the "Priest" chanted the Black Mass liturgy, the congregation periodically stood, prostrated them-selves, and returned to their benches. After 30 minutes, the "Priest" placed a holy communion wafer on the

"Living Altar's" chest and lifted the cup from her body. He tasted the wine and, in a violent gesture, flung the remaining red liquid across her nude lower torso. In a final sonorous plea, the "Priest" urged Satan to redeem his flock from "all good," from "all Godly virtue."

To Dockerill, despite the anti-Catholic provocations and public nudity, the demonic consecration was only symbolically offensive and relatively chaste. She was to learn that it was mere preparation for an entirely different kind of Satanic sex ceremony.

The following night Marian was invited to the mansion of a much talked-about and promiscuous Hungarian countess (probably Agnes Esterhazy) in Berlin West. Eighty guests arrived around midnight, decked out in high fashion. They were separated by gender and directed into two dressing rooms, where costumes and tables of intoxicants awaited them. Besides champagne and brandy, there were boxes of powdered heroin, cocaine, hashish, bottles of morphine, assorted pills, and hypodermic needles. Only a few of the women dabbled with the hard drugs. The others good-naturedly donned the party animal skins, loincloths, and togas.

In the brightly lighted ballroom, an orchestra played strange syncopated music. A huge drum overpowered the musicians with a relentless, frenzied thump. The crowd, mostly in solo positions, moved in jerky steps to the primitive percussive beat.

Left and Below:
The Black Mass Consecration, recreated by Marian Dockerill for the Hearst Syndicate, 1926

LOGENSCHUL-VORTRÄGE

GEHEIMWISSENSCHAFTLICHE STUDIEN

Heft 1

„KARMA UND ASTROLOGIE"

VON
EUGEN GROSCHE
DIREKTOR DER ESOTERISCHEN STUDIENGESELLSCHAFT
E. V. BERLIN

FRATERNITAS SATURNI'S SEX MAGIC RITE "GRADUS PENTAPHAE"

The room is illuminated in red. A black altar is covered with a white cloth, which has an inverted red Pentagram sewn on it. Over the altar is a five-branch candelabrum, which contains five, burning red candles. Between the altar and the council-chamber table is a flaming tripod. In the corners of the room, red candles flicker.

A hymn "In These Holy Halls" is played. A gong is struck five times.

The Master of the Chair, the Priestess, and the Master of Ceremonies wear red masks. All of the participants and observers are naked underneath their robes.

Tethered to a center platform was an oversized black he-goat. More than frightened, it seemed to be repulsed by the constant din and unnatural movement around it. The bucking animal bleated in counterpoint to the deafening tom-tom. When the music died down, a bearded man with a leopard skin covering his loins leaped to the wooden stage, and began to sing, in a deep bass:

> *"Give me the sight of the open eye,*
> *And the word of madness and mystery,*
> *O Pan! Io Pan! Io Pan! Io Pan! Pan Pan! Pan!*
> *The gods withdraw:*
> *To the great beasts come, Io Pan!*
> *Goat of thy flock, I am gold, I am god*
> *And I rave, and I rip and I rend,*
> *Everlasting world without end,*
> *In the might of Pan.*
> *Io Pan! Io Pan Pan! Pan! Io Pan!"*

The drunken celebrants responded with disjointed refrains of "Io Pan" and started to disrobe. Then the Dionysian-like festivities began in earnest.

Dockerill described the scene with some care: "I saw a woman turn like a tigress and sink her teeth deep into the shoulder of a man who leaped in front of her. He tore her hair until he broke the grip of her teeth and screamed; he began kissing her brutally. I saw others cutting each other with knives, and a man dragging a woman by her hair and striking her naked shoulders with a whip until they were streaked with blood. And finally, as the culminating horror, I saw a nude woman, with a dagger, leap upon the huge, now completely terrified goat, and cut its throat from ear to ear, so that the blood gushed out in a stream while men and women fought and clawed and tore at each other to bathe in the blood. [...] The mad orgy lasted until dawn." ("Confessions," March 27, 1926)

Aryan Love Cults and Barefoot Prophets

Over 200 mystic cults and secret societies were active in Central Europe during the interwar period. Most fell into distinct categories: Aryan brotherhoods, American-style Spiritualist organizations, "scientific" astrological circles, chic Satanist clubs, Freemasons, Gnostic associations, Buddhist and pseudo-Buddhist leagues, ascetic Sufi-like communes, Christian dissenters, Theosophical breakaway unions, Rosicrucians, and outlandish occult-political movements. Most groups had

SACRIFICED.
The Climax of the Pan-Worshiping Orgy Which Mrs. Dockerill. Witnessed in Berlin, When a Live Goat was Slain to Arouse the Mad Excitement of the Revelers.

their own insignias, liturgical rites, uniforms, publications, and often distinct cuisines. Altogether some two million Germans formally belonged to these non-conformist sects. Another eight million expressed interest in them, sometimes subscribing to a variety of journals or attending multiple services. Berliners veered to the most self-gratifying new-age religions.

Although the heyday of bizarre sectarianism paralleled times of economic crisis in Europe—the Inflation (1921–1923) and the Great Depression (1929–1933)—cultish examples of sex-frenzy could be found much earlier. One phallic-worshipping band surfaced in Schwarzenburg, a German-speaking district in Switzerland, around the 1890s. Founded by Johannes Binggeli, a dwarfish trance-author, the Forest Brotherhood proselytized incest as a

Above:
The Goat Sacrifice, by Panini, 1926

203

Master of the Chair: "Jallah! Greetings, my Brothers and Sisters. Are you prepared to enact the Five-fold Alpha ritual with a pure heart and without deceit?"

The Congregation: "We are!"

Master of the Chair: "Brother First Guardian, what is your duty?"

First Guardian: "To determine if we are all Masters of the 18°; if we all bear the sign and the know the grip."

Master of the Chair: "Execute your office!"

The First Guardian leaves his assigned position and listens to each member. Individually, they whisper the secret password in his ear. He returns to his station and replies, "To Me!"

The Congregation makes the sign of the Master and then the sign of the Magnus Pentalphae.

The First Guardian: "Venerable Master, all those present have made both signs of the 18°. No one here is uninitiated."

The gong is struck five times, followed by five rings of the silver bell.

The Second Guardian: "All is in order, my Brothers and Sisters!"

Master of the Chair: "Stand, my Brothers and Sisters, and proclaim the oath!"

The Congregation stands, extending their right fists with outstretched thumbs: "We all swear and vow to live and act according to the Holy Laws of the Five-fold Alpha. We will guard and retain the secrets and conceal them from outsiders -- even from our Brothers and Sisters who have not attained the 18°. Death and ruin to traitors! A curse upon their souls! Blessed be the true Chalice of Light, whose strength may preserve us from all temptation! Om!"

They sit.

Master of the Chair walks to the altar: "In Nomine Sator, Rahator, Etan! In Nomine Baphomet. Hal yac yin! Jallah! I call and invoke you, Forces of the Fire Element. Flow into my hands, my heart, and my brain! And give me the power to awake the Serpent!"

The Master of the Chair gestures to the Priestess' chair. She stands and walks to him in measured steps.

The Master of the Chair traces the sign of the Pentagram over her head and says: "Let the power of the Serpent, the ancient Dragon, awake in you, Daughter of Lilith. She raises up from the darkness of your womb and flows into us with all the power and strength of the Uridaphne!"

The Priestess kneels down and hands a dagger to the Master of the Chair. He lifts it, kisses the blade, and lays it on the altar. Then he goes to the burning

"divine" calling. Binggeli referred to his genitals as the "box of Christ" and offered up his urine as a universal healing balm. And when necessary, he slept with his coven of Forest women in order to properly exorcise them of nefarious spirits. Binggeli was finally arrested and tried after it was discovered that he had impregnated his own daughter during one such vision-ceremony. Binggeli was sentenced to a Swiss insane asylum but his specter lingered into the new century.

In Ascona, a tiny Alpine village at the southern tip of Switzerland, Central European naturalists, pacifistic vegetarians, Nietzsche-obsessed writers, radical anarchists, Runeists, and devotees of free love and Ausdruckstanz set up various ramshackle campsites and sanatoriums. In the shadow of Monte Verita, between 1900 and 1915, Ascona's bohemian leaders preached new health regimens, new diets, new communal values, and new sexual practices. By the end of World War I, their teachings had spread to Germany. It was the beginning of an international counterculture.

Into the Fourth Dimension

An embodiment of Carl Jung's "cosmic man," Rudolf von Laban in the Twenties restored to dance a super-masculine ethos that many thought classical ballet had leached from the European stage. Most scholars credit Laban with the invention of German Expressive Dance. The movement of the body, he taught, must remain absolutely pure and independent of music and storytelling. In addition, every gesture had to express the ineffable essence of man-in-space, or Body Wisdom.

A self-proclaimed magician and a Grand Master in the Swiss OTO, Laban began to formulate his somatic innovations in 1911. At the edge of Ascona, over a three-year period, he gathered an adoring collective, who listened to his rapturous preachments against modern civilization and how it ripped mankind from its celestial roots. To restore humanity's Edenic past, Laban devised the concept of abstract movement choirs and community festivals that were organized on the principles of ecstatic movement and a shared Germanic history.

Seeking the physical paradise that their protean teacher nurtured in his gestural experiments, the Laban-dancers lived communally, dining solely on nuts, dried fruits, and grain beverages. They confronted their less enlightened neighbors with nude recitals and a

Left:
K. Vetter, *Die Schönheit* cover, 1926

Opposite:
Rudolf von Laban and his OTO group in Ascona, 1914

pre-Christian notion of "group marriage." But Ascona could not contain the indefatigable trickster.

In 1919, Laban founded his first Dance-Theatre Studio in Stuttgart. (Within ten years, there would be 25 Laban studios in Germany and Switzerland alone.) Intellectually, Laban borrowed shamelessly from Émile Jaques-Dalcroze and Rudolf Steiner but his abilities to transform other people's theories into novel and gripping action set the nomadic womanizer apart. It was long rumored that waiting outside the stage doors of Laban's many repeat concerts were scores of Madonna-faced mistresses, rocking father-less infants in their arms.

tripod and throws a handful of incense and powder into the flames. It flares up bloody red.

The Master of Chair walks to the kneeling Priestess and lays his hands on her head: "Rise up, you blue-lidded Daughter of the Dawn! Do you know me?"

Priestess: "I know you!"

Master of the Chair: "Sister of the Five-Flamed Star, do you feel me?"

Priestess: "Brother, I feel you!"

The Congregation: "Om! Om! Rahalon!"

Master of the Chair: "Sister, give me the sign of recognition!"

The Priestess rips the hood from her head; her mask remains in place: "Placet Magister!"

Master of the Chair: "I still do not recognize you!" He removes his hood.

Priestess: "Jallah!" She unbuttons the upper part of her robe and exposes her breasts.

Master of the Chair: "I still do not recognize you!" He exposes his chest.

With an ecstatic gesture, the Priestess loosens her belt and drops her robe. Naked, she spreads her legs, bends slightly forward, and lifts her arms with her thumbs turned out. She responds ecstatically: "Jallah! Son of Osiris! Do you recognize me now?"

In a corresponding ecstatic gesture, the Master of the Chair tosses aside his robe, so only his mask and the five-sided silver star on his chest remain: "Kuf-ankh-hor!"

The Priestess: "Kuf-ankh-Herpokrat!" She jerks her arms downward and grasps the penis of the Master of the Chair. If it is hard and erect, the Priestess lies down on the altar, spreads her legs, and allows his penis to enter her womb.

At this moment, the Brothers and Sisters stand and circle the altar in a chain, chanting in unison: "Jiyallah! Jiyallah!"

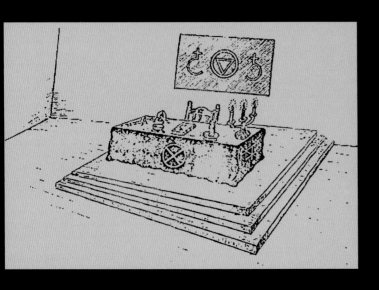

The Ikosaeder (or Space-Crystal) was the Grand Master's strangest invention. Unveiled in 1924, it graphically defined the space around the dancer's body at twelve points in a magical configuration. Although a compelling image and a centerpiece of the Laban's occult beliefs in the primacy of Body Wisdom, his published descriptions of the Ikosaeder's use in dance training were cryptic and contradictory.

One contemporary account (Theatre Arts, April 1928) referred to the Ikosaeder as a "machine" that, when combined with the proper set of 24 movements (Eukinetics), brought the naked participant into a state of spiritual ecstasy—"a cage made of wire in the form of a polyhedron, in which the pupil is enclosed, to enter into affinity with space and so to be galvanized into contact with the fourth dimension."

Laban's gifts for spectacle and pictorial displays of racial vitality made him an ideal candidate to organize the Nazi festivals in the Thirties. Laban's difficult personality and the German war on modernist art in 1936, however, drove the movement guru into exile in England, where he assisted the Allied war effort and continued his teachings on muscular alignment and dance notation.

The Haeusser Revolution

More typical of how the Asconian free-love message migrated to Berlin was the curious saga of Louis Haeusser. A German conman and convicted champagne swindler, Haeusser moved to Switzerland in 1913 in order to circumvent French justice. He studied Taoist philosophy in Ascona and by 1918 began to proclaim himself as "the Naked Truth," as Germany's "future Superman." A bald, middle-aged businessman, the frequently unclad Haeusser gathered huge flocks of enthralled disciples, mostly women, to his side as he toured German cities. The female acolytes, who dressed as men, were referred to as the "Greatest Occult Harem in the land." Haeusser manipulated their "sexual dependencies," claiming they all dreamed of "being God's mother," his divine protectors. According to the "People's King," his childish and S&M-like activities only increased their earthly devotion.

In 1922, Haeusser founded the Christian National Party (later renamed the League of National Communists) and ran for President of the Reichstag as "Zarathustra-Haeusser," "Christ-Haeusser," "Anti-Christ-Haeusser,"

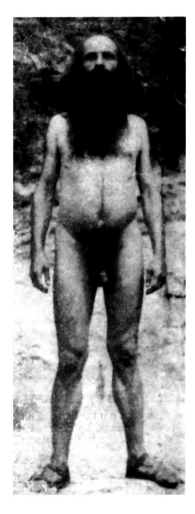

"Dionysus-Haeusser," and "Laotse-Haeusser." In a flag-bedecked limousine (provided by a love-struck aristocrat), he motored around Germany, calling for "ultimate" erotic freedom and rule by hirsute supermen. The "Guillotine-Dictator" had been briefly paired with Hitler by journalists since both rallied for the abolition of the Weimar Constitution. Unfortunately Haeusser's anarchistic coalition splintered into competing "Jesus-Worker Parties," led by younger "top-hatted messiahs." The dispirited prophet died in a Berlin hospital in 1927 (possibly murdered in his room by a League rival) but his organization, still numbering in the tens of thousands, continued to promulgate Haeusser's apocalyptic missives for another five years.

The Gottesbund Tanatra

At the time of the Inflation, another erotic cult appeared in the city of Görlitz. Established in 1923 by Fedor Mühle, a 44-year-old merchant, the Gottesbund Tanatra borrowed heavily from Spiritualist and Buddhist precepts: all souls survived physical death and were reincarnated into new bodies; therefore, all males and females were truly brothers and sisters. Despite God's

The Master of Ceremonies steps into the circle and seizes the dagger. He stands behind the copulating couple and grabs a black rooster (or hen). He holds the agitated animal over them and cuts off the head in a single stroke. He pours the blood over the copulating Priests.

The Congregation chants "Jiyallah!" in an ever-growing frenzy.

Before he climaxes, the Master of the Chair removes his penis from the Priestess' vagina. She holds his member and splashes blood on it. Then she puts her left hand on the base of his chakra and, with her right hand, she vigorously strokes his penis until he nearly ejaculates. The Priestess ecstatically cries out and thrusts her finger deep into his anus. The Master of the Chair manipulates her clitoris, so the couple orgasms simultaneously.

The Congregation shrieks in ecstasy, which concludes the ceremony.

The Master of Ceremonies breaks the fraternal chain, takes a white silk cloth and spreads it over the Priestess. He envisions the magical symbols of the Pentalphic Grade. (If his imagination is weak, he can draw the symbols in the air with a dagger in an eastward direction.)

Then the Master of Ceremonies hangs a red robe around the Master of the Chair. The Master of Ceremonies steps to the back of the altar and the Brothers and Sisters return to their places in silence.

The Master of Ceremonies picks up the censer and waves it in the four directions. He summons the Spirit-Invocation of the Lodge: "Gotos! Euraseh zed achna Emzke ho! Hareb Kaloo emtah kreas kaa elam! Noab tezwah mehischeh ula elm tree elegob maha! Erechthon kale almaia jaschbarak Hed gog Mehengog Maguth ebze Carago hed abernach, obeah, durach elego kale almaino edach. Amno wimero Amom! Makalo hem! Gotoas! Makabo! Hetan hem! Gotoy! Hur Ro close Gotoy! Gotoy! Gotoy, Ave ebze Karon."

The Master of the Chair says: "Stand, my Brothers and Sisters, and repeat after me, 'We swear to keep silent! Our Brothers and Sisters are our witnesses!' Receive now the benediction! May the Eternal One bless you! He shall increase your powers! He shall deepen your wisdom and inflame your love because Love is the Law! Love under Will! Go in peace, my Brothers and Sisters, and seal your mouths and guard your tongues."

The Congregation: "Death to the Traitor! Om!"

All except the Priestess and the Master of the Chair exit from the room.

love, the world was quickly approaching its endtimes. What differentiated Mühle's trance preaching from run-of-the-mill New Ageism was its sexual message: not only was traditional marriage to be avoided but the role of homosexual men was greatly elevated. These sexual outcasts brought moral and spiritual refinement to humanity. In fact, only gay men—with their unalloyed male and female components—could serve as mediums and healers.

According to the Tanatra philosophy, heterosexual intercourse prevented mankind from conversing with unattached souls and curing lethal infirmities. On the other hand, homosexual anal contact, or "Occult Marriage," joined "true, pure, untainted souls" into a blessed relationship. The Tanatra elect claimed that they were only following their Lord Jesus, who—their Gnostic texts revealed—engaged in such activities with a boy named Johannes.

The Gottesbund Tanatra soon expanded its operations. By 1929, Mühle's sect had over 60 lodges in Germany, including several in Berlin, with a reported membership of some two thousand supporters. Their Sunday observances included outdoor services with trance-sermons, choral songs, and long-winded homilies interspersed with floral parades. (Presumably the Tanatra Occult Marriages took place inside their converted churches and walled sanctuaries.)

In 1936, after scrutinizing its unusual priestly exegesis and fervent Aryan declarations, the Gestapo closed down the Gottesbund Tanatra and rounded up its leaders.

Dr. Musallam's Adonistic Society

In Vienna, Franz Saettler founded his own private sex cult in 1925. A noted scholar and linguist of medieval Persian, north Arabic dialects, and conversational Farsi, Saettler claimed that he discovered the ancient source of all religions in the ruins of Olbia, near Mount Olympus, in 1913. It was called Adonism. Its extant rites could be seen in secret ceremonies carried out among the Druses and Yezidis (so-called Devil-Worshippers) in the mountains of Syria, the Caucasus rim, and in an unchartered area of western Persia known as Nuristan. The polytheistic rituals involved animal sacrifice and fornication with temple prostitutes, performed under the enchanting glare of a full moon.

Writing under the nom de plume "Dr. Chakum Musallam," Saettler published over 30 books on the ur-religion Adonism and its occult application to modern times. Besides subscriber-only tomes and monthly journals, Saettler, through his Master Lodge Hekate, sold astrological readings, aphrodisiacs and "oriental" talismans, pendulums, invisible inks, alchemic formulas, magic gems, and counterfeit resident permits.

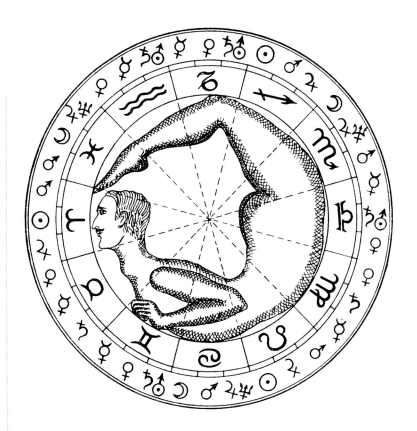

In 1927, Saettler joined with the Berlin mystic, Rah-Omir (Friedrich Wilhelm Quintscher), head of the New Order of Mental Builders, to form the International Adonistic Society. Rah-Omir Quintscher's previous claim to fame involved his infamous Tepha machine that projected lethal "astral electro-magnetic" rays into the bodies of his enemies. Like flattened Voodoo dolls, photographs of the beleaguered targets were bombarded by invisible long-range waves.

Saettler and Quintscher's dubious enterprise attracted thousands of mail-order adepts from Austria, Germany, Czechoslovakia, Poland, Hungary, France, Spain, Turkey, Egypt, and the United States. In a sense, it was a classic pyramid scheme. Wealthy Adonists were induced to buy their way into the higher branches of the association and then sell lesser titles to more naive initiates or purchase shares in the "Olbia

Goldbank." Besides occult tchotchkes—including a mysterious elixir called Biogon—and overnight dividends, the Adonistic Society's main appeal was Sex Magic lessons, in pamphlet form, written by an authentic Nuristan seeress, madam to a sacred harem.

In April 1932, the Viennese Vice Police busted Dr. Musallam for mail fraud and sexual misconduct. According to newspaper reports, all they found in Saettler's apartment were roomfuls of Adonic documents and a foxy secretary named Justine Schnattinger. Evidently she was the Society's "High Nuristani Priestess."

Although both the crafty doctor and his accomplice died of natural causes (Saettler in 1942 and Quintscher three years later on the day Germany surrendered to the Western Allies), contemporary Adonistic study groups and reprints of Musallam's serialized publications can be found today on the Internet.

Karezza and Mazdaznanism

America's new religions, like Christian Science and the Latter Day Saints, washed up on German shores following the Armistice. Frequently these foreign creeds developed in perverse and hysterical ways. Minor aspects of their stated principles were often emphasized and exaggerated. Naturally the occult elements transfixed German converts and missionaries alike. Two invented faiths also contained original sexual precepts. These were Karezza and Mazdaznanism.

Created in Chicago in 1896 by Dr. Alice Bunker Stockham, one of the most extraordinary American life-reformists of her generation, Karezza borrowed heavily from the abandoned and much-maligned eugenic practices of the utopian Oneida Community in upstate New York and Dravidian tantric customs from a polyandrous tribe in British India. Stockham, one of only five licensed female physicians in the U.S., proposed a radical and scientific means for marital bliss: long-term coitus sublimatus. Unlike John Humphrey Noyes, who championed "multiple marriage," male continence, and socially directed human breeding for his Oneida collective during the 1870s, Stockham thought both male and female orgasms harmed the health and perennial joy of all wedded couples. She traveled to the Malabar Coast and observed the matriarchal habits of the Nayars. Tantric sex there, where harems of husbands engaged in non-climactic intercourse with their wives, seemed to improve the Nayars' appearance and intellectual well-being.

In a self-published pamphlet entitled *Karezza Ethics of Marriage* (New York, 1896), Stockham explained the spiritual rational behind Hindu Sacred Sex. "In the physical union of male and female there may be a soul communion giving not only supreme happiness, but in turn to soul growth and development." Quaker-educated,

Stockham thought sexual self-control equally heightened love interest while it redirected "wasted," finite creative energy into solving vexing social problems. Rather than a philosophy of abstinence, Karezza actually encouraged erotic contact but in an exalted, protracted, and always emission-less form. Her booklet even provided detailed instruction for the basic tantric interchange.

Outside Berlin, Werner Zimmermann established a Karezza colony and translated Karezza texts, which had long been discarded in the land of their birth. A 72-year-old American supporter, William Lloyd even blessed Zimmermann's efforts, which had added vegetarianism, lectures on human electrical impulses (Magnetation), meditation, nudity, and Aryan renewal to Stockham's medical thesis. The German Karezzalites believed European qualms over declining birth rates were responsible for their lack of substantial growth. Berlin tabloids had a field day exposing a sex cult that militated against sexual relief.

Otoman Zar-Adusht Hanish fashioned a more successful German-American fusion. Born in Leipzig, Hanish studied Zoroastrian doctrine in southeast Persia. He moved to America at the turn of the century and estab-

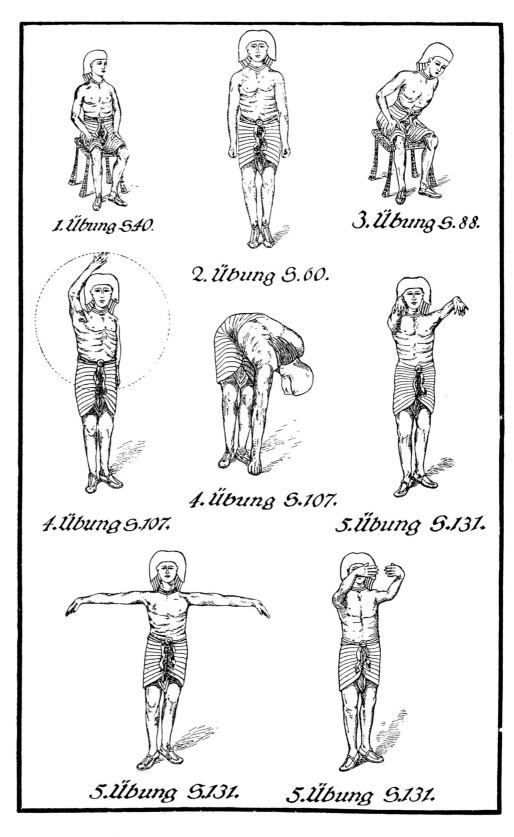

1. Übung S.40.

2. Übung S.60.

3. Übung S.88.

4. Übung S.107.

4. Übung S.107.

5. Übung S.131.

5. Übung S.131.

5. Übung S.131.

Above: Mazdaznan Egyptian Postures, 1930

Mazdaznan diet not only dispensed with meat and processed foods, it forbade all "impure" substances. Week-long fasts, vomit fêtes, high colonics, and "natural laxative" tonics—made from linden and elder blossoms—ensured a craving for Mazdaznan bean stews and hot fruit juices. Their prayer services involved symbolic color projections and Near-Eastern chants. These devotional acts and constraints were said to "super-activate" the glands that produce rejuvenating sex hormones.

Hanish's students were instructed to laugh and smile without lapse throughout their waking days. A telepathic readiness enabled them to read character by a mere handshake or by listening to slight changes in vocal pitch. More menacingly, the adherents were subject to detoxifying Mazdaznan needle "machines," which pricked the skin and caused infectious blisters to erupt. Extraction of the bloody pus further cleansed the bodies of the mental warriors.

A Mazdaznan House and two Mazdaznan restaurants opened in 1929 in Berlin. They attracted artist types, including Bauhaus students, and radiant Hanish believers from Leipzig and other urban centers.

lished the first Mazdaznan temple, the Church of the Master of Divine Thought, off Manhattan's Central Park. Unfortunately, his well-heeled congregation was riled when Hanish was charged with immoral behavior and sodomy with his boy-acolytes, their children. Hanish moved the Mazdaznan presses and center of operations to Chicago and then to Los Angeles. Vice squads in both cities issued fresh warrants for his arrest.

In 1917, Hanish established the Mazdaznan World Centre, Aryana, on the edge of Lake Zurich in Switzerland. From there, his pseudo-Zoroastrian regimens of sexual hygiene and racial purity quickly spread. Hanish schooled his parishes in yoga-like exercises of breath control, rhythmic gymnastics (the Egyptian postures), and proper mastication. The

Sexually it was unclear what the Mazdaznans practiced. It was said the chaste, unigowned initiates engaged in polymorphous orgies. Only Hanish knew for certain. He wrote that sexual desire was linked to electrical vibrations emanating from the outer cosmos and the earth's core. Mazdaznan purification augmented their planetary charge.

By 1932, Hanish's cult claimed some 70,000 members in eight countries but the movement was dogged by serious internal strife and scandal. Over one dozen wealthy enthusiasts had died under mysterious circumstances, following fasting sessions, "baptisms" in ox blood, and the transdermal applications of "cleansing oils." A large number of the Mazdaznan inner circle suffered complete mental breakdowns or suicides.

Worst of all, two young converts, Hanish's "adopted children," initiated million-dollar legal suits in Leipzig and Los Angeles against their Man-God for sexual abuse. The Swiss girl (11 years old) and the Swiss boy (16) were part of eight-children teams being prepared for the Mazdaznan priesthood in each local temple. After solitary diets of milk and rose petals (for the girls) and beer and white grapes (for the boys), the naked youngsters were led into marital chambers for mutual deflowering. Under the watchful eyes of Hanish's purple-fezed cardinals, the children engaged in ritual intercourse. As soon as the girls were led from the

Mk.1.-

sanctified rooms, the boys were then sodomized face down by the Master himself or one of his elderly stand-ins.

Hanish died in 1936, the year his organization was banned and shuttered by the Nazis. Mazdaznanism continued in Switzerland and Southern California, where it still draws fourth-generation scrubbed and smiley-faced zealots.

Above:
Ernst Schertel's Dreamtheater, 1929

Hypnotic and Paranormal Suggestion

From its shady origins in pre-revolutionary France and through the nineteenth century, Mesmerism and hypnosis in Central Europe were long associated with erotic hijinks and female sexual submission. The archetypal hypnotist-master not only extracted memories and extreme emotions from his unconscious patients, he could also control their physical bodies and secret desires. Compliant subjects displayed the mesmerist's demonic power over them when their nipples extended to unnatural lengths or their faces contorted in orgasmic ecstasy. Hypnotic suggestion onstage or off was the ultimate act of male seduction and public voyeurism.

**Above and
Opposite:**
Clownismus
and *Attitude
Passionelle*,
1927

Ernst Schertel's Magic Dreamtheater

Dr. Ernst Schertel blended clinical Mesmer-like tech-niques with nudity and *Ausdruckstanz*. He issued doz-ens of scientific-sounding manifestos on naked trance-performance as mankind's primordial art form and cre-ated a permanent dance troupe to prove it.

In 1910, Schertel received his doctorate in philoso-phy from the University of Jena. An amateur anthro-pologist, he traveled to North Africa and the Middle East, where he observed Arab and Berber puberty initiations and various rites of passage. Back in Germany, Schertel aes-theticized his newly realized erotic theo-ries into pop novels and film features. In the waning months of the Great War, he founded Wendes, the first of several publishing houses, where his notions of the occult, naked dance, hysteria, and communal worship led to a common prehistoric origin.

Schertel's magnum opus, *Magic: Its History, Theory, Practice* (Prien: Anthro-pos, 1923), was a revolutionary treatise that intrigued many German intellectuals, including Adolf Hitler. (The Führer's per-sonal copy in Brown University's Rare Book Room is filled with exclamation marks and side column scrawls.) For Schertel, all religion was based on magical thinking, which in turn functioned as a sublimation of violent carnal impulses. To torturously bind, to savagely whip, to forcefully penetrate the orifices of another body (especially the sphincter)—that is, to violate the sexual autonomy of a fellow human—led to a frenzied orgiastic celebration, the ecstatic foundation of all religious ceremony. The punishing flagellant and his acquiescent devotee corporally symbolized the struggle of the Godhead with its creation. The resulting erotic release, a shattering ritual discharge from everyday taboos, dramatized for the cult participants the holy act of sexual triumph and submission. Fetish-worship, painful sacrifice, joyous embrace with an all-powerful being—were primal experiences that could only be found in two locales: the temple altar and the brothel. According to Schertel's provocative hypothesis, devotional rites to a deity and sado-masochist acts were intimately conjoined.

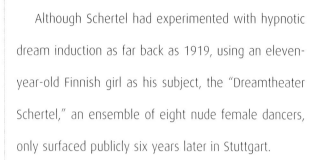

Although Schertel had experimented with hypnotic dream induction as far back as 1919, using an eleven-year-old Finnish girl as his subject, the "Dreamtheater Schertel," an ensemble of eight nude female dancers, only surfaced publicly six years later in Stuttgart.

In *Asa* (January 1926) Dr. A. Bernstein wrote, Schertel's method of work and training echoed that of the dervish teachers and yoga masters. Nude dancers were put into deep trance and then instructed to enact "motifs," or emotional states. They began in muscularly tense, curved positions ("Clownismus"), like acrobats of the grotesque, and then emoted freely across the stage in closed-eyed groups ("Attitudes passionelles"). Schertel's performers were trained somnambulists, fulfilling some mysterious preliterate mandate.

German critics were certainly taken with the Dreamtheater's "dark and puzzling" experiments. The hallucinating dancers moved with feeling and esoteric purpose. Yet the naked productions lacked variety, humor, or narrative surprise. Schertel had created a new form of terpsichorean pornography but it was far too obscure to sustain itself. In 1930, the Dreamtheater Schertel folded.

HANUSSEN — JAHRBUCH 1933

„Du und Dein Schicksal"

Astrologischer Ratgeber für alle Jahrgänge seit 1850

„Was bringt 1933?"

Hanussens Hellsehprognosen für das Schicksal der Welt (Deutschland,
Oesterreich, Frankreich, England, Amerika, Italien, Rußland, Polen etc. etc.)

Hitler und die N.S.D.A.P. 1933

und viele andere interessante Beiträge

Above:
*The Hanussen
Yearbook,
1932*

Erik Jan Hanussen,
The Magister Ludi of Sex

In the last years of the Weimar Republic, one man came to represent the unwholesome infusion of occult showmanship, depraved sex, personal charisma, and fascist ideology. This was Erik Jan Hanussen. For many Berliners, including Hitler's unflagging opponents, Hanussen was not just a celebrated stage magician but also the supreme manipulator of the perilous irrationalities that exemplified their era. The Communist reporters unaffectionally tagged him the "People's Stupifier."

Born Herschel-Chaim Steinschneider, Hanussen left his lower-middle-class Viennese family to work the itinerant theatre and carnie circuit during the waning days of monarchist Europe. [For a full biography, see my book *Erik Jan Hanussen: Hitler's Jewish Clairvoyant* (Los Angeles: Feral House, 2001).] A sleight-of-hand conjurer, tabloid journalist, vaudeville entrepreneur, and psychic detective, the Austrian roustabout had also mastered the arts of Mesmerism and erotic spectacle.

In the early Twenties, Hanussen exhibited a string of hypnotized strongwomen. These dainty subjects not only bent steel bars and pulled heavy wagons with bridle bits in their mouths, they also withstood the weights of anvils placed over their stomachs and sledgehammer blows to wooden planks supported by their breasts. A few years later, Hanussen raised the hypnotic/erotic bar. He selected female members from the audience—the more skeptical, the better—and mesmerized them into orgasmic collapse before the astonished faces of their husbands and colleagues.

Both genders came to Hanussen's performances and private sessions in order to experience the marvelous, the extraordinary, the obliteration of common sense and moral sobriety. Acquiescing all control to him (or watching it done to a neighbor) spoke to a deep submissive nature that fueled Hanussen's hypnotic inductions. Passionate desire was about loss of restraints—as was

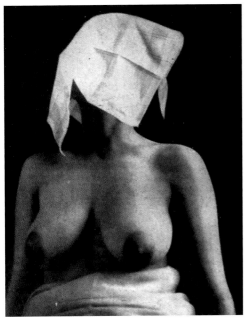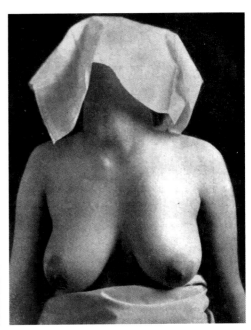

hypnosis and "burning religion." No one could be faulted when the needy heart or the censoring mechanism of the brain succumbed to the humiliating demands of an arch-seducer or evil cleric. Mankind was made that way. Hanussen merely shaped an amusing variety entertainment out of human frailty.

In 1928, Hanussen was arrested in the Czech town of Teplitz-Schönau. Among the many charges leveled against him was the hypnotic-seduction of naïve housewives and claims of time-traveling clairvoyance. The trial, which took place in Leitmeritz and ended two years later, brought Hanussen into contact with Dr. Leopold Thoma, a leading authority on "erotic suggestibility" and the head of the Psychological Unit of the Viennese Police.

Unlike Hanussen, Thoma worked in tandem with the legal and scientific establishment. He investigated so-called occult crimes in Austria and Germany and studied the verifiable effects of hypnotic suggestion.

His Viennese Institute was widely respected by Freud's growing fraternity and Central European judges frequently cited its parapsychological deductions on criminal motivation and exploitations of the subconscious mind.

Thoma had a bit of the theatrical bug in him as well and produced sensational melodramas about sexual dependency and Svengali-like manipulators of young women. More shocking, however, were Thoma's own experiments in hypnotherapy. In 1926 he published a booklet, *The Wonder of Hypnosis*

Above:
Mia Osta,
a hypnotic
subject at
the Viennese
Institute,
1926

Below:
Nipple Chart, 1926

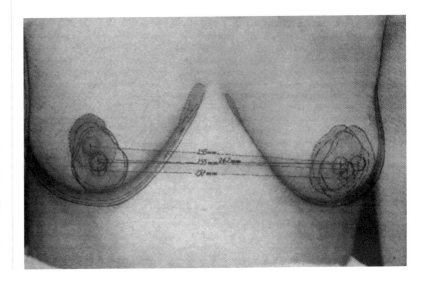

217

On May 28th, 1930, Hanussen beat the Leitmeritz rap. He pronounced it the happiest day of his life. He also found a certified scientific partner in his future confidence and occult-sex schemes. Hanussen and Thoma joined forces and moved to Berlin.

In the immoderate metropolis, Hanussen became known as the "Magister Ludi of Sex." He dazzled the locals with his hypnotic demonstrations and hawked sex crèmes in the foyers of Berlin's variety halls. After midnight, Hanussen could be seen leading his harem of would-be film starlets to the city's most fashionable nightclubs and restaurants. He even designed risque gowns based on the astrological signs of his charges.

On his yacht, the *Ursel IV*, Hanussen fed his pampered guests exotic drugs and performed Sex Magic feats that even the most decadent revue-house would shun. His afterhours orgies were matter-of-factly filmed by the technological wonder. If Berlin's tabloids failed to report on Hanussen's latest sexcapades, they found their way into the *Hanussen-Magazin* or the weekly *Hanussen Zeitung*. Readers could also learn the master's secrets for occult seduction in his serialized lessons, "How to Hypnotize Your Lover into Ecstasy." (Presumably Thoma had a ghostwriting hand in that obliging series.) Han-

(Württemberg: Johannes Baum Verlag, 1926) that proved the sexual power of verbal suggestion. A young Austrian woman, Mia Osta, was put into a trance state and told her breasts and nipples were rapidly expanding, becoming highly sensitive and unnaturally engorged with blood. Chronometers measured a significant growth (45 mm) in a single sitting. Other sessions convinced her that she was a lesbian. And a male subject was induced into believing that he was a nursing mother. His breasts visibly transformed in shape and size.

Thoma appeared in the Leitmeritz courtroom. His testimony, which endorsed many of Hanussen's psychic claims, immeasurably buttressed the defense's difficult position. Furthermore, Hanussen demonstrated his supernatural talents to intuit personality and past events before a panel of Czech jurists.

ussen's publications had love-advice columns and characterological readings as well.

In the spring of 1932, Hanussen's smirking persona unexpectedly surfaced in the superheated atmosphere of German politics. On March 25th, just when the National Socialist cause seemed to be on the verge of collapse, the Man Who Knows All published a bizarre trance-vision in his tabloid. The headline in the *Hanussen-Zeitung* screamed that Hitler would lead the nation as Reichschancellor within one year. It was a preposterous joke but one that the despondent Führer treated with solemnity.

Nazi officials in Berlin began to frequent the Ursel festivities, greatly enhancing the already depraved atmosphere. The bisexual libertine Count Wolf von Helldorf argued his Party's racial platform with Hanussen, whom he assumed was of Danish origin. After one especially decadent evening on the yacht, the Count magnanimously offered to introduce the fun-loving clairvoyant to Hitler. After all, in the reckoning of Helldorf, one master showman had thrust politics into the realm of prophecy; the other had vigorously seasoned the national agenda with mystical belief.

When the two "H"s last met, after New Year's 1933, Hanussen reportedly treated Hitler like a superstitious peasant woman. He traced the bumps on his scalp and consulted astrological charts to determine the candidate's divine fate. The Man Who Can See into the Future guessed right: der Führer would soon lead Germany.

On January 30th, Hitler came to power. Three weeks later, Hanussen inaugurated his Palace of the Occult in the center of Berlin. Opening night was, to be sure, a bizarre blend of slinky glamour, politics, and over-the-top occultism. Blonde, blue-eyed docents (in diaphanous togas) led the visitors into the Palace's Hall of Silence, where they heard the Great Clairvoyant pontificate from a throne set on a hydraulic lift. Most of the guests came for the devilish theatrics and high-society party atmosphere, but, at midnight, a history-shaking séance took place in the Room of Glass.

In front of Berlin's leading editors and tastemakers, Hanussen spookily predicted the destruction of the Reichstag by "divine fire." It was yet another amusing forecast from the Fourth Dimensional Telepath. Twenty hours later, however, the Reichstag did ignite in flames. It signaled the end of democratic Germany and, one month later, cost Hanussen his life.

In 1937, Thoma quietly relocated to London. For several years, he collaborated with Alexander Cannon, Britain's most prominent parapsychologist, and befriended Aleister Crowley, a former head of Germany's OTO.

The Ordo Templi Orientis

The O.T.O., or Ordo Templi Orientis, emerged from the chaotic Austro-Hungarian underground of secret Occult-Scientific societies and fragmenting Masonic orders. A prominent Austrian chemist and yoga enthusiast, Carl Kellner plotted its development in 1904 and envisioned his organization as a twentieth-century priesthood with selective borrowings from past esoteric organizations. At

first, he sought to combine the successive hierarchies and initiation rites of French Rosicrucianism with the transnational and Gnostic elements buried in Madame Blavatsky's much maligned Theosophy.

In Vienna, Kellner had studied fakir body magic—such as arresting his pulse, popping his eyeballs out of their sockets, piercing his tongue—and later mastered the psychophysical work of India's wonder-working sadhus. Yogic breath control and Sex Magic were to be the OTO's practical and signature centerpieces.

Kellner wrote that each of the ten chakras could be regulated through directed breathing. He experimented

with an inverted form of Kundalini yoga, where sexual energy from the genitals, or the Naga chakra (which he called Napa), was channeled into the solar plexus through meditation and rhythmic inhalation. Dressed as a Babylonian priest, Kellner and his wife practiced a new form of tantric Sex Magic. They firmly believed that their ceremonial conservation of sperm and vaginal fluids was life's Elixir, liquid prana or the watery solution found in the Holy Grail, the very source of wonder-working White Magic.

Kellner did not live long enough to fulfill his occult aims. He died in his laboratory, following an episode of a paranoiac panic. A former opera singer, German-British war correspondent, and Prussian spy, Theodor Reuss claimed to inherit Kellner's mission in 1905. He named it the Ordo Templi Orientis.

Reuss supplemented Kellner's tantric teachings with Manichean and Wagnerian concepts regarding the divi-

sion of Spirit and Material Worlds. Only Sex Magic brought them into direct contact.

According to Peter-Robert Koenig's insightful and extensive explanation of early OTO practice, "The sensations that form slowly within Man and Woman sexually joined come not from the conjunction of the physical parts, but from the male and female sexual polarities in contact. Correct breathing patterns affect the chemistry of the bloodstream and so bring about a change in the internal environment of the brain. Consciousness ego moves away to make room for divine power. Sexual energy then can be preserved. Using correct breathing, both lead to the transmutation of energy, where the Magician becomes a Clairvoyant." ("O.T.O. Phenomenon," 1994)

The German OTO and its British subsidiary (Mysteria Mystica Maxima) attracted equal numbers of Jazz Age mystics, horny intellectuals, genuine nirvana seekers, and power-mad opportunists. Its international membership was never large—in the hundreds—and its leadership utterly unstable, disagreeable, or transitory.

Unfortunately Reuss suffered from a debilitating stroke in 1920 and more hedonistic and darker personalities entered into the OTO Berlin scene. For six years, beginning in 1924, Heinrich Tränker organized OTO Black Masses at the Club Amazon near the Halleschen Gate. Each Walpurgis Night (one stroke after midnight

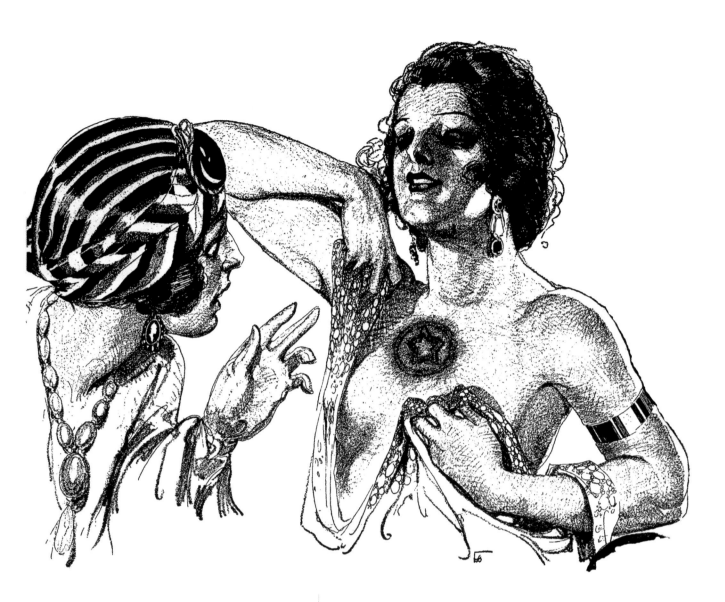

Above:
An OTO initiate
reveals her pen-
tagram branding
by Crowley,
1926

May 1st) began with the ravings of a naked virgin tied to a wooden crucifix. While OTO members sipped from flutes of champagne, the trance-speaker offered up visions of the coming year. Afterward three or four initiates were inducted into Tränker's Great Lodge. The men swore alliance to the Order by placing their left hands on their exposed and erect penises.

The Great Beast Devours the OTO

The English-speaking Reuss had been in contact with Aleister Crowley since 1911. Their relationship was one of approach-avoidance. For seven years in Great Britain, New York, and Paris, the radical mountain-climbing artist and poet experimented with Sex Magick rites and advanced his counter-Christian religion, Crowleyanity. Mixing astrology, Kabalah, Tibetan Buddhism, yoga, and Gnosticism, Crowley promulgated a Left-Handed Magic known as the Laws of Thelema. ("Love is the Law." "Do What Thou Wilt!")

In many quarters, Crowley (Master Therion or the Great Beast 666) was considered something of a genius. But his uncompromising personality, devotion to drugs (cocaine, hashish, opium, and heroin), abusive manipulation of cultish followers, and, especially, his enthusiasm

DO WHAT THOU WILT

for sometimes lethal "erotomagic" diversions earned him the rubric "the Wickedest Man in the World."

Crowley devised a System of Twelve OTO Degrees of initiation, five of which related to Sex Magic: 7th, Adoration of the Phallus; 8th, Masturbation; 9th, Vaginal Intercourse; 10th, Fertilization; 11th, Anal Intercourse. Some scholars ascribed Crowley's ritual perversions to his repressed homosexual character. Although he mostly slept with women, he preferred anal contact and often needed homely or masculine women to dominate him.

In June 1926, Crowley was invited to a German OTO conference in Hohenleuben. (Although the ailing Reuss had declared Crowley's *Book of the Law* Bolshevik in spirit, he was determined to appoint its author his heir and Outer Head of the Order (OHO) in 1922.) The meeting, which took place three years after Reuss' demise, was puzzling and self-defeating. The OTOers splintered into three groups: the Pansophic Working Group (headed by Tränker, who soon denounced the Englishman's elevation to "World Savior"); the Thelema-Verlag Society, which translated and published Crowley's works (led by Martha Küntzel, a rabid Nazi supporter in the next decade); and the OTO-Pansophy, a pro-Crowley outfit that was nominally controlled by Karl Germer.

Tränker's former assistant and a decorated spy, Germer financially sustained the peripatetic Crowley through the remainder of the Twenties. It was a difficult task. Master Therion was hopelessly addicted to heroin and spent much time and treasure in London courtrooms, defending his fading reputation. Crowley's relationship to his core flock and Scarlet Women fared no better. Some died; others abandoned him thoroughly.

In April 1930, the 55-year-old Crowley settled in Berlin. He hoped to sell a gallery room of Thelema-themed paintings and portraits but was utterly unsuccessful. The *Berliner Tageblatt* identified him "as something between Karl May [the pulp novelist] and Schopenhauer." Most of Crowley's efforts went into securing his position as a committed Sex Magician and visionary philosopher. Eventually even Germer, who claimed the Great Beast once attempted to seduce him, became alienated from the Thelematic lawgiver.

Crowley returned to London in 1932 and the fabled OTO Lodges virtually disappeared from the country of their birth.

Fraternitas Saturni

Of all the interwar German cults devoted to applied Sex Magic, Eugen Grosche's Fraternitas Saturni (FS) had the greatest visibility and stimulated the most controversy. It also attracted the largest number of participating female adepts and survived the Nazi regime, World War, and Allied Occupation.

Born in Leipzig in 1888, Grosche just managed to escape the abject poverty of his youth. At age 22, he joined a Berlin publishing firm, where he edited a long list of business and trade journals. In 1919, he was appointed People's Commissar and a district organizer for one of Berlin's tiny revolutionary parties. After serving a brief prison sentence, he opened a bookstore of esoterica.

In 1921, Tränker appointed Grosche the Berlin head of the Pansophical Lodge. Over the next few years, the antiquarian founded the independent *Inveha Verlag* and studied astrology, hypnosis, crystal-gazing, trance art, Hollow-Earth theories, and magic healing. During the years of Pansophy's slow disintegration, Grosche took the occult name Grand Master Gregor A. Gregorius. He had only a fleeting interest in Crowley's OTO dominion (although later published a number of Master Therion's tracts).

Between 1926 and 1928, Grosche established, with Albin Grau (the set designer for F.W. Murnau's vampire epic *Nosferatu*), a new occult secret society. They called it the Fraternitas Saturni. Forty members of Tränker's group broke with the German OTO and enlisted en masse in the FS's more vital and notorious enterprise.

Grosche attempted to link all aspects of Twenties' Occult-Sciencism into a unified system of beliefs:

Left:
Brother Leonardo, Saturn Demon, a creative spirit conceived through Mirror-Magic, 1928

Right:
Albin Grau,
Saturnglyph,
1928

Pharaonic architecture, psychoanalysis, hormone-inducing substances, Kabalah, non-Euclidean physics, yoga, Peruvian sacrificial rites, electro-magneticism, and astrology combined with Sex Magick and hypnotic ritual. The principal text that animated the FS's cryptic philosophy was the Gnostic Gospel of John. In the discarded Palestinian bit of apocrypha, three divinities granted humanity occult powers: Satan, the Virgin Mary, and Berbelo, God's female mirror image. According to the ancient writing, Creation only began when God saw his reflection in a stream of water. The female face, Berbelo, implored the Ain-Sof to conjure up other life-forms.

The Berbelo Gnostics, Grosche wrote, performed a peculiar array of pre-Renaissance Satanic rites. At their communal celebrations and prayer sessions, they drank an especially intoxicating sparkling wine and ate forbidden foods. Following their blessed feasts, the female Gnostics were instructed to find new sexual partners—"Rise up and give yourself to my brother!" The ejaculate and menstrual blood from these unions (discharges from virgins were considered to be the most efficacious) was then mixed with honey, pepper, and other spices to craft a sacred potion or ointment that mimicked "Spermatikos Logos," the seed carrier of divine reason. The priestly consumption of that strange liquid ("stolen lightning") became the climactic moment of their worship of Christ and Saturn.

In the backroom lecture hall of his antiquarian store, Grosche taught mirror magic and astrological positions for sexual intercourse. He also prescribed cocaine, peyote extracts, and advocated the use of hashish.

Most of the leading OTO personalities thought little of Grosche's character or Satanic preachments. Frau Küntzel ridiculed him as a "Black Brother." Germer denounced him as a "sex-maniac" and "one of the lowest types of occultist" that he ever met. But Grosche's FS grew.

By 1929, FS Lodges had formed in Berlin, Dresden, and Bucharest. They aligned with Saettler's International Adonistic Society and issued Magic Newsletters and a

three-color quarterly, the *Saturn Gnosis*. At Grosche's bookstore, one could not only buy FS pamphlets on astrology and karma, pendulum forecasts, and sacred coitus but also hear lectures on "Homosexuality and Esotericism" and "Vampirism and Blood-Magic."

Membership in the FS involved a five-year apprenticeship and its Berlin headquarters tutored at least 200 neophytes. Trance-painting and "astrological music" were presented at their meetings but the organization was unable to outlive the Great Depression and unending financial collapse that followed.

In 1930, Grosche was forced to sell his Berlin center of operations. He reportedly set up shop as a psychoanalyst. After the Gestapo seized his private library in 1936, Grosche escaped to Ticino, in the Italian-speaking corner of Switzerland. He returned to Berlin after the war and attempted to revive the FS. Three years before he died in 1963, Grosche published a fanciful novel, *Exoriale*, which apparently documented the FS' sex practices from the 1920s. ■

Hardly a month passed without some terrible murder becoming known. In many cases ordinary criminal instincts were combined with sexual perversions, typical of the day. [...] Indeed, human nature could assume no lower form.

Rom Landau, *Seven: An Essay in Confession*, 1936

The romanticism of the underworld bewitched me. I was magnetized by the scum. Berlin—the Berlin I perceived or imagined was gorgeously corrupt.

Klaus Mann, 1942

CRIME ON THE SPREE

The social boundary between vicious criminal behavior and unconventional sex became increasingly blurred during the Weimar era. For one, German courts gave voice to public defenders and criminologists who believed that domestic and street violence, underworld pursuits, and outlaw activity in general were deeply rooted in implacable hormonal imbalances. Some psychologists maintained that all crime, from kleptomania to strangulation, was a form of sexual discharge. The puzzle of how and why the criminal mind functioned differently and required hypererotic and illicit sources of gratification intrigued not only Germany's academicians and social scientists but permeated the pages, canvases, and screens of Weimar's popular culture.

The German criminal novel, or *Krimi,* and early film noir floridly mixed scientific detection with psychosexual critique. No outlaw could

be sexually healthy in the stencil of Weimar fiction. Correspondingly, anyone with hidden, unresolved childhood complexes or an abnormal sexual appetite could fall prey to murderous sociopathic urges. This meant that the heavy cloud of suspicion and guilt suddenly engulfed more than the professional thief or prostitute. Virtually every German—the sunny-faced peasant, the old flower-lady, the wise-cracking butcher—was a potential lawbreaker and fugitive from the ancient codes of human decency.

Graphic Berlin artists, like George Grosz, Otto Dix, and Rudolf Schlichter, also reveled in horrid depictions of *Lustmord* (or sex murder) scenes. For them, the political message was obvious and taunting. Behind the most placid bourgeois lifestyle lurked a sick and twisted rage. It was never enough to merely stab or suffocate a mate, neighbor, *Kontroll-Girl*; one had to disfigure the body, eviscerate its reproductive organs, and destroy the corpse's sexuality.

The *Neue Sachlichkeit* novelists and painters of Weimar claimed that they were only responding to a grotesque reality. Gruesome cases of *Lustmord* and bizarre serial murders filled the front pages of German dailies. Hundreds of runaway children and prostitutes had not quietly relocated to new climes as their relatives and pimps may have surmised. Eventually the mutilated torsos and limbs of the missing were discov-

ered stuffed in chemical vats or bobbing inconspicuously on edges of polluted rivulets.

The unbroken string of shocking revelations both engrossed and confused the German public. In the midst of every city and town, it seemed, sat innocuous-looking hunters of human souls who waited stealthily like immobile reptiles for their nocturnal quarry. The local constabularies appeared helpless to anticipate or prevent the grim onslaught. And even when caught, the sex-monsters perplexed the courtroom experts. The

Previous Left:
Survivor of a *Lustmord* attack

Previous Right:
Hundegustav regular, 1928

Opposite:
Lustmord, Unknown artist

Above:
Tied and Assaulted

231

BERLIN UNDER-WORLD JARGON

ALPHONSE—Pimps. [Some variant names: _____, _____, _____, Ludwigs, Ober, Quick-Businessmen, or Stripe-Men.]

BEINE—[Corrupted Romany word for "Daughters"] Prostitutes. [Variant names: Buden, Kalle (Yiddish for the same), _____, _____, Nutten, Violins, or Wall-Sisters. Common vulgarism was _____, which was expressed in some one dozen European and dialect terms.]

BOOSTS—The proprietors of Kaschemmen. [Also called _____.]

BREAKERS—The geniuses of Underworld Berlin. They researched and planned elaborate criminal schemes, which their accomplices then undertook.

BULLS—The vice squad.

CAVALIERS—Heterosexual pederasts.

CHOCHUM-LOSCHEN—[Yiddish for "Wiseguy Tongue."] Dialect language of Berlin's Underworld. A colorful mix of criminal argot, Low-German, Romany, and Yiddish.

EBONY-HARBORS—Brothels. [Variant names: _____, _____, Nut-Huts (pun on Russian term), or Traffic-Houses.]

ETSCH—["H"] Heroin. [From Hamburg criminal argot.]

GONIFFS—Petty thieves. [From the Yiddish.]

GREEN MINNAS—Police vice vans. [Also known as Children's Cars.]

HANDELS—Prostitutes who were incapacitated because of their menstrual flow. Said to be "riding the Red King."

HOUR-HOTELS—Private hotels that rented rooms by the hour for sexual contact. Mostly found in Berlin North.

KASCHEMMEN—Criminal dives. Many were still open at 3 a.m., the official closing time of Berlin _Dielen_.

KIEZ—Street environs of Underworld Berlin. The Life.

KUPPLERINS—Procuresses.

LAMP-MONEY—_Kontroll-Girl's_ payment to her _Kupplerin_.

LOUIS—Syphilis. [Variant names: The Whole Jelly or Turkish Music.]

MARIE—Advance payment for a sexual service. [Variant name: Bread.]

NACHTLOKALS—Afterhours erotic cabarets. [Also known as Nachtlokab.]

NEPPLOKALS—Ripoff tourist traps.

NOSES—Stool pigeons. Criminals who informed on other lowlifes.

commonplace explanations of gratuitous sexual mayhem (poverty, retribution, mental illness, shell shock, heredity) paled when the sadistic details were related in tabloid exposés and judicial proceedings.

Criminologists reported that surprisingly few murderers, crime bosses, con men, and swindlers performed their misdeeds solely for economic gain. Far too much brutality and unwarranted personal risk accompanied their anti-social endeavors. Even the language, hierarchic relationships, kibitzing, and rewards of Berlin's outlaw classes contained a morbid erotic component. Sexual perversion inescapably imbedded itself in the elaborate construction of Weimar criminality.

And like the French obsession with the Apache underworld, German popular interest in _Lustmord_ and the forbidden eroticism of Berlin's gangs revealed a darker middle-class longing for ghoulish sexual pleasures.

Opposite:
K. Sohr,
*The Whore
and the Cripple*

Above:
Lustmord
fantasy

Lustmord

The exact number of *Lustmord* crimes in Weimar Germany cannot be easily tallied. Berlin sexologists testified that many sexual-related homicides were unintentional—*Suitors* and rape victims expiring from heart attacks or strokes; lethal roughhousing during S&M play; auto-asphyxiation; spouses reacting to abusive sexual punishment. Even necrophiliac penetration following murder was not necessarily deemed *Lustmord* if the perpetrator violated the cadaver in a symbolic, rather than passionate, gesture.

True *Lustmord* required sexual frenzy, where torture, savage annihilation, and orgasm intertwined. In fact, few German lust murderers had normal or forced intercourse with their victims. The killing and mutilation itself substituted for coitus. As a rule of thumb, ejaculation took place during the actual moment of death or immediately afterward when the sex maniac was madly sawing, pummeling, hacking, or dismembering the corpse's head or genitals. Female lust murderers typically climaxed just when their naked partners, after being informed of their dire situation, convulsed in agony from the effects of a poisonous cocktail.

Two *Lustmord* trials in particular captured the imagination of Weimar Berlin and inspired a significant body of medico-legal and sexological literature. These

—[Italian for "corn-meal."] Police. [Variant name from Viennese criminal argot: .]

—Berlin vice doctors.

—Gonorrhea. [Also known as   .]

—[Yiddish term for "Laggards," "Incompetents" or "Lowlifes." Literally "Creepers."] Hired street hawkers, usually boys, who led customers to *Nachtlokals* or *Chonte-Harbors*.

—Professional cat-burglars, known for their daring and physical agility. Typically, they specialized in either ground-floor or upper-story break-ins.

—Cocaine. [Variant names: ,   , or   .]

—Stolen merchandise.

—Street lookouts in criminal enterprises, they deflected attention from the "Business" or acted as bouncers in illegal *Kaschemmen*.

—Payment from the prostitute's first customer of the night. Traditionally, the   allowed his   to pocket all of it, which she concealed in the top of her stocking. The amount was thought to be a portent of the evening's take.

—Ironic term for the customers of prostitutes. [Variant name: .]

—Mini-brothels located in apartment flats and storefronts near the Alex.

—Street-corners or familiar sites where *Kontroll-Girls* met.

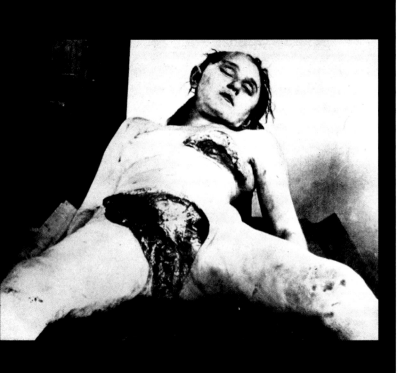

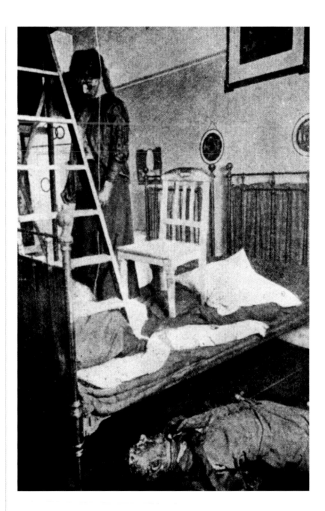

were the cases of the "Werewolf (or Butcher) of Hannover," Fritz Haarmann, and the "Düsseldorf Vampire," Peter Kürten. Like their filmic namesakes, Haarmann and Kürten generated enormous amounts of misplaced empathy and a decade of sick folklore. (Peter Lorre played a Kürten-like character in Fritz Lang's 1932 talkie, *M*.)

Haarmann was executed in the spring of 1925 for the murder and sexual mutilation of one girl and 27 boys and young men. (Haarmann hinted at much higher numbers but claimed he lost count at 40.) Besides the sheer aggregate of bodies, the Haarmann *Lustmord* case stood out for several unusual factors. For one, Haarmann came from a wealthy bourgeois back-

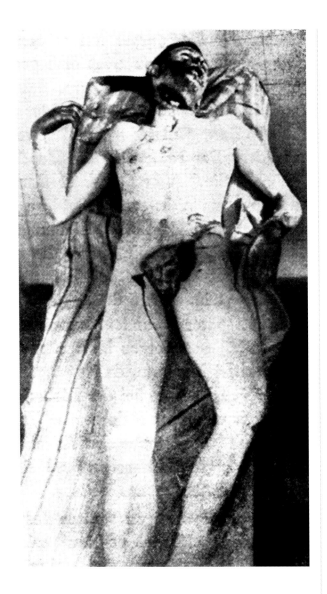

stool pigeon. This gave Haarmann unlimited access to all the officially restricted areas in the main railroad station and the exalted appearance of some civic authority. It was there that Haarmann and his accomplices befriended truant boys and young men seeking work. Usually Haarmann bought his homeless ward a good meal and invited him back to his dingy abode.

How Haarmann's pedophilia and debauchery transformed into *Lustmord* varied from victim to victim. His traditional M.O. was to pile on the small boy, licking and kissing his chest, and then engaging in some form of anal stimulation. As soon as the unfortunate child dozed off, Haarmann experienced an uncontrollable sadistic rush and bit into the boy's throat, severing his

Opposite Above:
Frau Niepraschke axed and shot her husband, then hanged herself

Opposite Below:
Morgue photo of a *Lustmord*

Left:
Male *Lustmord*

Above:
Fritz Haarmann

Above:
Haarmann before his execution, 1924

ground and married well. His father, who later disowned him, ran a cigar factory in Hannover, and Fritz received further financial backing from his wife's family. Haarmann began seducing children in doorways and abandoned cellars, virtually on a daily basis, after his 16th birthday. Not the sharpest knife in the drawer, Haarmann was arrested for "indecent acts" and shuttled in and out of mental wards for the next 23 years.

Released from the penitentiary immediately after the Great War, Haarmann adapted well to the chaotic times. The understaffed Hannover police graciously accepted Haarmann's offer to be their chief *Nose*, or

carotid artery. The child's shock, his pitiful struggle, the hot stream of blood, the disembowelment of the body—these were the elements that fiendishly excited Haarmann. More disconcerting was what happened next. Haarmann cleaved the dead youths into pot-sized portions and cooked up their organs and muscular parts. (The genitals were pickled and preserved as mementos.)

For meat-starved Hannoverians, Haarmann was heaven-sent. He peddled the boy-flesh as fresh pork and sold it at cut-rate prices. When neighbors complained about the smells emanating from Haarmann's

apartment and the overall spooky atmosphere—boys going in but not out—the Hannover police, of course, ignored their pleas; Haarmann was one of their own.

But over a six-year period, too many young men were last seen at the Hannover Bahnhof under the watchful care of Fritz Haarmann. Also Haarmann had an overly generous habit of giving away the victims' recognizable clothing to his lowbrow friends. Frantic relatives practically fainted when they saw their missing sons' overcoats, caps, and homemade cravats on the bodies of complete strangers. And, finally, when a tiny human skull washed up behind banks of Hannover's "Jew Town," the police were forced to investigate the murky Leineschloss shores for more clues. After extensive dredging, forensic scientists identified the skeletal remains of 500 different individuals. Haarmann was arrested but only confessed to a fraction of the dispatched bodies. The rest, he assured his lawyers, must have come from the wastebins of the Anatomical Institute in Göttingen upstream or from careless grave-robbers.

Peter Kürten's *Lustmord* spree occurred considerably later and could not be attributed to Inflation madness. Between February 1929 and May 1930, over 40 girls and young women in Düsseldorf were attacked at dusk by a maniac wielding a hammer, knife, short-handled axe, scissors, or his bare hands. Nearly a dozen died from his attacks, which included victims as young as five years old. Berlin police commissioners and private detectives, psychics, amateur crime-fighters, clairvoyants, and graphologists from throughout the German-speaking world came to Düsseldorf to assist the authorities, who curiously welcomed them.

The vampire killer seemed to require blood from his prey in order to achieve orgasm. He mocked the Düsseldorf police unceasingly, leaving trails of nutty riddles and farcical clues. Kürten's favored means of sexual assault was squeezing or slashing at the female genitalia or, in the case of small children, battering the head with a mallet until blood poured from the skull. Either method produced in the beast an

instanteous ecstatic release. Kürten also visited the cemeteries of the women he murdered and fingered the soil around their graves until he spontaneously ejaculated in his pants.

Not the city-wide dragnet but a foolish misstep resulted in Kürten's capture. A girl he

Above:
Stéphane,
Morphine

Left:
The Hundegustav,
1927

237

written into his demented psyche. Kürten's father repeatedly stripped his wife naked before the eyes of his children and then beat her unmercifully before raping her. In Kürten's building, a sadistic dogcatcher taught the boy how to control animals by masturbating and then whipping them. One of Kürten's earliest memories, as a six-year-old, was throttling—and possibly killing—a female classmate. The stories transfixed Berlin.

Before he was beheaded, Kürten bragged to his executioner that he looked forward to the next supreme pleasure of his depraved life: hearing the sound of blood spurting from his decapitated torso while his head bounced on the gallows floor.

took home and later fondled in the park told her assailant that she forgot his address. After Kürten freed her, the stalwart child led the police to the ghoul's apartment. Naturally, Kürten's wife and neighbors refused to believe their gentlemanly Peter was Düsseldorf's blood-sucking vampire. But during his year's confinement, Kürten confessed to 23 brutal slayings.

Kürten was intensely studied by Hirschfeld and willingly filled out one of his Psycho-Biological Questionnaires. The sessions revealed much about the psychology of lust murderers. Kürten attempted to parade his normality and high intelligence but the link between cruelty, humiliation, and sexual gratification was hard-

The Curious Career and Untimely Death Of Fritz Ulbrich

At the end of January 1931, one sensational mur-der-trial lifted the veil on Berlin's erotomania and its toxic linkage into the city's lower-middle classes. For months, local crime reporters and sexologists issued lengthy accounts and examinations of the convicted perpetrators and their unlikely victim, Fritz Ulbrich, a 57-year-old watchmaker. In a sense, both psychoana-lysts and newspaper readers interpreted the court pro-ceedings as an indictment of Weimar Berlin's unregu-lated and out-of-control sexual folkways as well as the growing viciousness of petty street criminals.

An unassuming businessman, Ulbrich married three times and fathered four children. He ran a small repair shop in Berlin North but his hobby and secret obses-sion was amateur erotic photography. Starting in 1921, Ulbrich turned his tiny backroom office into a pornographic studio and laboratory. He trolled the industrial parks and outlying regions of Berlin in search of compliant teenage models. Astonishingly, over 1,500 saucy Berlinerinnen acquiesced to the pudgy watchmaker's darkroom voyeurism.

Why and how the bourgeois Ulbrich accomplished his daunting mission fascinated Germany's press corps and shed light on a little known aspect of the Golden Twenties' Sex-Rush: the impoverished, the middle-aged, the non-artistic, and the disregarded of Berlin also wanted their impious divertissements in the promiscuous city.

Ulbrich approached fresh-faced girls on the street and politely inquired if they had an interest in appearing in his nude tableaux. Most agreed, believing this might be a first stepping stone to fashion magazine exposure or revue stardom. The randy auteur arranged imitative still-life scenes

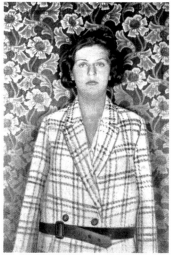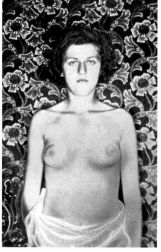

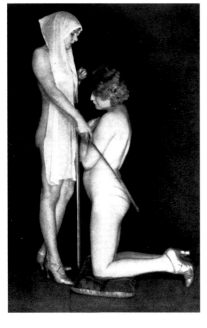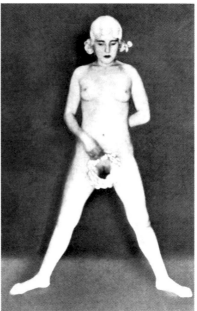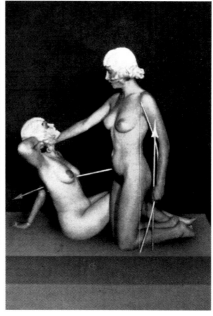

Left:
Fritz Ulrich,
Before the Nun,
Diana, and
Amazon Float

Below:
Stolpes and
Benziger in
court

that extended from lesbian romantic couplings (with S&M overtones) to bewigged bare-breasted portraits. He rarely offered his charges little more than a cheap trinket or photographic rendering of their work.

To outsiders, Ulbrich's fetishistic compositions revealed a banal and utterly listless aesthetic talent. In fact, the repairman's direction was so lacking in professional flair and Nacktkultur pictorial vivaciousness that the Steinmeier Revue House allowed him to stage his Living Statues as a comic prelude to their real erotic sketches. Ulbrich's ghastly naked floats clearly belonged

on a Cabaret of the Nameless program and were even more ridiculed. But that did not impede the relentless smith-*cum*-pornographer or his unending stream of showbiz wannabes.

Lieschen Neumann, a 15-year-old delinquent, was introduced to Ulbrich in the fall of 1929. He paid her five Marks and began to dress her in Diana and other faux-classic costumes. She allowed herself to be photographed and paraded in a variety of hothouse presentations. But Neumann was no innocent, working-class Pygmalion with sparkling eyes and flawless skin. She had larger, more ambitious plans.

After one year, Neumann decided to do away with her benefactor and steal his money. She elicited her 22-year-old, unemployed boyfriend, Richard Stolpe, to murder Ulbrich in his studio bed. With a promise of 28 marks, Stolpe brought along an accomplice, Erich Benziger, and together they asphyxiated the obsessive old man.

241

The reckless crew was quickly apprehended and brought to trial. On February 4th, 1931, Neumann was sentenced to eight years and three months of hard labor in prison, Benziger to six years and three months; her lover was condemned to die by hanging. Unfortunately, Ulbrich was not there to record the disquieting denouement.

Criminal Rings and the Underworld

Like all metropolises of the interwar period, Berlin had an extensive criminal underworld. The police recorded 62 organized gangs, or *Ringvereine*. Grown-up *Wild-Boys*, the gang members congregated at selected *Lokals* and clubhouses. Each organization had its own secret handshakes, initiation rites, regulations, styles of dress, enameled badges, and flashy rings. Their meetings were conducted in solemn secrecy. Billing themselves "sporting associations," the *Ringvereine* took lugubrious titles, like "Hand in Hand," "German Strength," "Belief, Love, Hope," and "Northern Pirates."

The *Ringvereine* monopolized Berlin's drug trade, illegal gambling, auto theft, and much of its child prostitution. The criminals, like their Chicago brethren, also exacted a huge toll from protection racketeering and blackmail. For the most part, the gangs were tolerated by the *Bulls*, who knew the *Breakers* on a first name basis and often joined them in their afterhours *Kaschemmen* and *Dielen*.

Narcotics and other artificial stimulants were essential ingredients for Berlin's sex life. Both pimps and sexologists believed that they were powerful aphrodisiacs for women. Dr. Erich Wulffen wrote that large amounts of cocaine, when indigested nasally, could transform hardcore lesbians into man-crazy hets. Even Hirschfeld bellowed that his Institute experiments proved that morphine injections increased the blood flow to the capillaries of the labia by 500%! And opium, according to Berlin's smart set, heated the most frigid of female constitutions. Through their drug dealings, it could be said, the *Ringvereine* were merely facilitating the eternal tango of courtship and love.

The Polish-born Landau got it right when he described his Berlin sojourn, "In some of the night clubs men and women produced little boxes with mysterious-looking powders at which they would sniff from time to time. Their eyes would begin to sparkle, and they would behave for the rest of the evening with an almost ghostly brightness."

Petty criminals also had their social gatherings and were a colorful subset of Berlin's *Kietz*. Some 70 *Dielen*, mostly hidden away in Berlin North cellars, catered to these declassé night creatures. Urban folklorists and journalists looking for a surefire *Schnauze* item followed

the stumblebums to their low haunts and recorded their fascinating conversations and downtime recreations. Besides, unlike their organized colleagues, these semi-professionals stole, traded, drank, played, fought, and obscenely gossiped in the open. One plucky travel agency advertised post-midnight tours of criminal clubs in "darkest Berlin." German and British tourists too hip for the Topp and Eldorado excursions must have been the intended clientele.

Architecturally the *Kaschemmen* could not have been easy on the eye. Dimly lit and crammed with mismatched junk furniture, the places seemed fit only for the *Screens*, assorted riff-raff, and their *Brides* who

trafficked in *Sohre* there. In the bottom-grade "Café Dalles" the tin cutlery resting on the tables was attached to long iron-chains, which in turn were stapled to the restaurant walls, preventing most utensil theft. When a customer exited and the table setting needed a fresh-up, one of the Dalles' employees hoisted a huge vat filled with greasy broth and rinsed the used spoons and plates in it. None of the regulars complained.

A few of the criminal *Dielen* had more inviting atmospheres. The "Sing-Sing" was constructed like a prison dining hall and featured mock executions in a wooden electric chair, a punishing apparatus which only existed in the New World. Other dives provided

music and cabaret entertainments. Mostly, it was the denizens of Berlin's underworld that attracted outsiders. At the "Blue Stocking," one could meet such *Kietz* luminaries as "Boot-Job Else," "Hedwig with a Cold Hand," "Snot-Faced Adolf," and "Singer-Franz," who ranted that he once sang at the Komische Oper.

The "Hundegustav Bar" hosted another unlikely Dick Tracy crew. The *Beinls* included "All-Tits," "Cocaine-Betty" (to be differentiated from her archrival "Cognac-Betty"), "Bottom-Girl Ede," the three Elses ("Dance-Else," "Jew-Else," and "Sexy-Else"), two Ernas ("Cement-Erna and "Wacky-Dance Erna"), two Metas ("Puffy-Eyes Meta" and "English-Meta") and two Trudes ("*Bubikopf*-Trude" and "Pockmarked Trude"). The male characters had even more cartoonish monikers: "Big Dick" (or "The Breuslauer"), "Apache-Erich," three Emils ("Harem-Emil," "Soldier-Emil, and "Brown-Emil"), "The Anti-Franz," "Doll-Brained Hermann," "Jewface," "Pickles-Julie," two Karls ("Muttalo-Karl" and "Raven-Hair Karl"), "Long Leo," "Insect Paul," two Piepels ("Basher-Piepel" and "Robber-Piepel"), "Madman-Robert," "Shithead" (everyone's favorite raconteur), and three Walters ("Halitosis-Walter," "Palace-Walter," and "Soldier-Walter").

The *Ringvereine* brothers and the barely intelligible street toughs had their time in the sun. Vice Commissionaries with a literary bent and columnists glorified in their rituals and jargonistic babble. The lawbreakers had their own judicial systems and public ceremonies. When a *Ringvereine* member died, all of Berlin North was treated to a funeral procession that rivaled in complexity and ornateness that of a reigning Balkan monarch. But like the rest of wicked Berlin, it came to an abrupt end. In January 1934, Hitler's SA-troopers cordoned off whole sections of the city and those found on the old police lists of convicted felons were dispatched to Dachau. ■

COCAIN

Mondaine u. demimondaine
Skizzen von

F. W. KOEBNER

v. Puttkamer

GROTILGO VERLAG BERLIN

A WORLD IN FLAMES

Adolf Hitler was officially appointed Reichschancellor on January 30th, 1933. It was virtually the last gambit in a vain scheme by the Nationalist and reactionary leaders to tame and discredit their Nazi opposition. President of the Weimar Republic, the revered 83-year-old Field Marshall Paul von Hindenburg, assured his right-wing partners that Hitler could do little but hysterically seethe and storm without a Nationalist Socialist majority in the Reichstag. But on February 27th, the Reichstag itself was destroyed by arson.

That night the Berlin police seized a Dutch Communist fanatic who confessed to the criminal deed. In order to prevent the so-called Marxist uprising, Hitler demanded from von Hindenburg emergency dictatorial powers. Anti-Nazi members of Hitler's cabinet—in a spasm of panicked confusion—acquiesced to the Führer's petition. They knew it would bring an end to Weimar's constitutional democracy.

So began Hitler's Third Reich and the path to world catastrophe.

Unfortunately, the facts of the time don't much support this tempting Puritanical thesis.

Few Germans or foreigners living in Weimar Berlin saw the moral linkage between the city's tawdry hijinks and the calamitous events of 1933. After all, it was the progressive citizens of Sodom on the Spree who fought the fascist menace with the utmost ferocity. All the political and media tools in their possession, however, could not overcome Nazism's deep mystical appeal to the distressed farmers of Schleswig-Holstein and other provinces far from the fleshpots of the Friedrichstadt. Hitler's consolidation of power resulted from a confluence of

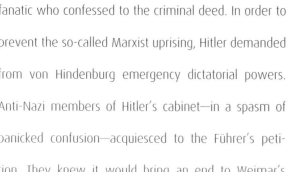

many unforeseen factors, including the staggering folly of the Communist and central-right opposition parties, who themselves promulgated extremist programs to eradicate Berlin's conspicuous demi-monde.

Michael Davidson, an old Berlin hand, challenged the conventional postwar wisdom in his erotic memoir of the Thirties, *The World, the Flesh and Myself*: "There must be people who believe that Hitlerism was a stern reaction to this 'German decadence,' or alternately regard the Nazi Party itself as a foul edifice of degeneracy—in either case blaming Germany's blatant homosexuality for the Hitler tyranny. Both assumptions are false."

Nazi Cleansing

The erotic world of Weimar Berlin crumbled by degrees. Already in the spring and summer of 1932, there were serious attempts by the Socis (Berlin's reigning Social Democrats) to ban most pornographic publications and seal the doors to the most flagrant transvestite clubs. Even Koch's nudist Berlin clinics were shuttered before the November 1932 elections.

Gay leaders equivocated over the impending Nazi threat. Hitler's second in command, SA-Führer Röhm, had been ridiculed as a pederast in the leftist press and many of his Storm-Trooping cohorts were rumored to be aficionados of boy-love as well. Hirschfeld, who had the most

Sinful Cities
of the **Western World**

Hendrik De Leeuw

A revealing and documented study of an
international traffic in womanhood

to lose from a Nazi-led government, defended Röhm's orientation. Papa declared it was Röhm's thuggish politics that should be combated, not his sexual escapades. Other Militant Homosexualists welcomed the jack-booted Nazi warriors as fellow revolutionaries. Most Berliners were in state of denial or shock at the prospects of a "Brown Germany." Hitler was kitsch incarnate.

The March 5th, 1933 elections, held five days after the Reichstag conflagration, handed the Nazis their final civic victory. Now legal guardians of the nation, National Socialist private militias proceeded to "cleanse" Germany of Jewish and Marxist elements. They started with Hirschfeld's Institute of Sexology.

On May 6th, SA-men and students from the School of Physical Fitness ransacked the Institute's library and vandalized the main buildings. After pouring ink over the archival files, smashing the exhibition cases, and playing soccer with erotic artifacts, the loyal *Hitlerjungen* gathered 100,000 books and manuscripts to fuel an evening bonfire at the Opernplatz. A brass band played throughout.

One Danish observer, with the infortuitous name Frederik Böök, shared his unusual condolences over the death of wicked Berlin: "Nor does it disturb me in the least that the youth of Germany burned the whole of the Sexual Science Library which was attached to the University under the name Magnus Hirschfeld Institute, and if a few irreplaceable collectors' treasures have thus been destroyed, I shall not shed a tear. If by this means the knowledge of a few particularly interesting sexual aberrations has been lost—so much the better." (*An Eyewitness in Germany,* Lovat Dickson: London, 1933).

Other Nazi actions against Weimar's inequity were difficult to fathom. The embarrassing issue of prancing queers at the helm of the mighty SA was deflected by the Führer for close to two years. Anglo-Saxon journalists perceived the Storm-Trooper's "sissy" interests and Hitler's shrill voice and mannerisms as evidence of a weak and sexually confused administration. But the Brit's mocking prognosis changed after June 30th, 1934, when Captain Röhm and the bulk of the SA leadership were executed in a day-long bloodletting, known as the "Night of the Long Knives." Although Hitler rationalized the messy purge as a purifying sexual measure, straight enemies from the old Nationalist coalition and recalcitrant Nazi intellectuals were liquidated too.

Early Nazi edicts against homosexuality were uncertain and inconsistent. While legistrators in 1935 amended Paragraph 175 to include all forms of male sex contact, lesbian behavior was utterly ignored in the

pamphlet-sized document. Prominent Aryan gay artists, like the Ausdruckstanz pioneer Harald Kreutzberg, continued their international careers unabated. In 1934 the bisexual actor Gustaf Gründgens received a commission to head the venerable Berlin Staatstheater, where he produced eleven Reich-approved seasons. Even Wilhelm Bendow, the swishy transvestite comic, enjoyed a National Socialist following at his own cabaret house in Berlin East. The government-approved *Grieben's Guide Book* for the 1936 Nazi Olympics magnanimously placed "Bendows Bunte Bühne" on the "highly recommended" list for nighttime pleasures.

Above:
Wilhelm Bendow, *Magnesia, the Tattooed Lady*, 1927

Left:
Harald Kreutzberg, 1935

Right:
Portrayal of
healthy Nazi
sexuality,
SA-Mann,
SS-Mann, and
Nazi labor militia
man, 1933

Nazi Sex

Generally, Christian, non-leftist Berliners accommodated themselves to the Nazi Revolution with surprising ease. One week after Hitler's ascension to the Reichs-chancellery, the formerly liberal Rumpelstilzchen marveled at the colors of the Nazi flag and how dreadful the old national pennant looked. Once again, Davidson captured the overall mood of the city, "The ordinary people I knew—wage-earners, unemployed, little artisans, door-to-door hawkers, people employed in 'vice'—loathed Hitler and the Nazis; but the antagonism of most went no further than their private conversation and half of these quickly changed sides after January 1933."

Berlin's sex industry contracted and nearly disappeared throughout the summer months of 1933. *Kontroll-Girls* and *Fohses* abandoned the Friedrichstadt and Kudamm storefronts. Most migrated to Berlin North or bowed out completely. Other *Beinls* followed suit. By spring of 1934, only 20 or so brothels remained in Berlin and these were high-class joints for tourists, ranking Nazis, and soldiers on leave. "Café Aryan"

ADMIRALSPALAST

HENKELL

Heinz Weber

REVUE
Parade der schönen Frauen

Sonnenschein für Alle

Above:
Program cover,
Sunshine for All,
1939

offered gay, cross-dressed, and straight shows for the exorbitant fee of 20 American dollars but that bit of Weimaria was closed down after the last Olympic tourists departed.

One madam, Kitty Schmidt, kept her fancy establishment running by reluctantly agreeing to collaborate with the local Gestapo, who maniacally turned the "Pensione" into a wired love nest. The thousands of hours of taped recordings between the Nazi-trained sex-workers and foreign diplomats proved militarily worthless but provided a needed thrill for the erotically deprived spymasters. In 1942, Kitty was forcibly retired, her pensione cleared out, and with it the last authentic remnant of Weimar sexuality vanished.

Revisionist History

In the first years of the Reich, Nazis continued their grand spiritual mission to demolish the vestiges of Weimar culture. A surprising number of the German intelligentsia and professionals acquiesced to the Brown Revolution in the mid-Thirties. They assisted in the book-burnings, Aryanization of publishing and media outlets, confiscation of Jewish property, and the establishment of censoring boards. The mass arrests, incarcerations, and physical violence were left to others. But to effectively obliterate Berlin's fabled erotic past, Nazi ideo-

logues also needed to construct a new historical narrative to thoroughly demonize the former sex capital.

Before 1933, the Jews were targeted by the Nazis and their Nationalist allies as an insidious political and financial foe of the German people. The election posters told it all. Behind the façade of democratic rule, the parasitic Jewish race and their leftist minions controlled the destiny of the mighty nation. These cowardly power brokers secretly profited from Germany's ills and humiliations. Jewish sexual perfidy—as violators of Aryan

women, ritual murderers, traffickers in white slavery, abortionists, homosexual pederasts, purveyors of pornography—was a minor electioneering theme during the Weimar era.

In 1927, Julius Streicher's virulently anti-Semitic Nazi newspaper, *Der Stürmer* had only 14,000 subscribers.

Ten years later, its circulation approached one-half million copies, making it one of the most popular journals in the Reich. *Der Stürmer* and its sister publications advanced the preposterous Nazi theory about Jews and Berlin: Babylon-on-the-Spree was the invention of the accursed Jews. Graphic color illustrations showed hid-

eous Jewish businessmen, doctors, lawyers, film directors, even pastors (concealing their Hebraic origins) as lust murderers, dope peddlers, and defilers of Aryan youth. Decadent Berlin was a Jewish and homosexual paradise and therefore a Germanic hell.

Streicher's relentless propaganda, itself a form of pornography, found more and more adherents as the real Weimar Berlin receded into history. The Prussian metropolis was an evil place. Eternally evil. For the German people and the nations who defeated them in 1945 after a superhuman struggle, Streicher's distorted image remained. And endures. ■

A DIRECTORY OF EROTIC

The following listings were compiled by the author from approximately 200 sources, most of which appeared in the late Weimar period between 1927 and 1932. Descriptions in the 1931–1932 Weimar Berlin guidebooks—the last to appear—frequently mimicked earlier accounts and were likely "borrowed" renderings. Occasionally, a contrary situation arose; some travel digests were widely at odds with one another over their assessment of the actual scope of depraved activity in a featured *Diele* or entertainment environment. (When in doubt over which report to believe, I generally accepted the more salacious account.) The 50 locales described here represent between five and ten per cent of all the known erotic or nighttime establishments in Weimar Berlin. **Solid-numbered establishments are included on the map.**

GIRL-CULTURE VENUES

1 Cabaret of the Nameless

2 Café Braun

3 Haller-Revue

4 Haus Vaterland

5 Heaven and Hell

6 Kakadu Bar

7 James-Klein Revue

8 "Resi"

9 Restaurant Hackepeter

10 Rio Rita Bar

11 Stork's Nest Cabaret

12 Weisse Maus

AND NIGHTTIME BERLIN

HOMOSEXUAL VENUES

1. Adonis-Lounge
2. Alexander-Palast
3. Bürger-Casino
4. Cabaret of the Spider
5. Cosy Corner
6. Karls-Lounge
7. Monte-Casino
8. Moustache-Lounge
9. The Passage
10. Zauberflöte

LESBIAN VENUES

1. Aukula-Lounge
2. Café Domino
3. Café Dorian Gray
4. Café Olala
5. Hohenzoffern-Café

7. Meyer-Stube
8. Taverne
9. Toppkeller
10. Verona-Lounge

NUDIST VENUES

1. Berlin Association of Free Body Culture
2. Birkenheide
3. Body Culture School of Adolf Koch
4. Free Sunland
5. New Sunland
6. Territory Adolf Koch

SEX MUSEUM

1. Dr. Magnus Hirschfeld's Institute of Sexology

TRANSVESTITE VENUES

1. Eldorado
2. Eldorado (New)
3. Mikado Bar
4. Monocle-Bar
5. Silhouette

UNDERWORLD VENUES

1. The Blue Stocking
2. Hundegustav Bar
3. Red Mill Cabaret
4. Sing-Sing

WEIMAR NAZI VENUES

1. Café Aryan
2. Pension Schmidt

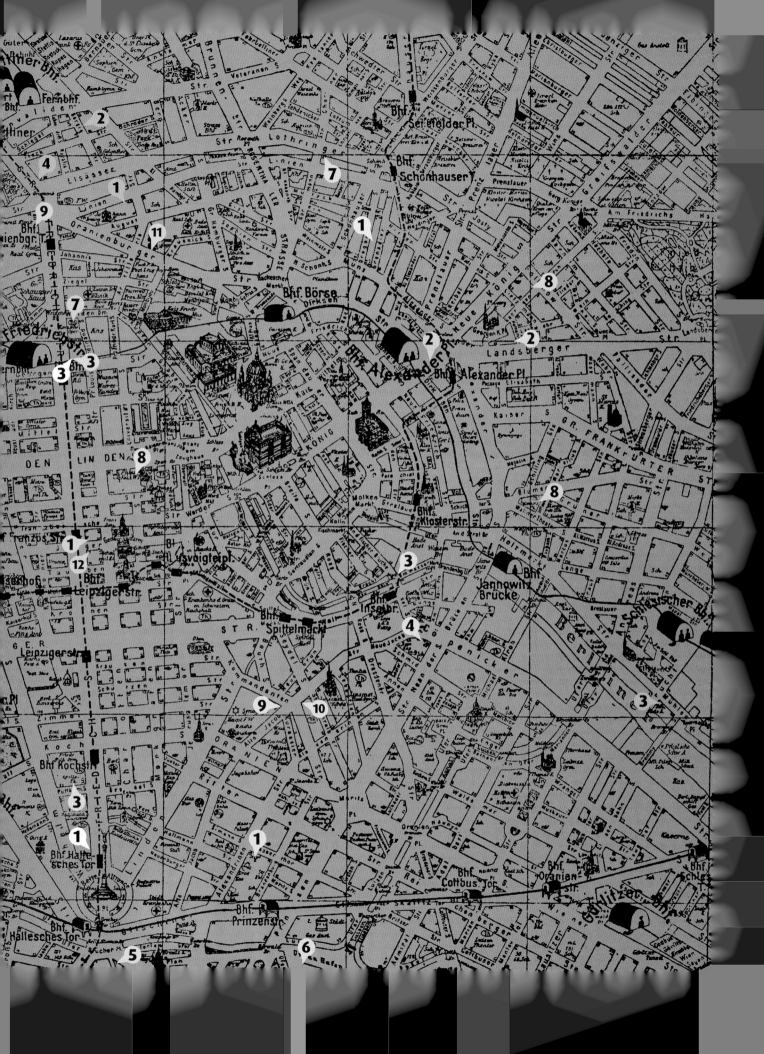

GIRL-CULTURE VENUES

Area: Center of FRIEDRICHSTADT.

Atmosphere: Clamorous, malevolent, sadistic. "Typical Berlin bad taste."

Clientele: Thrill-seeking middle-class Berliners bent on slacking their brutal, anti-social impulses.

Decor: Standard small cabaret space with tables and 98 chairs. Wine and champagne are served.

Entertainment: Fifteen ten-minute amateur acts are introduced by the acerbic conférencier "Elow" (Erwin Lowinsky) over the course of an evening. Selected for their utter lack of performance talent, weird physicality, and astounding naiveté, the "artistes" are further deluded by Elow into believing that they are about to receive their big show-business break.

Typically, the clueless entertainers try to imitate the work of established cabaret personalities and proceed to humiliate themselves completely in their numbing attempts. While audience members drunkenly interrupt and boo the wretched losers, Elow unctuously takes the part of a kindly uncle or philanthropist and encourages the amateurs to ignore the vicious Philistines and continue their rotten singing, juggling, storytelling, impersonations, or poetry recitals. Sometimes Elow "directs" a trio of the most unskilled performers in a scene from a well-known German classic.

tors frequently target the slowest-moving performers with crumpled programs and coins. (Naturally the audience's murderous insults and constant jeering are sometimes misinterpreted by certain simpleton-"stars" as yet another stormy accolade that affirms their exalted status.)

Unusual: The truly mentally unstable, ranting megalomaniacs, and near-cripples are "the Nameless'" favored victims. Aggressive specta-

CAFÉ BRAUN Alexanderstrasse 1 1928–1934

Area: ALEXANDERPLATZ. Concealed in an alley around the corner from the Alex. [Formerly the BEROLINA.]

Atmosphere: Sexy. Fast moving. "American" tempo. Crowded at all hours.

Clientele: In-the-know, bohemian types.

Decor: Standard restaurant dance-club with band stage and bar. In the back are outdoor "love porticos," for extreme privacy. These are normally packed and available for two additional marks.

Entertainment: Dancing and interacting with the restaurant staff.

Unusual: All the restaurant employees (except the beautiful bar maid) are dead ringers for world leaders and film stars. The hooked-nose doorman wears a monocle and looks and behaves exactly like the British premier Lord Chamberlain. The waiters, scurrying by the jam-packed tables with plates of wurst and steins of beer, seem to be wax-museum figures of Harold Lloyd, Marshal von Hindenburg, Prime Minister Briand, and many others. Each brings a specialty dish from his country, like the Hirohito Pineapple Bowl or Reparation Brandy.

In addition, every band member wears a facial mask of an international celebrity and performs an appropriate musical solo/monologue from his "country."

HALLER-REVUE Friedrichstrasse 101/102 1923–1929

Area: FRIEDRICHSTADT. At the THEATER IN THE ADMIRALPALAST.

Atmosphere: Most extravagant of the Revues. True reflection of the topsy-turvy eroticism of contemporary Berlin. Everything in American rhythms.

Clientele: Elite Berlin crowds. Foreign tourists. Seating varies between two and three thousand.

Decor: Lush accommodations with VIP sections. Elegant dining and dancing available in the

Edith Schollver   Dolores Twins   Hella Kürty   Original-Lawrence-Tiller-Girls   Kurt Lilien

Admirals-Kasino and Admirals-Lounge. The venerable Admiral-Baths are also in the same building.

Entertainment: International variety revue with some 50 fast-paced acts. Emphasis is on outsized glamour, lewd pictorialism, and female beauty. Famous for its Empire Girls (also known as the Lawrence-Tiller-Girls). Trained in London and New York, these 24 precision dancers ("Often copied—never equaled!"), blend—in both real and parody forms—"Fordism," gaudy French flesh-peddling, and the crystalline regimen of equestrian military drills.

Each production is led by an accomplished MC and includes juxtapositions of common cabaret numbers with naked dance and highbrow musical and dance pieces.

HAUS VATERLAND Köthener Strasse 1-5   1922–1936

Area: The entire POTSDAMER PLATZ.

Atmosphere: Exciting, international. Ersatz. Fun tourist trap, expertly designed for around-the-clock party ambiance. The "Department Store of Restaurants" is open until 3 a.m. and can serve 6,000 diners. For non-German-speakers "the jolliest place in Berlin."

Clientele: Mostly free-spending German provincials and foreign tourists, except during winter holidays when native Berliners dominate. A substantial coterie of Half-Silks make this their early-evening haunting grounds.

Decor/Entertainment: Overwhelming and grandiose architecture, combining Baroque and modernist styles. Entrance fee to the madhouse is 1 mark. The central lobby is broken up by an impressive series of color-light fountains and leads to the Palmtree Room, the Palace's Variety show (admission is another 3M).

The upper four floors are connected by ugly marble staircases, which direct the crowds into twelve restaurant "environments":

313

30063 Potsdammer Platz at Night, the Center of
Berlin's Gay Night Life, Germany.

1) LÖWENBRÄU: A Bavarian Biergarten, seating one thousand celebrants. At one end is a man-made lake, replicating the mountainous Bernese Oberland. Buxom barmaids in traditional dress serve Bavarian beer while young men in green waistcoats and short knickers stroll through the restaurant, yodeling to one another. A Bavarian orchestra and revue of female chorines, an August clown, a family of jugglers, and a parody of some South German dance (like the Munich Cauliflower Feast) is staged every night.

2) GRINZING: A Viennese café (set outside the imagined city) with wooden trellises separating the tables. Diners look out on the fantastic diorama of Old Vienna and the Danube River. A *trompe-l'oeil* of the central railway station is activated with tiny electric trains crossing miniature bridges and mechanical boats sailing beneath. The three-man Biedermeier orchestra plays Strauss waltzes and other familiar Viennese fare. Comic washerwomen's quartet is the chief attraction.

3) WILD-WEST-BAR: A saloon (specializing in pre-Prohibition American cocktails) is located on an alcove and surrounded by a striking vista of rolling prairies and cactus. Patrons enter through swinging doors. Folk-singing cowboys in oversized ten-gallon hats serve as waiters. They carry order-pads in their revolver hosters and alternate with an American jazz band as the musical accompaniment. Scantily-clad cowgirls perform Shimmys and sing American hit songs, which are available on 78 RPM disks. Blackface minstrel show rounds out evening.

4) SPANISH BODEGA: A huge Iberian inn jutting out from one wall. Bathed in a bordello-red spotlight is a Gypsy girl with a flower in her hair and dagger in her stocking hem. She sits provocatively on a wine casket and dances with customers on request. Other female Gypsy dancers join her when the mandolin orchestra starts up. Green-uniformed hussars serve as waiters.

5) RHINELAND WINE TERRACE: A cavernous room gives the three-dimensional illusion of the Rhine riverside. Quarter-sized paddle-boats float past a diminutive castle-ruins, where a singing troupe performs Rheinish folk songs. On the hour, a five-minute, artificial storm magically showers rain on the delighted customers.

In addition, there is a dimly lighted Turkish Café with cushions and short-legged divans; the Csarda, a "Hungarian" pastry restaurant set in Old Prague with zither music; an "open-air" Tuscan plaza; a student beer-cellar from Old Heidelberg; a Japanese tea garden; a sailors' galley inside a rocking Bremen ship; and finally a smart Berlin café, which opens as an independent restaurant onto Königgrätzerstrasse.

Unusual: Advertised as "An Inexpensive Holiday Trip!" Kempinski's Vaterland also provides, in its Palmtree Room, a nightly floor-show of big-name variety acts and the Vaterland-Girls. Altogether, there are 12 bands, 24 girls, and 50 separate cabaret numbers in this famous abode.

Area: BERLIN WEST. Across from the Memorial Church and the ROMANISCHES CAFÉ.

Atmosphere: Glamorous, expensive. Always an erotic buzz here. Risqué posters and illuminated signs promise a sophisticated evening.

Clientele: Old-family scions, up-and-coming politicians, playboys of every sort, the elite of Berlin's nightlife. "The longest-legged women" of Berlin and highest-paid Minettes can be found in the powder-rooms here.

Decor: A doorman, dressed like Saint Peter or a mustached Satan, directs guests to their choice of two adjoining dining areas, partitioned into "Heaven" or "Hell." Both spaces of the nightclub face the "Cabaret-Montmartre" stage.

Bathed in a mysterious dim blue light, the walls of "Heaven"

are lined with wooden angels, framed manuscripts, sacred statuary, and miniature palm trees. The white-faced waiters, "garçons of Heaven," are dressed like angels (with gauzy wings and halos) and greet the customers with Lutheran appellations. Scroll-like menus, bowls of holy water, and votive candles are placed on the tables. Religious music from an organ is played intermittently.

"Hell" is illuminated in a phosphorescent red glow and its walls are plastered to resemble that of a burning cavern. Dressed as red imps, the waiters here scurry around a boiling cauldron and torment the orchestra and diners alike with iron triads. When delivering the food to the "sinners," the devilish imps always describe the dishes' individual punishing qualities: "This bockwurst will seal your intestines for 20 days!"

Entertainment: Elaborate naked revues from the Cabaret-Montmartre are presented every evening at midnight. Under the direction of French choreographer Madeleine Nervi, as many as 50 showgirls appear in musical presentations of the "Beautiful Body Unveiled." Themes of the Montmartre evenings normally veer to Parisian-style perversity, like "25 Scenes From the Life of the Marquis de Sade" or "The Naked Frenchwoman: Her Life Mirrored in Art." Staging is professional and considered the highest caliber.

Unusual: Saint Peter and Satan often surface in their designated areas to give appropriate and amusing exegesis during the performance.

KAKADU BAR Joachimstaler Strasse 10   1920–1936

Area: BERLIN WEST. Corner of Kurfürstendamm.

Atmosphere: Exclusive if slightly tacky. Free admission for the well-dressed. A foot fetishist's paradise. Open until 3 a.m.

Clientele: Stockbrokers, artistic types. Police officials, Italian tourists, foreign journalists. Always *Nuttes* in revealing American-style flapper outfits. (Some wearing red-white-and-blue sparkling foil in their hair.)

Decor: Mock Tahitian/German Samoan furnishings. Small tables under palms. Lush red lighting. The blue and gold bar is advertised as the longest in the city. Fireplaces in the small lounge are kept burning at all hours. Nearby are newly-acquainted couples, smooching heavily in chaise-longue chairs and sofas.

Entertainment: Bar, vegetarian restaurant, dance palace, and cabaret, all in one place. The Barberina-Cabaret has a full program consisting of five acts. Typical evening consists of an acrobatic dancer, a sketch artist, a comic monologuist (no political humor, thank you), a female dance trio, and an eccentric sailor dance. A jazz orchestra for pre- and post-show dancing. The cocktail bar is reputed to have the most ravishing and scintillating barmaids in Berlin West.

Unusual: Over every dining table is a parrot in a cage—the logo of the establishment. When a customer wishes to leave, he merely taps his water-glass with a knife. This signals the bird to squawk, in a grating old man's voice, "The bill! The bill!" Regrettably, the parrots have an uncontrollable tendency to let their droppings fall on the plates of first-time or inattentive patrons.

JAMES-KLEIN REVUE   Friedrichstrasse 104a   1922–1930

Area: Upper FRIEDRICHSTADT. At the KOMISCHE OPER near the FRIEDRICHSTADT train station.

Atmosphere: Crass. Expansively lewd. A touch of Inflation Era madness mixed with Parisian Music Hall nudity. One critic referred to a James-Klein-Revue as "a pornographic magazine come alive."

Clientele: Middle-class Berliners. German and foreign tourists.

Decor: Big revue house, seats 1,200.

Entertainment: Mostly lavish nude tableaux—or "meat shows"—arranged around a comic theme and led by a well-known conférencier like Paul Morgan or Hans Albers. Characteristic sensational poster ads: "1,000 Completely Nude Women!" or "500 Sweet Legs!" *Take It Off* was promoted as an "Evening Without Morals in 30 Pictures, Enacted by 60 Priceless Naked Models." [Actually only 24 scenes and 42 females appear in the program.]

Unusual: Any activity that is sexually over-the-top in Berlin is frequently labeled a "miniature Klein-Revue."

"RESI" (RESIDENZ-CASINO)   Blumenstrasse 10   1927–1936

Area: BERLIN EAST. Southeast of ALEXANDERPLATZ.

Atmosphere: Always a bit giddy and self-consciously naughty, like a secretary's bridal shower that is interrupted by a bachelor party down the hall. A veritable institution for promiscuous, middle-class hijinks.

Clientele: Out-of-towners, local bureaucrats, and "Merry Widows" intent on fun. Lots of flirtatious women. (Ratio of single females to males is usually 5 to 1!) Dance floor can accommodate 500 couples.

Decor: Weird: outwardly decked out in a lavish, Parisian fin-de-siècle style but surrounded by modern technological surprises. Building is partitioned into a main room, loges, private cellar, four bar-counters, orchestra pit, and miniature Luna-Park gallery (with a carousel ride for fun-addled adults). Ballroom ceiling is made of reflective glass and painted in Japanese motifs.

Entertainment: One hundred whirling mirrored globes on poles open in rhythm to the bands and colored water displays cre-

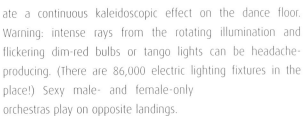

ate a continuous kaleidoscopic effect on the dance floor. Warning: intense rays from the rotating illumination and flickering dim-red bulbs or tango lights can be headache-producing. (There are 86,000 electric lighting fixtures in the place!) Sexy male- and female-only orchestras play on opposite landings.

Food: Horrid Prussian fare.

Unusual: Two hundred private telephones are fixed to numbered tables and balcony stations. These encourage audacious patrons to engage in across-the-room introductions or in anonymous, suggestive chats. Guests can also choose from among 135 pocket items and have them shot, through air compression, across the Resi ceilings and handrails, where they are delivered to netted baskets hanging from the numbered tables.

FLOOR PLAN
and Gift Stations

ACHTUNG!
Der Klosterkeller und die Nummern
10, 84, 13 haben keine Rohrpoststation

RESTAURANT HACKEPETER Friedrichstrasse 124   1924–1933

Area: BERLIN NORTH. Near the ORANIENBURGER TOR.

Atmosphere: Merry. Biergarten mood.

Clientele: Working-class men and women mostly. Local gourmands and curious downtowners in the evening. Devoted *Nuttes* and female fans of Jolly in attention-getting blouses and dresses.

Decor: Typical Upper Friedrichstrasse restaurant.

Entertainment: An unshaven hunger-artist named Jolly sits in a glass booth with a water glass in one hand and a cigarette in the other. While Hackepeter's diners devour their carnivore delicacies, Jolly chain-smokes and sips seltzer water.

Food: Famous for its pig's leg special (boiled, deep fried, and then covered with a sticky cream sauce) in addition to steak-with-fried-eggs and Hackepeter.

Unusual: At the top of the hour, a midget in a tuxedo bellows into a megaphone the exact units of time that Jolly has gone without food. Nearby a dark-suited attendant makes certain none of Jolly's devotees disturb the artist's concentration or that any morsel is secreted in the glass cage. At Jolly's insistence, his lair is guarded around the clock by bonded observers.

RIO RITA BAR Tauentzienstrasse 12   1931–1934

Area: BERLIN WEST. A few steps from the Memorial Church.

Atmosphere: Packed chic bar and "intimate" nightclub. Cultivated and elegant. Friendly.

Clientele: Sex-obsessed artists, playboys, British journalists. Top-drawer German diplomats, monocled Ruhr industrialists, and foreign businessmen traveling incognito. Table-Ladies—mostly of the demonic German or Spanish aristocratic variety.

Decor: Simple, American-designed with dazzling panels in cream and gold. Entrance is through the long bar-foyer into a nightclub area surrounding an eight by ten-foot dance floor. Murals illustrating the life of the Spanish dancer, Rita, and soft tablelights (covered with dark glass spikes) break up the dance room, giving it a warm intimacy. Two private, plush V.I.P. rooms, scented in orange blossom, are located in the back.

Entertainment: Tangos begin at 9 p.m. Blind pianist heads the well-regarded jazz band. Beautiful and exotic-looking hostesses, dressed in the latest French fashions, sit at tables laughing at customers' jokes and repeating obscene gossip. Their job as Table-Ladies, fetish-attired Geishas, is to make certain that bottles of overpriced champagne and plates of fresh peaches are in constant circulation.

Unusual: Much-in-demand Table-Ladies double as kinky *Minettes*. Clients pay the head-waiter for "their time off" so the playful ladies may leave the club for a few hours or retreat to one of the back private rooms. Excellent place for the purchase of high-grade opium and cocaine.

STORK'S NEST CABARET Oranienburger Strasse 42   1923–1931

Area: BERLIN NORTH. Near the ORANIENBURGER TOR. (Formerly the CHANTANT SINGING HALL.)

Atmosphere: Sordid dive. Drunken, madhouse ambiance when the performance begins. (Said to be the model for the cabaret scenes in the 1930 film *The Blue Angel*.)

Clientele: Greatly mixed: working-class but conservative patrons, local students, soldiers, some colorful criminal types.

Decor: Outside is a marquee of yellow and red lights and a glass case displaying revealing photographs and boastful reviews of the evening's attractions. Inside, the tables, chairs, wall fixtures, benches, and stage are all at least a generation old. On the stage is a semi-circle of chairs, facing the audience.

Entertainment: In sequence, each cabaret performer leaves her chair and moves downstage to replace the last entertainer just as she is completing her solo. Audience members traditionally send up steins of beer to the chanteuses when they have completed a number.

Photographs of the performers are hawked after each act.

A normal evening consists of a few touring stars: Lola Niedlich, "the Prize-Winning Torch-Singer, Three Times Engaged at Marienbad" (in her photo the sexy Lola demurely holds a doll in her arms); a coquettish toe-dancer named Charlotte Corday, who feebly attempts to engage the audience in tête-à-têtes; a transvestite-ventriloquist Paul Schiephacke, who can't get started—this trio is in addition to the half-dozen frumpy regular artistes in garter belts and lacy skirts hitched up to their crotches. The female singers specialize in prostitute songs, patriotic war ditties, and other standard cabaret fare.

Tourists: A few slummers from downtown, some of whom will exit sans billfolds, watches, and wedding rings.

Unusual: Customers can purchase seats on the stage during the performance or meet privately with the cabaret stars in a succession of side-rooms. There, after port or cognac, negotiations for sex, usually of the manual variety, take place.

Area: Center of FRIEDRICHSTADT.

Atmosphere: Wicked, often raucous. Expensive. Customers who wish to conceal their identities are given the choice of a black or white half-mask to wear.

Clientele: Traveling salesmen on expense accounts, elderly gentlemen from the provinces, underworld kings with small harems of *Nuttes*, lesbian groupies, and Berlin intellectuals.

Decor: Beautiful 98-seat cabaret space with a curtained dance stage.

Entertainment: Naked or "Beauty" dances are presented in close proximity to audience. Productions usually last about one hour and begin at midnight. A typical evening consists of a disingenuous—and hysterical—introduction by the director, disclaiming any pornographic intent: "We come here for Beauty alone."

Unusual: Anita Berber, high priestess of the Inflation Era, performed here until she smashed an empty champagne bottle on a patron's head. Berber had a devoted following because she enacted something other than Naked Dances; she recreated her disturbing sex and drug-induced fantasies. These nude dance-dreams were executed with a chilling realism and activated by dark, metatrophic impulses. When harangued by drunken spectators, Berber had been known to spit brandy on them or stand naked on their tables, dousing herself with wine while simultaneously urinating.

HOMOSEXUAL VENUES

ADONIS-LOUNGE Alexandrinenstrasse 128   1924–1933

Area: BERLIN SOUTH. East of the HALLESCHES TOR.

Atmosphere: Sullen Boy-Bar. Often referred to as "the Pits." Familiar down-and-out clubhouse mood. Quiet, desperate until Tree-Stumps or tourists appear, which create an eddy of excitement. Like Calcutta beggars, the Adonis urchins hustle around the newcomers' tables and follow them into the street when they exit.

Clientele: Short-haired, blonde Wild-Boys, sailors, and pot-bellied Tree-Stumps. Sugar-Lickers around dinner time. Favorite word-of-mouth spot for British queers living on the cheap.

Decor: Discreetly blackened-out façade. Entrance is shielded by a somber curtain hanging from a flimsy shower rod. Inside the smoky room are bare tables, separated by paper arbors, and a bar-counter. Hanging from the ceiling are paper garlands and monstrously oversized cardboard grapes. Two walls are covered with cheap landscape paintings. Sparse lighting.

Entertainment: After 3 p.m., sentimental songs are pounded out on an antique piano by the resident drunk. In the center of the tiny room is an open area for one or two "dancing" couples. Watered-down drinks complete the nightmarish environment.

Women and Straight Men: Never.

Unusual: The lads here do not qualify as professional Line-Boys. Too much cynicism and despondency. The Wild-Boys listlessly lean against the naked walls or slump over tables. All eyes face the entrance way,

in a half-hearted attempt to attract the attentions of a Sugar-Licker. The Boys here usually trade sex in the toilet for beer, wurst, coffee, or—more frequently—cigarettes. Good place, however, to obtain inexpensive cocaine and rolled balls of opium.

Sonnabend, 10. Juni 1922 — Gesellschaftsklub Alexander E. V.

1. Groß. Strandfest

Ende Sonntag früh.   Ende Sonntag früh.   Ende Sonntag früh.
Strandanzug erwünscht. — Festpolonaise durch den illuminierten Naturgarten.

ALEXANDER-PALAST Landsbergstrasse 39   1921–1930

Area: BERLIN NORTH. On ALEXANDERPLATZ. (Formerly the ALEXANDER-PALAIS.)

Atmosphere: Upscale. Expensive.

Clientele: Mostly mature, middle-class gay couples in tuxedos and top hats; elderly shopkeepers, frock-coated clerks, and even policemen. Their quaint and courtly manners are a reflection of their conservative, sometimes monarchist, political affiliations.

Decor: Gigantic American ballroom for 150 couples.

Entertainment: Big Band and cabaret stage. Dancing from 9 p.m. to 1 a.m.

Unusual: AP offers monthly Transvestite Balls, which welcome non-transvestite guests. Separate lesbian nights are also offered.

BÜRGER-CASINO Friedrichgracht 1   1927–1932

Area: FRIEDRICHSTADT. At the edge of the Spree by SPITTELMARKT.

Atmosphere: Located in an isolated tract by the river, the BC can only be discovered through the reddish glow of its outdoor marquee. The riverfront district around the bar is quiet, serene, and virtually abandoned at night. Inside, the air is saturated with clouds of blue smoke. General mood is upbeat and highly flirtatious.

Clientele: Blonde Line-Boys (many in schoolboy outfits that expose their knees and upper chests) crouch at the bar with their beer and smoke cigarettes. Stiff-collared merchants and state officials in expensive suits. The Line-Boys here are clean and great teases.

Decor: Tables separated by high garlanded trellises. Standard bar with many hidden corners.

Entertainment: Live piano music. The middle-class men dance with boys; the Line-Boys with each other. Little space for ballroom-style dancing, so there is much intentional bumping, touching, and lingering glances. Lots of suggestive, girlish movements on the dance floor.

Women and Straight Men: None.

Unusual: Many of the Line-Boys appear in freshly laundered sailor outfits since that is a basic taste of their customers. Sexual contact takes place at a nearby pier.

CABARET OF THE SPIDER Alte Jakobstrasse 174   1922–1925

Area: BERLIN EAST. South of SPITTELMARKT.

Atmosphere: Wacky. No admission.

Clientele: Mostly petty bourgeois, mature gays. Aunties.

Decor: Painted on a wall inside is the sign of the lounge: a crouching spider resting snugly in her web.

Entertainment: Saturdays and Sundays at 7 p.m., a floor show is presented. A few of the announced acts: "Luziana, the Mysterious Wonder of the Earth—Man or Woman?"; Liselott from the Mikado; the Alhambra-Duo, a song-and-dance team of male twins; or Gert Bathé as a man.

Women and Straight Men: None

COSY-CORNER Zossener Strasse 7   1927–1932

Area: KREUZBERG. South of the HALLESCHES TOR. (Formerly NOSTER'S RESTAURANT.)

Atmosphere: Hard-drinking boy-bar. On cold nights, *Bubes* sit around the pot-bellied stove with their sleeves rolled up and shirts unbuttoned to the waist. In summer, the same wide-eyed boys sport high-cut lederhosen.

Clientele: Rough-trade *Bubes* (working-class Line-Boys) and their adoring Tree-Stumps. Aspiring British writers led by Christopher Isherwood.

Decor: Homely. Former neighborhood restaurant. Blacked-out windows. A leather curtain conceals the entranceway from the inside. Photographs of boxers and cyclists are pinned up above the bar. That overheated stove.

Entertainment: Drinking and card games.

Women and Straight Men: None

Unusual: The toilet stall is an open space without partitions or cubicles. Instead there is a long urinal trough, where the *Bubes* can innocuously display their penises and pretend to urinate before titillated Suitors.

KARLS-LOUNGE Karl Strasse 5 1921–1926

Area: BERLIN NORTH. South of the Hospital complex. (Formerly Café-Restaurant CEMENT-CELLAR.)

Atmosphere: Private, underground. Very crowded and boisterous. Heavy, depressed mood. Surprisingly free of tobacco smoke and alcoholic beverages. Closes sharply at 2 a.m.

Clientele: Young Line-Boys, nearly all beardless in crisp, tailored sailor outfits. Coolies and Tree-Stumps on the make. Hectic groups of Bad Boys are constantly entering and then abruptly leaving for street action or other lounges. (Many are dealing cocaine in the clubs.)

Decor: Stripes of wax paper cover the inside entrance to the "Cement Cellar." In the first room is a massive bar and a dusty glass liquor cabinet. A dim inner room is primitively decorated with jeweled lampshades (made from the cloth of old coats) and jewel-studded walls covered with mismatched paintings of men's portraits and tiny porcelain tchotchkes.

Entertainment: At a broken-down baby grand piano, shoved into a corner, a pianist and fiddler play. Regulars, like "Pretty Benno" and "Karlo" waltz between the tables. Other couples dance in the shadows against the bejeweled walls.

Food: Plates of Hungarian pastries and lemonade only.

Women and Straight Men: Why bother?

Unusual: Testy old waiters are dressed in nautical uniforms, identical to the teenage *Line-Boys* they serve. Alcoholic drinks are not are served to customers but drugs, especially cocaine and morphine, are freely traded and used at the tables.

MONTE-CASINO Planufer 5 1923–1933

Area: KREUZBERG. South of the HALLESCHES TOR. (Formerly RESTAURANT HEIDEBLUME.)

Atmosphere: Bizarre. "Unorthodox." Falls into no set category. Closes at 3 a.m.

Clientele: On weeknights, lower-middle-class men with their Hausfraus in tow, some gay men and transvestite couples. On weekends, lots of British and Dutch "straight" tourists (both male and female) searching for the "authentic Berlin."

Decor: Dilapidated strip club with an elevated dance stage. Bar on the side.

Entertainment: Amateurish transvestite revue—surprise: the girls are really boys. Dances and songs are performed by eight or nine effeminate Line-Boys, ranging in age between 14 and 18. Some of them appear to be undernourished. Professional piano accompaniment. Hunky blonde teenager "Pretty Adolf" acts as energetic conférencier.

Women and Straight Men: Strong word-of-mouth has made this de rigueur for heterosexual foreign couples.

Unusual: Monte-Casino is owned by a "kind-hearted" drag queen with a stable of obliging Line-Boys. They orally service the working-class customers in backroom cubicles while the young dancers prance on the cabaret stage. The ever-patient customer-wives sit in the hall and drink beer (across from the tables of other lonely Hausfraus) and take in the entertainment.

MOUSTACHE-LOUNGE Gormannstrasse 2 — 1929–1933

Area: BERLIN NORTH. Corner of ROSENTHALER PLATZ.

Atmosphere: "Celebratory." Noisy. Heavy drinking of Pilsen with unconstrained displays of affection and sexual bravado throughout.

Clientele: This is the outpost for Society Men—40- to 60-year-olds with magnificent moustaches and facial hair. Every kind and color of hair-lock is here, from slight blonde Van Goghs to full Santa Claus beards. Long bushy sideburns and Kaiser Wilhelm moustaches predominate. The Society Men are a cross-section of middle-class Berlin: accountants, publishing types, small business owners. Also a goodly number of non-hirsute Line-Boys after midnight.

Decor: Large beer-hall room lodges some 200 animated drinkers. Half at tables, the others around the bar. In the back is a tiny stage, festooned with flowers.

Entertainment: One lonely transvestite chanteuse.

Women and Straight Men: None.

Unusual: Good pickup place for Line-Boys, charging 2 or 3 marks (about $12). Lots of sex between the Society and the boys in the toilet stalls.

Overheard Pick-up Lines: "Mine is bigger than yours!" (pointing to waxed moustache)

THE PASSAGE Between Unter den Linden and Friedrichstrasse — 1919–1934

Area: Center of FRIEDRICH-STADT.

Atmosphere: Creepy, old fashioned, the refuse of a previous century. "A synthesis of Byzantinism and pornography." Musty old shops where one can buy dirty French postcards, glass transparencies of the Madonna, meerschaum pipes, or an amber necklace for the wife. Discount stores, tired travel agencies and peepshows but each establishment lacking in earnest business prospects.

Clientele: Purveyors of the various shops and cafés but also—from 9 a.m. to 3 a.m.—the main thoroughfare for desperate Doll-Boys and their customers.

BERLIN, Passage zwischen Friedrichstraße und Unter den Linden

Decor: Faded glass-covered arcade supported by marble-paneled iron columns. A strange Wilhelmian imitation of a Renaissance market. Prewar signs and unintentionally disturbing window displays.

Entertainment: THE ANATOMICAL MUSEUM, open until the late evening, advertises exhibitions "Devoted to the Improvement of Mankind. No Children Admitted!" Inside are cases of antique mannequins engaged in horrific rituals and surgical operations; also prominent are displays of real body parts ravished by venereal disease and sexual organs representing the world's "races."

WORLD-PANORAMA is a stereoscopic emporium, where as many as 25 viewers can sit around a huge wooden cylinder of peepholes and watch three-dimensional images of naked people from exotic climes. A pornographic cinema theatre, the "STAR" does a small tourist business in the late afternoons and evenings.

Food: Several cafés, all filled with Doll-Boys and their free-spending Suitors.

Unusual: The competition among the dirty-faced Doll-Boys is so great that many Tree-Stumps are able to offer them less than a mark for an hour's engagement. By 6 p.m., there are over 70 hardened Doll- and Line-Boys posing in the vicinity of the "STAR-KINO" alone. Another 80, with their hands in their pockets, mill around the Behrenstrasse exit. (The Line-Boys wear peaked schoolboy hats and short pants to appear considerably younger.)

ZAUBERFLOTE Kommandanstrasse 72 1926–1933

Area: FRIEDRICHSTADT EAST. "One minute from SPITTELMARKT."

Atmosphere: "The Most Beautiful Dance Emporium in Berlin." Wild, "American," aggressive, noisy, fun.

Clientele: Both gay men and lesbians on separate floors. Each of the dance halls can accommodate over 1,500 merry-makers.

Decor: Three stories: An enormous dance hall for lesbians on first floor, "the American Dance Palace." Second and third floors, the "Florida Dance Hall" (with sweeping pink lights) and "Oriental Casino," a lounge area, are exclusively for gay men.

Entertainment: Brassy orchestra plays on balcony above dance floor, both jazz and German folk dance music—for group dances that resemble gay square dancing, which frequently results in lovers' disputes.

Women and Straight Men: Absolutely forbidden by opposite groups.

Lesbian Floors: Aggressive, "masculine" mood among the *Bubis* with lots of drunken brawls over available *Mädis*. Flower-sellers inside provide on-the-spot gifts for public apologies by *Bubis*. On New Years, a great costume ball, "The Silver Spider," is given and at midnight the Princess of the Moon releases a gigantic balloon on the roof.

LESBIAN VENUES

AULUKA-LOUNGE Augsburger Strasse 72   1924–1933

Area: BERLIN WEST. Near NOLLENDORFPLATZ and the Hotel Eden. [In 1929, renamed the GEISHA BAR.]

Atmosphere: Hot, weird, loud. The *Bubikopfed* maître d', who greets the guests, is attired in male/female garb: a man's blue sportscoat, which reveals her breasts, an officer's leather tie, and provocative short skirt.

Clientele: Chic lesbians—mostly blonde, elegant *Garçonnes* wearing high male collars and ties. Foreign tourists and their hired *Nuttes*.

Decor: Permanent "Japanese Cherry Blossom" theme—artificial snowballs affixed to overhanging cherry-tree branches. Dim Japanese paper lanterns and table lamps. Red sofas and cushions line the walls, which feature crude erotic cartoons drawn in green and black.

Entertainment: Upbeat, contemporary dance music played on piano by eccentric former Russian prince. A female lead-dancer performs solo pieces.

Men: Yes. Many voyeurs.

Unusual: Taking in the action are carloads of Japanese and Chinese tourists, who sit silently with high-heeled German *Nuttes* in the "Tokyo" section.

CAFÉ DOMINO Marburger Strasse 13   1921–1930

Area: BERLIN WEST. South of the Memorial Church.

Atmosphere: "The Intimate Bar of the West." Sensuous, hard. A smoky pick-up bar, resembling that of straight men. Specialty aphrodisiac drink is called "Cherry Cobbler."

Clientele: Exquisite, wealthy *Sharpers* (many in tuxedo/short skirt combinations). (This is their haunt.) Lots of jewelry and expensive perfume. Slim-hipped *Mädis* in shiny silk hose—always a few feigning shock by the same-sex surroundings. Parties of head-turning *Gamines* on the weekends. *Dodos* and some straight men.

Decor: Bar area completely illuminated in red light. Double rows of champagne-filled tables. The tiny spaces between the tables provide a shadowy area for seductive foxtrots and anonymous touches.

Entertainment: "Hot American jazz" on piano. Later in the evening, Romanian singer, Jonescu, leads a "Gypsy Band." "Naked" dancers from Eastern European troupes perform at midnight.

Gertie, the brunette hostess in a sleek tuxedo, helps establish the lush mood by dancing with patrons and then pairing off horny *Sharpers* and *Dodos* with sweet-faced *Mädis*.

Men: Plentiful in the late evening but willfully ignored by Domino regulars.

Unusual: On the nearby Tauentzienstrasse corner, an old Jew advertises Domino's evening theme—like "Sapphic Nights" or "Japanese Flower Festival"—on a hand-drawn sandwich board. Intrigued male clients, many just recovering mentally from nearby Boot-Girl sessions, are frequent habitués of the midnight shows.

CAFÉ DORIAN GRAY Bülowstrasse 57   1927–1933

Café Dorian Gray

BÜLOWSTRASSE 57

Telephon: Kurfürst 6321

Ist und bleibt

der intime Treffpunkt
der
vornehm. Damenwelt

Jeden Freitag die be-
liebten Damen-Elitetage,
verbunden m. Programm-
wechsel der
Bunten Abende

Area: BERLIN WEST. West of the POTSDAMER Train Station.

Atmosphere: Usually very hot. Loud, airy. Advertised as "The Intimate Nexus of the Ladies-World."

Clientele: Mostly lesbian couples, especially fun-driven *Garçonne* pairs. On special occasions, like Wednesday "Sado-Masochist Nights," transvestites of both genders are welcomed. ("Gentlemen" are required to pay twice the admission.)

Decor: Artistic café interior in front. Real flowers on the tables. In backroom, cheap but elaborate silken drapery, Japanese paper lanterns, beads, veils, palm trees.

Entertainment: Live tango music and an annoying male violinist who goes table to table, hovering around until he receives a tip.

Food: Good Viennese kitchen.

Men: Rambunctious gay men (organizations of *Bad Boys*) reserve the spacious backroom for private parties on Thursday, Saturday, and Sunday nights. [Curiously, both lesbian and gay clubgoers come dressed in similar leather blouses/shirts and fetishistic sailor costumes.]

Unusual: An imposing, humorless doorman makes certain that patrons have come to the correct lesbian or gay function. Friday nights are billed as "Elite-Women's Day"; weekday lesbian evenings have themes like "Wild Night," "Bavarian Alpine Feast," "Rhineland Wine-Growers Holiday," or "Three Days in the Wild West."

CAFÉ OLALA   Zietenstrasse 11

Area: BERLIN WEST END. Near NOLLENDORFPLATZ.

Atmosphere: Loud laughter, but creepy, empty inside. Imitation Parisian café. Flirtatious lesbian waitresses in French maid outfits add some sparkle.

Clientele: As many straight men looking for a cheap thrill as hard-drinking Girl-Friends, Tauentziengirls, and Hot Whores.

Decor: Filthy windowpanes and generally messy tables.

Entertainment: Banal *chansons* play on scratchy phonographic disks.

Unusual: A special corner for Salvation Army Girls and Tauentziengirls. The mother-and-daughter teams are on the vigil for interested pedestrians and pass the time stealing each other's schnapps before braving the streets.

HOHENZOFFERN-CAFÉ   Bülowstrasse 101   1921–1933

Area: BERLIN WEST. Near NOLLENDORFPLATZ.

Atmosphere: Easygoing, somewhat faded. Formerly known as the HOHENZOFFERN HALL (then the "H-LOUNGE"), this is the oldest established lesbian café in Berlin.

Clientele: Downhome "married" lesbian couples. The *Bubis* wear neckties, collars, and conservative men's jackets and converse heartily with other another. The *Sweet Mommies* quietly sit between their "men" and engage in small talk with other *Mädis* as they nurse cups of coffee.

Decor: Blacked picture windows to hide the interior room. Large restaurant-style booths and padded chairs.

Entertainment: Occasional box-step, social dances. Pop music performed by a gay duo on violin and piano (or accordion).

Men: Tolerated.

Unusual: Sometimes straight men dance with attractive *Mädis*—always first requesting permission from their respective *Daddies*.

Area: BERLIN WEST. East of WITTENBERG PLATZ.

Atmosphere: Exclusive. Brazenly lesbian. Always packed. Fixed sign on entrance: "CLOSED FOR PRIVATE PARTY." At the front desk are two identically dressed, over-sized *Bubis*, who wear noticeably huge diamond rings and thickly applied eyeshadow. On their laps are two lissome *Gamines* in translucent silk blouses. Both *Bubis* methodically rub the giggling girls' nipples while one *Bubi* dutifully checks the reservation list. (An enduring and memorable image for all first-time male guests.)

Clientele: Very selective. Usually no more than 60 customers at any one time. Favorite hangout for lesbian artists, intellectuals, singers, stage actresses, and film stars. Lesbians working for Max Reinhardt's theatre organizations often stage birthday celebrations here.

Decor: Blacked-out picture windows. A relatively small room but decorated stylishly with a traffic light flashing red over the dance floor.

Deep comfortable chairs in the corners and erotic lesbian paintings (donated by wealthy patrons) hanging on the walls.

Entertainment: Both hot jazz and sentimental love songs performed by professional male pianist. Crowd frequently shows its appreciation by clapping in time to the music. Also visiting opera stars or Russian actresses will be encouraged to sing arias or specialty lesbian songs in their own tongue.

Men: Not admitted unless accompanied by a lesbian habitué. Even with invitation, males are quickly disregarded by women after formal introductions.

Unusual: Mali, one of the owners, is a beautiful Jewish *Garçonne*-type who insists on dancing with each of her female clientele. Ingel, her partner, is a vivacious *Gamine*. Together they create an aristocratically refined if outrageously promiscuous mood.

MEYER-STUBE Xanterner Strasse 3   1927–1928

Area: WILMERSDORF. South of the Kurfürstendamm. Adjacent to Berlin publishing conglomerates.

Atmosphere: Serious, intellectual. Moody.

Clientele: Regular crowd of famous journalists, novelists, graphic artists, and businesswomen. Mostly *Dodos* and their saucy *Garçonne* companions. Also unattached *Sharpers* at the bar.

Decor: Immaculate bar-counter. Ten tables set with linen and flowers.

Entertainment: Phonograph plays sentimental tangos.

Men: None.

Unusual: A pick-up joint for high-achieving lesbians. Except for plucking a cat's hair from a stranger's blouse or brushing a thigh, little overt physical contact. Lots of heavy shop-talk and networking here, capped off with a serious glass of Calvados or imported rum.

TAVERNE Georgenkirchstrasse 30a 1927–1930

Area: BERLIN NORTH. "Two minutes from ALEXANDERPLATZ."

Atmosphere: Extremely downscale except on Saturday and Sunday nights. Crude. Beery smell. An aura of frustration and menacing sadism. Sign on the door warns that the bar is closed for a "PRIVATE PARTY."

Newspaper promotion: "WHERE TO MEET LESBIANS? WHERE IS IT SEXY? HERE AT THE TAVERNE!"

Unusual: Public necking and general bad behavior—humping displays by exuberant *Bubis* (pointing to bulging objects in their pants), jeers and Biergarten challenges brought on by inebriation, frequent attempts to cop feels from the preening *Mädis*, and related boorish activity. Like rutting moose, some aggressive *Bubis* are easily provoked from symbolic fisticuffs into real physical combat.

Clientele: Elderly, burly *Bubis* usually in singles or doubles. Troublesome, flirtatious *Mädis*.

Decor: Disgusting. Outer foyer looks like the waiting room of an abandoned train station. Main parlor consists of distressed furniture, an orchestra platform, and a ladies' bathroom.

Entertainment: Very loud, overpowering jazz band, led by the one-eyed "could be a woman/could be a man" Charly. Hefty blonde chanteuse, Gerda sings current hits.

Men: None.

TOPPKELLER Schwerinstrasse 13 1923–1932

Area: BERLIN WEST. Near NOLLENDORFPLATZ.

Atmosphere: Dangerous, fun, sexy. Bohemian. Normally packed and difficult to get in on Friday nights. Regarded as a lesbian "Show-Bar" or "Stock Exchange," it is an excellent place for female encounters.

Clientele: Lesbian groups, top-of-the-line actresses (entering after shows), singers, famous dancers, foreign tourists, *Gougnettes*, Hot Whores, unusually striking young *Garçonnes*, straight males in search of whipping and bondage sessions, curious married couples, S&M prostitutes.

Decor: The main room itself is surprisingly unattractive and filled with beer-hall tables and dim lights. Hanging from the ceiling are paper garlands of herons. Scribbled on the walls is phony graffiti, like a message of personal congratulations to the Ladies Club Pyramid from Mussolini. There is also a proscenium stage with ten holes cut in the fore-curtains for the late evening revue of the "Prettiest Female Calves," knees, ankles, or feet.

More elegant space at the back of the club decorated with erotic murals and cutouts of entertainers and the hostess Gypsy-Lotte.

Entertainment: A lively four-piece brass band and—for one year—a cabaret show. Lesbian games, line dances, and contests are held through the night.

Especially popular is the ritual dance, the Black Mass, executed exactly at twelve o'clock. Led by a stunning Amazon in a black sombrero, the lesbian participants (holding full cognac glasses) form a circle around her as they obey her strict commands to kneel, stand, drink and fondle a fellow celebrant.

Men: Straight men are especially welcome—since they are reputed to be the premier drinkers and spenders. During the day, many are handed risqué flyers, asking them to participate in the selection for the "Most Attractive Female Legs" competition or "Best Breasts in Berlin" (of any sex) contest.

Unusual: *Gougnettes*, glamorous Half-Silks, and Dominas do a thriving heterosexual trade here, discussing their skills and negotiating fees for next-day sessions. Reserved tables of foreigners and formally-clothed married couples at the back of house are particularly welcome draws for these professional ladies. (Police reports claim that on weekdays close to 50% of the female spectators are actually high-end sex-workers.)

VERONA-LOUNGE Kleiststrasse 36   1919–1931

Area: BERLIN WEST. East of WITTENBERG PLATZ.

Atmosphere: Usually pleasant and chic in the early evening but erotic mood often turns tense with outrageous public scenes of lesbian courtship. Berlin Vice Police sometimes harass Verona patrons by monitoring their entrances and exits.

Clientele: Despite being advertised as "the 'Love Domicile' for All Girl-Friends," the Verona is considered an afterhours headquarters for dominant *Gougnettes*. Also "serious" lesbians meet here, demonstrating intellectual support for their radical Sisters. Interested straight women and voyeuristic male artists.

Entertainment: Lesbian orchestra conducted by comic MC Harylett. Hot cheek-to-cheek tangos and contemporary social dancing.

Men: Sophisticated types admitted when accompanied by a lesbian entourage but treated as passive onlookers once inside. Waitresses will often regard them as nonentities.

Unusual: At the end of their commercial day, *Gougnette* patrons meet here for open sexual displays of conquest and submission. *Gougnettes* are easily recognized by their heavy makeup and characteristic attire—stylish men's hats, long fur coats, patent-leather footwear, and specially tailored skirts that are sharply upturned in the center to reveal the tops of their glossy, sheer silk stockings.

NUDIST VENUES

BERLIN LEAGUE OF FREE BODY CULTURE (FKK) Wilhelmstrasse 119/120 1920-1936

Affiliation: Nationalist (FKK). Led by anti-Koch doctor, Artur Fedor Fuchs. Official journal, *Nacktsport*.

Atmosphere and Philosophy: Class-oriented but pointedly progressive. Aryanism married to holistic principles of natural health.

Clientele: General mix of upper- and upper-middle-class Berlin. Bald aristocrats (noticeably wearing their wire-rim glasses or monocles), flaccid matrons in red bathing caps. A few attractive young women. (Jews, homosexuals, and Marxist types gently discouraged.)

Health Regimen: No alcohol. Most members religiously imbibe a special Bulgarian cultured-milk drink.

Separation of Genders: Implied. Modest display of breasts and male genitalia.

Studios: The Lunabad facility in the Lunapark on Sundays is reserved for FKK members. Naked air baths, sunlamp treatments, and curatic massages are offered. On Tuesdays, the Association rents the monstrous Wellenbad building, which features several indoor beaches and two powerful wave machines that mimic North Sea currents. Every ten minutes, a lifeguard issues a mock-serious warning to swimmers, "The waves are coming!"

Unusual: Nude members maintain Prussian protocol in the bath and restaurant, where one can observe formal greeting rituals, such as bowing and hand-kissing; even the military habit of clicking (barefoot) heels when meeting a superior is common here. Refined and sanitary-minded naked dinners use silver tongs to pick up sugar cubes and breakfast rolls.

BIRKENHEIDE Brandburg Motzen Lake Camp   1924-1933

Affiliation: Strictly apolitical. Undogmatic. Founded by the free-spirited Charly Straesser. No membership cards, personal questionnaires, nor cultural, ethnic, and class restrictions.

Atmosphere and Philosophy: Hedonistic and pleasure-oriented. Strong libertarian tenor. Guests have certain work obligations to help run the camp but may engage in any chosen activity after that. No rules regarding diet or dress. Organizational codes of "purity and cleanli-ness," athletic beauty, or civic belief are ignored and often parodied.

Clientele: A community of "New People." Young, vivacious, attractive Berliners, including many 175ers. Former-Wandervogel types. Wealthy actresses and their companions. Some nonconformist families with children. (Voyeurs toting cameras, and thrill-seeking bourgeois patrons not admitted.)

Decor: Extremely rustic, except for an outdoor coffee shop.

Health Regimen: Basically laissez-faire. Lots of medicine ball games, tennis, volleyball, free-form gymnastics, popular social dance. Sun bathing and swimming. Nude exercises and competitive games, like mud-wrestling, enacted in a playful atmosphere.

Separation of Genders: None.

Unusual: Public homosexual contact and inter-generational sex is common here and adds to the aura of unfettered carnal freedom.

BODY CULTURE SCHOOL OF ADOLF KOCH Friedrichstrasse 218   1920–1932

Affiliation: Socialist ("Free Men, Union for Socialist Life Reform and Free Body Culture in the Alliance of People's Health"). Official journal *Körperbildung/Nacktkultur.*

Atmosphere and Philosophy: Fun blended with didactic study. Koch's instructors pontificate that vigorous hygiene, Bode-like exercises, and nudity are all married to good health. Lectures are often laced with pedagogical and therapeutic terminology. Utopian, spiritual mood.

Clientele: Thousands of working-class and unemployed families. [Over 300,000 members in 1932, of which the out-of-work comprise almost half. Payment is 5% of annual salary, if any.] Lots of children. Among adults, many overweight and unattractive bodies. "Pendulous breasts and Zulu hips" noted among mature female members. Homosexuals and lesbians welcome.

Health Regimen: Two-hour sessions: 8 p.m.—public showers and freestyle warm-ups; 8:30—special group rhythmic gymnastics (synchronized to tiresome children's songs on piano or drumbeats); 9 p.m.—nude bathing in municipal swimming pool.

Separation of Genders: All sexes and ages mixed, except during morning exercise sessions. Designated political lectures related to the Women Question.

Studios: Headquarters in the two floors of the Apollo Theater. Friday night meetings in the Berlin State Bathhouse.

Unusual: Everyone is addressed, as in Kindergarten, in the familiar case ("Du").

Affiliations: Seemingly apolitical with a Nationalist slant ("Free Sunland Union" and the "Concerned Community of Free Sunland and Naked Sports"). Overseen by Dr. Artur Fedor Fuchs, editor of *Nacktsport*.

Atmosphere and Philosophy: Upscale. Strangely erotic. Restricted to well-paying members and guests. (Each participant must present a passport-like booklet that establishes his or her political beliefs.) Relatively little overt propaganda, but nudism is promoted as a healthful and vital aspect of pre-Christian German life.

Clientele: 6,000 paid-up members. Lots of middle-class denizens in family units and office groups. Unconventional Nationalists, who often gather by a far corner around the radio in the evening. Many aristocrats and social butterfly types, including gigolos and "Merry Widows" from the Resi. Also a place for UFA film stars, like Willy Fritch and Lilian Harvey. A few American tourists.

Decor: Entire encampment surrounded by wooden fences and Gothic *Verboten* signs. Mock primitive within. Sandy, pine-studded meadows. Two "fuck" cabins in the woods, three chalets, a restaurant, and an outdoor changing room, each covered in a characteristic rough-hewn oak.

Health Regimen: No smoking, liquor, or beer. Heavily sports-directed—organized swimming and diving, javelin-tossing, medicine-ball throwing. Nude tennis and volleyball being the most popular intersex group activity after swimming. Massages and facials offered.

Separation of Genders: During mornings, segregated activities for mature men (horseshoe-pitching), young men (boxing), women (gymnastics), and children (handball). Mixed activities after lunchtime. Groups of men in well-oiled bodies by the sea often register—to outsiders—a strong homoerotic sensation.

Unusual: Males and children walk around the compound completely naked but class and celebrity status of females is indicated by tiny accouterments, like chic bathing-hats, pearl earrings, and fine gold necklaces. Many wear distinct, French silk footwear for protection from pebbles.

Affiliation: Militantly apolitical. Founded by Fritz Gerlach. Member of Reichs Union for Free Body Culture and Life Reform, a consortium of organizations opposed to Koch and Fuchs' tendentious beliefs. ("German Light-Bathing Society" and the "League for Free Life Reform"). Journal *Licht-Luft-Leben*.

Atmosphere and Philosophy: Sexy and vibrant. "'Happiness—the imposed order of the day!"

Clientele: Smart set, including members of the British Embassy staff. Young suntanned, sports-group types. Beautiful boys and girls. "Fatties" and photographers banned.

Decor: Agrarian and unpretentious.

Health Regimen: Nude sports—ball-tossing, swimming, bathing. Sun bathing, family picnicking, open campfires, folk singing, and boating.

Separation of Genders: None.

Unusual: Displays of physical affection and romantic attachments allowed.

Affiliation and Clientele: Same as Koch's Berlin schools.

Atmosphere and Philosophy: Socialist, non-sexual. Family-friendly. Utopian, a bit of paradise for the underprivileged.

Clientele: Mostly workers from North Berlin and its suburbs. Unemployed and homeless youth who can make the trek to the Territory are allowed one free week of food and lodging.

Decor: Cabins and tents are surprisingly cozy but set cheek-by-jowl like an Edenic slum. Trails, stone pathways, swimming areas, and exercise grounds are scrupulously forged from native materials.

Health Regimen: Nudists sign on for one- or two-week sessions. In addition to attending Socialist lectures and gymnastic classes, they are expected to do practical work, like baking bread, building cabins, digging sanitation ditches, and erecting fences. No smoking or alcoholic drinks. Cheap vegetarian meals are offered: fresh milk, butter, vegetables, whole-grain breads, and a sticky root-vegetarian goulash.

Separation of Genders: None.

Unusual: All campers must fill out a detailed "Free Men" questionnaire about their personal lives and political orientation. Teenage boys, in addition, are required to write about their most vivid sexual fantasies. A female counselor then meets with them in order to assess the likelihood of any embarrassing, spontaneous arousal. Boys who experience erections or other signs of "unnatural" excitement are sent to a special clinic for therapy.

SEX MUSEUMS

DR. MAGNUS HIRSCHFELD'S INSTITUTE OF SEXOLOGY Beethovenstrasse 3 1919–1933

Area: A beautiful and isolated area of the TIERGARTEN. One block south of the Spree.

Atmosphere: Dignified and seemingly scientific. A quaint throwback to the Wilhelmian era. Yet beneath its finely polished veneer, the Institute is a citadel of revolutionary and astonishing beliefs. Directly over its massive portal is an inscription in Latin, "Sacred to Love and Sorrow."

Clientele: Curious Berliners, foreign tourists, including many artistic celebrities, and groups of international social reformers, anthropologists, physicians, and psychiatrists.

Decor: Three adjacent buildings on the former Radziwill and Hartfeld estates—some 65 rooms in all. In the Prince's central mansion, the basement is divided into domestic, kitchen, and office spaces. Main floor consists of a reception area (with one room filled with mementos of Queen Louise and Napoleon) and small consulting and waiting rooms. Second floor is cleaved into Magnus Hirschfeld's living quarters and the Museum of Sexology. The top floor houses various laboratories and an X-Ray studio.

The second building houses several outpatient clinics and a large lecture hall. Here counseling for venereal disease, birth control, marriage difficulties, frigidity, impotence, and gender exploration is conducted. The Institute's records and scientific library (which includes Europe's largest collection of graphic and literary pornography) is held in a smaller courtyard unit.

Entertainment: The Museum is open to the public and contains thousands of erotic artifacts and pictorial materials, categorized according to Hirschfeld's unique sexual taxonomy. The masturbation machines and mechanical sexual aids from everywhere, including Oceania and Southeast Africa, are a public favorite. Also of special interest are the 1,200 fantasy drawings by convicted *Lustmord* prisoners and 8,000 selected photographs and cherished items from the collections of Berlin foot and hand fetishists.

Unusual: Sex manuals and magazines, scientific literature, traditional aphrodisiacs from Asia and Africa, and erotic stimulants, which were developed in the Institute, are sold at the Museum counter. Many of the Institute's employees fall into Hirschfeld's "transitional" spectrum of "not male/not female" categories. "Female" and "male" hermaphrodites, transvestites, transsexuals, and other Intergrades cook the meals and assist with the Museum activities and demonstrations.

TRANSVESTITE VENUES

ELDORADO Lutherstrasse 29   1926–1932

Area: BERLIN WEST. "Face-to-face" with the SCALA Variety theatre.

Atmosphere: Wild ballroom excitement on weekends. Ostentatious but thoroughly titillating. Flyers in tourist cafés advertise: "International Trade, Interesting Nights." The air itself is dense with clashing fragrances: French perfumes and the unmistakable scent of the powdered female body.

Clientele: Berlin high society, adventurous foreign tourists, provincial artists and writers, *Dodos*, and beautiful Ladies in evening finery. Uncommonly attractive *Demi-Castors* and *Fohses*—competing with a like number of cross-dressed knockouts.

Decor: Huge banner over entrance proclaims: "HERE IT IS RIGHT!" Nearby are two oversized frescoes that show Ulysses being beckoned by gorgeous Circes (of course, in drag) and the trial of Paris, who hesitates between a trio of male Graces.

An eccentric series of pseudo-homilies are posted in the foyer and at the hat-check room. One reads: "Don't Worry about the Cold of Winter/ Here You Can Warm Your Hands!'

Lou, a Valentino-lookalike maître d', leads the customers to the main dining room, where there are several dozen packed tables pushed to the left and right sides of the dance floor. More frescoes of nude hieroglyphic figures are painted on the walls. Garlands hang everywhere and stringed balloons float from the tops of champagne bottles. A large cabaret stage adjoins the far wall.

Entertainment: The effusive orchestra, costumed in unisex silk blouses, plays provocative and haunting songs from French and Argentinean repertoires. Major amusement is the difficult task of assigning a biologic gender to the dancing couples, most of whom are convincingly made-up transvestites.

A lavish floor-show is presented at midnight. Typical production consists of five or six numbers: "Sweet Carlo," an androgynist, twirling boy is introduced to stormy applause; then a courtly diva sings (in shrill falsetto) a medley of risqué Parisian *chansons*, which concludes with a baritone finale. This is followed by a comical trio of rumba dancers in drag, who play out a Latin love-triangle. Lastly, Lou, the Andalusian maître d', appears in a turban, naked except for a bra and skimpy G-string. She/he executes an exotic, totally believable "naked" ballet. With the striking of the last percussive note, Lou throws her turban in the air, revealing a distinctly pomaded male mane.

Unusual: There are two service bars: a long American counter near the entrance with a row of femme bartenders (including a poor, stranded 21-year-old English-speaking girl). Over the counter is a disturbing series of S&M photographs. The second bar is at the rear. It is ministered by a jocular bartender, who insists on kissing every lady's hand. Despite the telling Eton haircut, this character is so obese that it is impossible—even for Eldorado regulars—to determine his/her sex.

Overheard conversation:
Society Matron to transvestite dancer: "Are you really a man?" Falsetto reply: "I am whatever sex you wish me to be, Madame."

ELDORADO (New) Motzstrasse 15   1928–1932

Area: BERLIN WEST. Near NOLLENDORFPLATZ.

Atmosphere: Even more glamorous and fashion-driven than the first Eldorado. Magazine advertisement: "Original Or Not—We Are Ready!"

Clientele: Serious male and female transvestites, usually in parties of four to ten. French and Scandinavian Ladies on holiday. Also lots of staid international travelers, due to a clever campaign of promotion in straight hotel guides and the powerful inducement of free admission.

Decor: "HERE IT IS RIGHT" marquee re-appears over the club doorway. On the Motzstrasse side of the building, there is a garish mural that exhibits this Eldorado's philosophy. A series of cartoonish drawings of dancing couples unfolds, beginning with a man clasping a woman; second image is a man waltzing with another man; then a woman with a woman;

next a ridiculous cross-dressed pair; a threesome doing a polka; and finally a man romantically embracing a frisky, perverse poodle.

Inside a Chinese motif prevails: standing copper gongs and sketches of opium-smoking Chinamen on the walls. More spacious seating than in the Old Eldorado.

Entertainment: Hot dance orchestra, the Bernd Robert Rhythmics. Weekends feature female impersonators, like the ostrich-headressed Muguette (in a tribute to French Music-Hall chanteuse legend Mistinguett). Still, drinking and intersexual gawking are the evening's cardinal activity.

Unusual: The opening of a second Eldorado created a pressing social problem among Berlin's stylish Ladies: which to patronize. As always, there is an elegant solution—begin the evening at Lutherstrasse 29 and then slowly migrate here for unbridled fun and games.

MIKADO BAR Puttkamerstrasse 15 1907–1933

Area: FRIEDRICHSTADT SOUTH. East of ANHALTER Train Station.

Atmosphere: Jokey. Comic-aggressive. The oldest extant transvestite club in Berlin. Once the center of organized male homosexual activity.

Clientele: Attractive drag queens (flagrantly sauntering back and forth from the Ladies Room), tantalized provincials, and heterosexual tourists. Some masculine women in suits (conspicuously using the Men's Room).

Decor: Tacky Oriental furnishings with Japanese lanterns and hanging beads over doorway arches. Flashing red traffic light illuminates the dozen tables.

Entertainment: The Baron Sattergrün (known simply as the "Baroness") on piano and a violinist play tango ballads and dance music. Transgendered illusionists dance with one another. A complete transvestite revue is offered on weekends.

Unusual: Four or five assertive divas with short-cut dresses and rubber breasts go table to table, demanding the straight males dance with them. Tourists amuse themselves, guessing which powdered patrons are biological females. Every night, a few transvestite prostitutes manage to usher confused heterosexual admirers to their nearby apartments.

MONOCLE-BAR Budapester Strasse 14 1929–1933

Area: BERLIN WEST. Near NOLLENDORFPLATZ. (Formerly the political cabaret KÜKA).

Atmosphere: Militantly gynocentric. A hefty female transvestite at the door makes certain males do not enter. (He/she holds a riding crop in one transgendered hand.

Clientele: Mostly cross-dressed *Dodos* and *Garçonnes* in pants. A few *Mädis* and daring married women.

Decor: Rows of hard, wooden benches against the walls, tables, a cabaret stage.

Entertainment: All-girl orchestra performing an up-to-date international repertoire. Cabaret acts are introduced by conférencière Lola Gray.

Area: BERLIN WEST. Near NÜRNBERGER PLATZ.

Atmosphere: Calm, self-assured. Blanketed in a blue haze of cigarette smoke. The cynosure of worldly sophistication. Maître d' unerringly knows who is a suitable guest and who does not belong.

Clientele: The most cosmopolitan mix in Berlin: film stars (notably Conrad Veidt, Anita Berber, and Marlene Dietrich—circa 1925), wealthy transvestite first-nighters, and in-the-know foreigners. Many *Bubis* in natty smoking jackets and marcelled hair, "giving off sparks like virile gigolos." *Mädis* wrapped in long sequined dresses. Seated at one of the front bars is always a string of 20-year-old Ladies with large gazelle-like eyes and dresses that emphasize their tiny waists and foamy, soft artificial breasts.

Decor: Long narrow room illuminated by dim pink lights and red Japanese paper lanterns. Two counters on either side of the foyer; each bar is "manned" by three youths in white silk shirts, matching signet rings, and slicked-back hair. Every so often, one of the narcissistic bartenders stops in the midst of preparing a martini and admires himself in a mirror over the opposite booth.

Small nightclub with limited floor seating in the back. Sofa-like chairs are arranged against the walls. Along the secluded second-floor balustrade, there are a dozen partitioned areas, consisting of low-lying tables with sunken leg spaces underneath.

Entertainment: Dapper-looking orchestra. Dancing on a long red carpet spread over parquet floor. Most customers come here for the dining and private socializing although rhapsodic female impersonators perform in the early evening.

Unusual: This is the only Berlin club where male and female transvestitism is a natural, if elevated, form of erotic display. The darkened and comfortable surroundings on the balcony are ideal spots for midnight trysts. Little in the way of commercial sex.

UNDERWORLD VENUES

THE BLUE STOCKING Linienstrasse 140 1923–1933

Area: NORTH BERLIN. Behind the St. Johannes Evangelical Church. (Also called the LINIEN-CELLAR.)

Atmosphere: Extremely friendly, if a bit on the wild side. Each patron is checked out or greeted by Karl, the elder of Berlin's Spanners. He sits studiously on a wooden block outside the Kaschemme. Only Karl's clicking approval opens the cellar door for approaching customers.

Clientele: Wealthy Crackers and their colleagues, pickpockets, mulatto prostitutes in revealing blouses, boxers, assorted cocaine addicts; hand-job whores; cocky Alphonses; suspicious Polish-Jewish smugglers, and sickly Gravelstones. After 1:30 a.m., the "Hub of Berlin's Lowlife" begins to heat up.

Decor: Fifteen or so bare tables and a bar-counter. Dim, blue lighting.

Entertainment: A droopy zither-player intermittently plays a few chords. Singer-Franz (a late-evening patron who claims he once sung with the Komische Oper) provides obscene ditties while his *Kalle*, the refined Cold Ente, and her promiscuous rival, Bootjob-Else, flash their tits.

Tourists: Not if Karl can help it.

Unusual: This is the best place to come for underworld gossip. The Stocking's *Boost*, Uncle Hans, knows all and tells all. Also, Hans specializes in settling petty disputes among his oft-feuding customers.

HUNDEGUSTAV BAR Borsigstrasse 29 1921–1933

Area: BERLIN NORTH. Near STETTINER Train Station. (Formerly the BORSIG-CELLAR.)

Atmosphere: Air thick with mischief but friendly. Place picks up considerably after 3 a.m. Hundegustav, the *Boost*, and his wife attempt to make everyone feel at home. A waiter, who wears a white coat over his nightshirt, also helps maintain order.

Clientele: Gangster bar habitués: pickpockets, assorted Grids, *Kontroll-Girls* and their *Louies*, sadistic Johns, German-speaking Africans from the Cameroons, a few homeless types. All the Berlin Police Commissioners (the Bulls) and City Public Defenders like to make a showing here afterhours as private citizens and have their own tables.

Decor: An old coal cellar with tables and chairs.

Entertainment: A trio of musicians: a guitarist, a banjo player, and a piano/accordion-player vocalist. Spectators also sing along and play percussion at their tables. Execrable, homemade Berlin North imitations of tango and Charleston music.

Tourists: Good number of thrill-seekers—although the neighborhood is a bit on the dangerous side. Outside are always a few limousines and hired cars. (Police usually raid Hundegustav's the day after any reported violent hold-up.)

Unusual: Dive named after the *Boost* Gustav, who once worked as a dogcatcher. Also rumored that he still enjoys eating dog meat. Hence the name "Dog-Gustav."

RED MILL CABARET Mühle Strasse 49 — 1919–1929

Area: BERLIN EAST. 200 feet south from SCHLESSISCHER Train Station.

Atmosphere: Lowest of the low. Disorderly and crowded after 9 p.m. Tumultuous every night. (Said to be the inspiration for Bertolt Brecht's *The Three Penny Opera*.)

Clientele: All deadbeat underworld types, especially *Ludwigs*, Grids, cocaine dealers, marriage-swindlers, and *Kontroll-Girls*.

Decor: Old restaurant cellar.

Entertainment: Music by the "Armchair Orchestra." Starting at 10 p.m., a cabaret. This normally consists of six standard acts: a dopey over-the-hill chanteuse; a "quick-poet," who creates clever rhythms from audience suggestions (almost all obscene); a "husband-and-wife" dance-team; a Bavarian folk singer; a neighborhood ventriloquist, and Jack, the Escape-King, who demonstrates how to slip out of regulation police handcuffs and other arm and leg restraints.

Tourists: Occasional.

Unusual: Lots of drunken behavior, culminating in shouting and inane threats to the cabaret performers, who are called "Shits," "Garbage," "Pimps," "Fart-gas," and "Bulls." The headwaiter Erich does a heavy trade in loan-sharking and high-quality cocaine transactions.

SING-SING Chausseestrasse 11 — 1927–1933

Area: BERLIN NORTH. Near the ORANIENBURGER TOR. (Sometimes referred to by its old name, the CAFÉ ROLAND.)

Atmosphere: Rough. Bizarre. The cauliflower-eared Spanner is dressed in a prison guard's uniform and menacingly slaps a rubber truncheon against his palm. Only open from 1 to 6 a.m.

Clientele: Real gangster-types, Grids, pickpockets, big-shot pimps, *Kontroll-Girls*, petty thieves, hangers-on, lovesick *Nuttes*. Many tough-looking ex-cons with shaved heads and tattoos.

Decor: The entire establishment is designed like a hideous prison restaurant-*cum*-execution chamber. (Largely based on the actual dining quarters of the Berlin penitentiary at Plötzensee.)

The windows are outfitted with thick iron grills, the tables are made of heavy wood, and waiters wear stripped and numbered convict uniforms. Against the main wall stands a crude replica of Sing Sing's electric chair.

Entertainment: Each night, usually between 2 and 3 a.m., a customer is selected to be executed on the Iron Lady. As soon as the "condemned" is seated and placed behind the "Swedish curtains," which conceal his face, a mad ruckus ensues throughout the restaurant with whistles, obscene jeering, much banging and stumping of boots. A particularly convincing victim, who squirms in realistic agony, is often encouraged to face the coup de grace several times before his delighted public.

Food: Prison fare. All the cutlery and dishware are regulation cell-block tin. (Not worth stealing.)

Tourists: Acceptable if subdued in dress and respectable of the real cons, who look with disdain on anyone with less than one year's hard-time incarceration. Unattended coats, wallets, passports, and wrist-watches are sometimes outsiders' involuntary contribution to this jaunty, underworld milieu.

Unusual: For many of Sing-Sing's regulars, the bar brings back nostalgic memories of their bittersweet years in the pen. The unpredictable and nasty-tempered Spanner, the resentful waiters, even the poorly prepared menu, the gaffed games, counterfeit money, and strange companionship all hark back to a simpler, if more difficult, environment. Police occasionally collar petty criminals here, especially those with well-connected rivals or loser types who are just plain homesick for authentic institutional living.

WEIMAR NAZI VENUES

ARYAN CAFÉ Dragonerstrasse 10 — 1933–1934

Area: BERLIN NORTH. (Formerly the site of the CAFÉ PARIS.)

Atmosphere: Outside building—creepy, perverse, secretive. Brusque Spanner with a bulldog face and huge scar on right cheek scrutinizes potential customers. Those selected must then negotiate several doors inside a hallway until they enter a tiny booth, where a black man questions them through a peephole. Inside: perverse, carefree, saturated with the smells of cigar smoke, imported liquor, expensive perfumes, facial creams, sweat, and strong disinfectant.

Clientele: Men in tuxedos, *Minettes*, stylish *Nuttes*, smugglers, crime bosses and other underworld types.

Decor: A cocktail lounge in front for "business," leading to a huge banquet room. Displayed on the wall there are erotic drawings (grossly detailed renditions of heterosexual and gay copulation) and pornographic photographs, which are separated by Prussian blue drapes. Each framed picture hangs loosely from the ceiling and, when moved, reveals a peephole to one of three naked cabarets.

Entertainment: For 20 American dollars, visitors have unlimited access to all three shows: a) a luxurious transvestite revue with libidinous (rather than comic) overtones; b) a masochistic bacchanalia, featuring a Domina flagellating a brutish-looking SA-Mann type to orgasm; and c) a Nordic-looking couple (she is blonder and taller) who perform intercourse while a female voice from an instructional phonographic record pedantically explains the joys of the wedding night.

Unusual: The rapturous performance of the "married couple" concludes sharply with the gramophone's final admonition: "Heil Hitler!" Under a mystic bluish light, the nude statuesque Aryan pair take a curtain call.

PENSION SCHMIDT ("SALON KITTY") Giesebrechtstrasse 11 — 1930–1942

Area: BERLIN WEST. Near the Kurfürstendamm.

Atmosphere: Highbrow, relaxed, extremely upscale bordello. Kitty Schmidt, the charming, fiftyish madam, has created a good facsimile of a turn-of-the-century Parisian literary salon-*cum*-brothel. Reputed to be the best establishment of its kind in Berlin.

Clientele: High society, musicians, flush bureaucrats, German army officers on leave, foreign embassy types, occasionally a few randy heads of state—usually Italian or Romanian dignitaries.

Decor: Old-fashioned Wilhelmian foyer and drawing room with refined, bourgeois furnishings: Persian carpet, velvet curtains, grand piano, Art Nouveau knick-knacks. Seven bedrooms, all tastefully arranged with overhead mirrors, bidet, and sink. Clean sheets and bedding.

Entertainment: German canapés, beer, French wine, champagne, coffee, and hard liquor are available in the foyer. Customers are handed photographic books, where they discuss with Kitty their predilections (usually by hair color) and select among 20 striking women. Kitty then telephones the chosen prostitute, who quickly outfits herself in the desired attire, walks to the nearby Salon, and is introduced to her "suitor" in the drawing-room. Typically, after drinks and small talk, the pair is directed to a numbered room.

Clients are encouraged to order more food and drink in the bedroom and partake in post-coital socializing with other customers and winsome prostitutes in the foyer. The (often extraordinary) bill is settled discreetly with Kitty in her office.

Unusual: In late 1939, the Berlin SS added a dozen "prostitute-spies" to Kitty's stable and installed 120 electrical bugs in an elaborate espionage scheme. Over 24,000 wax disks were used to record "sexual interrogations" of loose-tongued Axis diplomats and Wehrmacht officers.

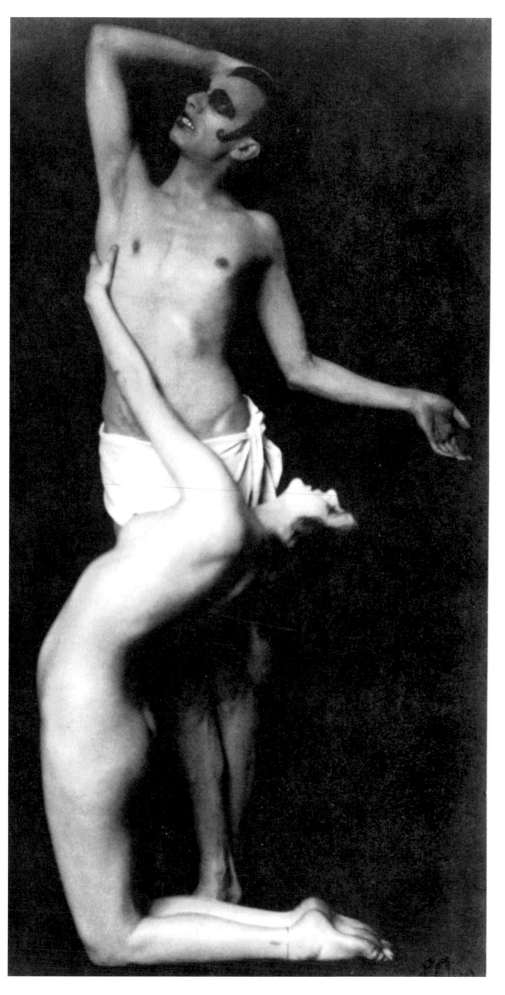

The visual material of this book is from the author's private archive.

The vast majority of the erotic art work reprinted here was confiscated from the original legal owners—mostly Jewish-owned agencies and publishing houses—and then "Aryanized" by the German government in 1933 and 1934.

The cover photograph is typical. It first appeared in *Die Aufklärung* (April 1929, 1:3), a monthly "Sex and Life Reform" journal edited by Magnus Hirschfeld and Marie Krische. In March 1933, the Nationalist Socialist authorities not only organized the physical destruction of Hirschfeld's Institute, they also appropriated Hirschfeld's extensive intellectual properties and disbursed them to various German institutions. The University of Cologne, for instance, still acts as the copyright owner of this photographic image. Today when it assigns publication rights for the "Masked Woman," it does so without any recognition or attribution of its 1929 sources.

Each individual graphic in *Voluptuous Panic* has a complex artistic and legal history. Some appeared in Weimar periodicals and *Sittengeschichten* simultaneously. Others found their way into foreign journals via official Nazi photo agencies after 1933. Readers wishing additional information on any specific illustration may contact Feral House directly.

Opposite:
D'Ora, Droste and Berber in Martyr dance, 1922

Left:
Berlin kiosk, 1926

SELECTED BIBLIOGRAPHY

GUIDEBOOKS AND CONTEMPORARY ACCOUNTS

John Chancellor, *How To Be Happy in Berlin*. London: Arrowsmith, 1929.

Le Crapouillot, Paris: April 1931 (Issue on Berlin).

Hendrik De Leeuw, *Sinful Cities of the Western World*. New York: Citadel Press, 1934.

Ernst Engelbrecht, *15 Jahre Kriminalkommissar*. Berlin: Peter J. Oestergaard Verlag, 1926.

——, *In den Spuren des Verbrechertums*. Berlin: Peter J. Oestergaard Verlag, 1930.

Ernst Engelbrecht and Leo Heller, *Kinder der Nacht*. Berlin: Hermann Paetel Verlag, 1925.

Jay Gay, *On Going Naked*. Garden City, NY: Garden City Publishing Co., 1932.

Charles Graves, *Gone Aboard*. London: Ivor Nicholson & Watson, 1932.

Daniel Guérin, *The Brown Plague*. Durham and London: Duke University Press, 1994. Translated and introduced by Robert Schwartzwald.

Leo Heller, *So siehst aus Berlin!* Munich: Verlag Parrus & Co., 1927.

Joseph Hergesheimer, *Berlin*. New York: Alfred Knopf, 1932.

Magnus Hirschfeld, *Sittengeschichte der Nachkriegzeit*. 2 vols. Leipzig: Verlag für Sexualwissenschaft Schneider & Co., 1932.

Kennen Sie Berlin? Stettin: Verlag F. Hessenland, 1929.

Alfred Kind and Julian Herlinger, *Flucht aus der Ehe*. Leipzig: Verlag für Kulturforschung, 1931.

H.R. Knickerbocker, *Germany—Fascist or Soviet?* London: John Lane, 1932.

Rom Landau, *Seven: An Essay in Confession*. London: Ivor Nicholson & Watson, 1936.

"Losa," *Sexuelle Verirrungen*. Berlin: Auffenberg Verlagsgellschaft, 1930.

Netley Lucas, *Ladies of the Underworld*. Cleveland: Goldsmith Publishing, 1927.

Frances and Mason Merrill, *Among the Nudists*. Garden City, NY: Garden City Publishing Co., 1931.

Curt Moreck, *Führer Durch das "Lasterhafte" Berlin*. Leipzig: Verlag moderner Stadtführer, 1931.

——, *Kultur-und Sittengeschichte der Neuesten Zeit: Das Genussleben des Modernen Menschen*. Dresden: Paul Aretz Verlag, 1929.

Above:
Delhi,
The Stallion

Walter Polzer, *Sexuell-Perverse*. Leipzig: Asa-Verlag, 1930.

Ruth Margarete Roellig, *Berlins Lesbische Frauen*. Leipzig: Bruno Gebauer Verlag, 1928.

Louis-Charles Royer, *Let's Go Naked*. New York: Brentano's Publishers, 1932. Translated from the French by Paul Quiltana.

Rumpelstilzchen [Adolf Stein], [*Gesammelte Schriften.*] 15 Vols. Berlin: Brunnen-Verlag, 1920–1935.

Roger Salardenne, *Hauptstädte des Lasters*. Berlin: Auffenberg Verlagsgellschaft, 1931.

Bernhard Schidlof, *Prostitution und Mädchenhandel*. Leipzig: Lykeion, 1931.

Francis Scott (editor), *Halbwelt von Heute*. Leipzig: ASA-Verlag, 1927.

——, *Prostitution*. Berlin: ASA-Verlag, 1927.

——, *Das Lesbische Weib*. Berlin: Pergamon-Verlag, 1933.

Charly Straesser, *Jugend Gelände*. Thüringen: Self-published, 1926.

Eugen Szatmari, Berlin: *Was Nicht im Baedeker Steht*. Munich: R. Piper & Co., 1927.

"WEKA" [Willy Pröger], *Stätten der Berliner Prostitution*. Berlin: Auffenberg Verlagsgellschaft, 1930.

Conrad Wel, *Das Verbotene Buch*. Hannover: Verlag Paul Witte, 1929.

GENERAL HISTORICAL AND SCHOLARLY BOOKS

Wolf von Eckardt and Sander L. Gilman, *Bertolt Brecht's Berlin: A Scrapbook of the Twenties*. Garden City, NY: Anchor Press, 1975.

Bilder-Lexicon. 4 vols. Leipzig: Verlag für Kulturforschung, 1928–1931.

Susanne Everett, *Lost Berlin*. Chicago: Contemporary Books, 1979.

Otto Friedrich, *Before the Deluge: A Portrait of Berlin in the 1920s*. New York: Harper & Row, 1972.

Thomas Friedrich, *Berlin Between the Wars*. New York: Vendome Press, 1991.

Alex de Jonge, *The Weimar Chronicle: Prelude to Hitler*. New York and London: Paddington Press Ltd., 1978.

Anton Gill, *A Dance Between the Flames: Berlin Between the Wars*. New York: Carroll & Graf Publishers, 1993.

Anton Kaes, Martin Jay, and Edward Dimendberg (eds.), *The Weimar Republic Sourcebook*. Berkeley, Los Angeles, London: University of California Press, 1994.

Walther Kiaulehn, *Berlin: Schicksal einer Weltstadt*. Munich: Biederstein Verlag, 1958.

Bärbel Schrader and Jürgen Schebera, *The "Golden" Twenties: Art and Literature in the Weimar Republic*. New Haven and London: Yale University Press, 1988. Translated by Katherine Vanovitch.

MEMOIRS AND BIOGRAPHIES

Luigi Barzini, *The Europeans*. New York: Simon and Schuster, 1983.

Hans Blüher, *Werke und Tage*. Munich: Paul List Verlag, 1953.

Michael Davidson, *The World, the Flesh, and Myself*. London: Arthur Barker, 1962.

Sefton Delmer, *Trail Sinister*. London: Secker & Warburg, 1961.

Gerald Hamilton, *Mr. Norris and I*. London: Allan Wingate Ltd., 1956.

Christopher Isherwood, *Christopher and His Kind, 1929–1939*. New York: Farrar, Straus, Giroux, 1976.

Leo Lania, *Today We are Brothers*. Boston: Houghton Mifflin Company, 1942. Translated by Ralph Marlowe.

Ludwig Lenz-Levy, *The Memoirs of a Sexologist*. New York: Cadillac Publishing, 1954.

Klaus Mann, *The Turning Point*. New York: L.B. Fisher, 1942.

J.H. Morgan, *Assize of Arms.* New York: Oxford University
 Press, 1946.
"PEM" [Paul Markus], *Heimweh nach dem
 Kurfürstendamm.* Berlin: Lothar Blanvalet, 1952.
Curt Riess, *Das Waren Zeiten.* Vienna-Munich-Zurich-
 Innsbruck: Verlag Fritz Molden, 1977.
Charlotte Wolff, *Hindsight: An Autobiography.* London,
 Melbourne, New York: Quartet Books, 1980.
Carl Zuckmayer, *A Part of Myself: Portrait of an Epoch.*
 New York: Harcourt Brace Jovanovich, Inc., 1970.
 Translated by Richard and Clara Winston.
Stefan Zweig, *The World of Yesterday.* New York: Viking
 Press, 1943.

DIRECTED STUDIES

Michael Andritzky and Thomas Rautenberg (eds.),
 "Wir Sind Nackt und Nennen Uns Du." Giessen:
 Anabas, 1989.
Peter Auer, *Adlon.* Vienna: Wiener Verlag, 1997.
*Eldorado: Homosexuelle Frauen und Männer in Berlin
 1850–1950.* Berlin: Edition Hentrich, 1984.
Fritz Giese, *Girlkultur.* Munich: Dephin-Verlag, 1925.
Goodbye to Berlin? 100 Jahre Schwulenbewegung. Berlin:
 Verlag Rosa Winkel, 1997.
Magnus Hirschfeld, *Geschlectskunde.* 5 vols. Stuttgart:
 Julius Puttmann, 1926–1930.
——, *Sittengeschichte des Weltkrieges.* 2 vols. Leipzig:
 Verlag für Sexualwissenschaft Schneider & Co., 1930.
Peter Jelavich, *Berlin Cabaret.* Cambridge, MA, and
 London: Harvard University Press, 1993.
Alfred Kind, *Die Weiberherrschaft.* 4 vols. Leipzig: Verlag
 für Kulturforschung, 1931.
Jürgen Lemke (ed.), *Gay Voices from East Germany.*
 Bloomingdale and Indianapolis: Indiana University
 Press, 1991. Translated and edited by John Borneman.
Allan H. Mankoff, *Mankoff's Lusty Europe.* New York:
 Viking Press, 1972.
Peter Norden, *Madam Kitty.* London: Abelard-Schuman,
 1973. Translated by J. Maxwell Brownjohn.
Harry Oosterhuis and Hubert Kennedy (eds).
 *Homosexuality and Male Bonding in Pre-Nazi
 Germany.* New York: Harrington Park Press, 1991.
Hans Ostwald, *Sittengeschichte der Inflation.* Berlin:
 Neufeld & Henius Verlag, 1931.
Norman Page, *Auden and Isherwood: the Berlin Years.*
 New York: St. Martin's Press, 1998.
Ernst Schertel, *Der Erotische Komplex,* 3 vols. Leipzig:
 Parthenon, 1932.
——, *Der Flagellantismus als Literarisches Motiv.* 4 vols.
 Leipzig: Parthenon, 1929–1932.

Leo Schidrowitz, *Sittengeschichte der Geheimen und
 Verbotenen.* Leipzig: Verlag für Kulturforschung, 1930.
Claudia Schoppmann, *Days of Masquerade.* New York:
 Columbia University Press, 1996. Translated by Allison
 Brown.
Karl Toepfer, *Empire of Ecstasy.* Berkeley and Los Angeles:
 University of California Press, 1997.
Charlotte Wolff, *Magnus Hirschfeld.* London: Quartet
 Books, 1986.
Knud Wolfram, *Tanzdielen und Vergnügungspaläste.*
 Berlin: Edition Hentrich, 1992.
Heinrich Wörenkamp and Gertrude Perkauf, *Erziehungs.
 Flagellantismus.* Vienna: Verlag für Kulturforschung,
 1932.

Above:
Delhi,
Breaking In

Following:
Das Magazin,
1931

**Following
Opposite:**
*Illustrirte
Zeitung,* 1930

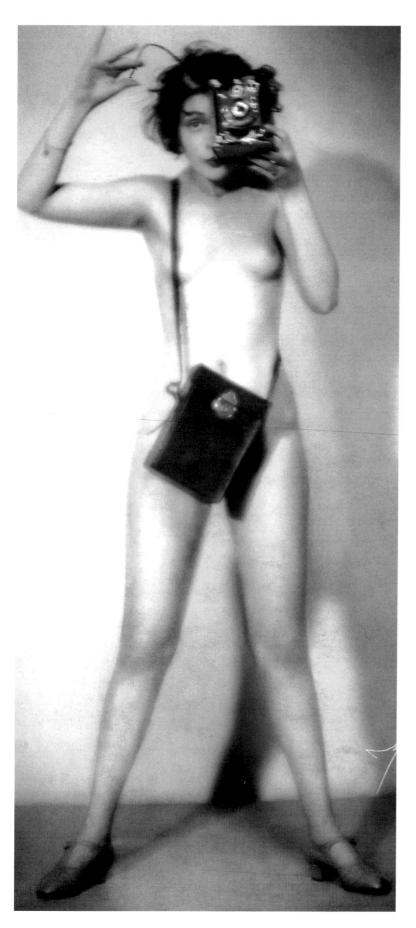

ADDED BIBLIOGRAPHY

Marian Dockerill, *My Life in a Love Cult: A Warning to All Young Girls*. Chicago: Better Publications, 1928.

Stephen Flowers, *Fire and Ice*. St. Paul, MN: Llewellyn Publishers, 1990.

Mel Gordon, *Erik Jan Hanussen: Hitler's Jewish Clairvoyant*. Los Angeles: Feral House, 2001.

Eugen Grosche, *Karma und Astrologie*. Berlin: Orient Berlin, 1930.

Ottoman Hanish, *Mazdaznan Atem– und Gesundheitspflege*. Leipzig: Mazdaznan Verlag, 1930.

Francis King, *Sexuality, Magic, and Perversion* [1971]. Los Angeles: Feral House, 2003.

Richard Kaczynski, *Perdurabo*. Tempe, Arizona: New Falcon, 2002.

Rudolf von Laban, *Choreographie*. Jena: Eugen Diederichs Verlag, 1926.

Ulrich Linse, *Barfüssige Propheten*. Berlin: Siedler Verlag, 1983.

Rudolf Olden, *Das Wunderbare*. Berlin: Rowohlt Verlag, 1932.

Alexander Pilcz, *Über Hypnotism, Okkulte Phänomene, Traumleben*. Vienna: Deuticke, 1926.

Theodor Reuss and Aleister Crowley, *O.T.O. Rituals and Sex Magick*. Thame, UK: I-H-O Books, 1999 [Edited by A.R. Naylor. Introduced by Peter R. Koenig].

Theodor von Rheine, *Massage-Institute*. Berlin: Private Edition, 1932.

——, *Stiefel-Mädchen*. Berlin: Private Edition, 1932.

Ernst Schertel, *Magie: Geschichte, Theorie, Praxis*. Prien: Anthropos, 1923.

Paul Scheurlen, *Sekten der Gegenwart*. Stuttgart: Quell-Verlag, 1930.

Alice Bunker Stockham, *Karezza Ethics of Marriage*. New York: Private Edition, 1896.

Montague Summers, *Geography of Witchcraft*. London: Routledge & Kegan, 1927.

Lawrence Sutin, *Do Want Thou Wilt*. New York: St. Martin's Press, 2000.

Cornelius Tabori, *My Occult Diary*. London: Rider and Company, 1951.

Leopold Thoma, *Wunder der Hypnose*. Württemberg: Johannes Baum Verlag, 1926.

Erich Wulffen and Felix Abraham, *Fritz Ulbrichs Lebender Marmor*. Vienna-Berlin-Leipzig: Verlag für Kulturforschung, 1931.

Also see Peter-Robert Koenig's website, http://user.cyberlink.ch/~koenig/hallo.htm

JOURNALS AND MAGAZINES

Die Aufklärung, Berliner Illustrirte Zeitung, Berliner Leben, Berolina, Die Dame, Der Eigene, Freikörperkultur und Lebensreform, Figaro, Form und Farbe, Die Freudinnen, Die Garçonne, Hanussen-Magazin, Ideal-Ehe, Illustrirte Zeitung, Der Junggeselle, Jugend, Körperbildung/Nacktkultur, Lachendes Leben, Licht-Land, Lustige Blätter, Das Magazin, Magazin für Alle, Pegasus, Der Pranger, Der Querschnitt, Reigen, Die Schönheit, Simplizissimus, Tempo, Uhu.

MEL GORDON is professor of theatre arts at University of California at Berkeley and author of *Dada Performance* (New York: Performing Arts Books, 1986); *Erik Jan Hanussen: Hitler's Jewish Clairvoyant* (Los Angeles: Feral House, 2001); *Expressionist Texts* (New York: PAB, 1987); *The Grand Guignol: Theatre of Horror and Terror* [Revised Edition] (New York: Da Capo Press, 1997); *Lazzi: the Comic Routines of the Commedia dell'arte* (New York: PAB, 1982); *Meyerhold, Eisenstein, and Biomechanics: Revolutionary Acting in Soviet Russia* (Jefferson, NC: McFarland Press, 1996) [co-written with Alma H. Law]; *Mikhoels the Wise* (New York: Gateway Press, 1982); and *The Stanislavsky Technique: Russia* (New York: Applause Books, 1988).